To
with me.
Betty Richards

MW01282065

Ardis Heights

BY

Betty Richards

authorHOUSE®

AuthorHouse™
1663 Liberty Drive, Suite 200
Bloomington, IN 47403
www.*authorhouse*.com
Phone: 1-800-839-8640

First published by AuthorHouse 7/16/2008

ISBN: 978-1-4343-3661-3 (sc)

Library of Congress Control Number: 2008900972

Printed in the United States of America
Bloomington, Indiana

This book is printed on acid-free paper.

ACKNOWLEDGEMENTS

I would like to thank my first writing teacher, Jeannine Hathaway, who introduced me to the joys of writing. To the women in my critique group who suffered patiently and helpfully through the countless revisions of this book, Coleen Johnston, Myrne Roe, Sharon Jesik, Linda Gebert, Emily Bonavia, Dianna Kitch, and Margalee Wright, a grateful thank you. To my friend and editor, Alta Brock who advised and encouraged me, to all the wonderful writers at the Kansas Writers Association who give so generously of their time and talent and, last but not least, to my children and husband who have supported me in my struggles over the years to get this book written, I owe a debt of gratitude.

FOR MY CHILDREN
Susan, Mimi, Jinx and Matt
who grew up in a different world

"Our greatest glory consists not of never falling—
But in rising every time we fall."

Ralph Waldo Emerson

1929

CHAPTER 1

He didn't know whether to consider it the beginning or the end. He only knew that once it started it was like a fungus that began between his toes and quickly spread up his body while there was no way of stopping it. He could only stand helplessly by and watch it envelope him and all those around him. It began without warning, like a storm that comes up suddenly, unexpectedly, a downpour that wouldn't stop until it had almost washed away the familiar world.

Thursday, October 24, 1929 had started as a day like most for Dr. John Swinson. Men, women and children came from miles around seeking his help with sore throats, crossed eyes, and various other ailments of the eyes, ears, nose and throat. At 5:30 that afternoon he said goodbye to his last patient. He went through his usual routine of washing his hands in the small sink that hung on one wall of his inner office, then putting instruments in the sterilizer. Before leaving for home he cracked the door of his examination room and made a final check of his waiting area. All the chairs that lined the wall of the long narrow room were empty. He opened the door wider and smiled at the woman occupying the reception desk.

"Looks like that's all for today, Mildred."

Mildred was a rosy cheeked woman in her mid-fifties who had been his nurse- receptionist for over twenty-five years. She smiled back at him from where she sat putting away files. "Yes, looks like it, Doctor."

"You run on home then. I'll see you tomorrow. Have a good evening and tell Henry hello for me."

"Okay. You, too." she said and opened the drawer where she kept her purse.

He turned and reentered his office, exchanged his white doctor's coat for his suit jacket and Stetson hat, and left by the back door. He hummed to himself as he walked down the long hall to the elevator which would take him down the six floors to the lobby of the First National Bank Building. He nearly always hummed when he was on his way home. His medical practice was an important part of his life but the very thought of his farm in Ardis Heights made him want to sing.

He'd grown up on his family's farm in east Texas and as a small boy, sitting on a stool in their dilapidated old barn milking the cows, he'd dreamed of some day owning a farm with a modern dairy barn and all the latest milking equipment. For many years this dream had been delayed by marriage, medical school, and raising four sons and a daughter but was now a reality.

Out on the street, people passing by smiled and greeted him with "Hi, Doc." He smiled back and had something to say to everyone. When he rounded the corner at the end of the block, his eyes lit up as he caught sight of his new dark blue Packard Roadster. Its gold fenders and running board sparkled in the sunlight. He brushed the hood with his fingertips on his way to the driver's side and stopped short when he spotted a speck that marred its perfect surface. Removing his handkerchief from his pocket, he rubbed it clean, then took a second to admire his work before getting in the car.

The drive from downtown Greenville to his farm was a little more than five miles through lush countryside. Indian summer was in full bloom and the sun shown brightly and warmed the rich black soil on either side of the road. In the near distance, trees lined the banks of the Sabine River which snaked its way across the land and autumn seemed to be lighting a torch, setting the oaks and sumac on fire with color.

When he arrived home and turned into the driveway that cut though the green lawn by the side of his house, he sat for a while, admiring his surroundings. A smile crossed his face as he reminisced about the day he'd found this farm and came bounding into the house where they lived in town, flushed with excitement. Dandy, his wife of over forty years looked up and nodded when he entered.

"Guess what, Sweetheart! I found it today. I finally found the perfect one," he announced, foregoing his usual greeting.

She was setting the table for supper and was only half paying attention to what he was saying. Absent mindedly she asked, "You found what, Papa?"

"Our farm."

She stopped and looked at him, holding the plate she was about to set down. "What farm? What are you talking about?"

Filled with elation he answered, "You're not going to believe it. This farm has everything. There's a large lake and several ponds and the Sabine River runs across the back of the land and…"

"Wait a minute! Slow down, Papa. Just where is this perfect place you've found? And what does it have to do with us?"

"It's out in Ardis Heights. I can hardly wait for you to see it. You're gonna love it! Of course we can't move right away. We have to build a house first, but…"

"Stop! Now just you wait a minute. No need for you to go any further. I'm not leaving this house in town to go live in Ardis Heights. Move our beautiful teenaged daughter to Ardis Heights? Have you lost your mind?"

This stopped him for a moment while he tried to think of a good argument. He knew the Ardis Heights community was not very fashionable. In fact, it was considered to be a little seedy. He couldn't help but notice that down the road in one direction from the farm was the Jones' place; a rundown gasoline station that everybody in town knew was a cover for bootleggers and gamblers. On the other side of the road a short distance away was a tourist court where most business was done in the light of day. However, he wasn't going to give up. He wanted this place. After a short silence, he begged,

"Dandy, please wait before you make up your mind. Will you at least go with me to look at it?"

"No. No. No. Don't ask me again. No!" With that she turned her back to him and returned to setting the table.

A week passed and he brooded, hanging his head and speaking only when spoken to. Finally she broke down. "Okay. Stop moping around like a dog with it's tail between it's legs. Let's drive out and I'll take a look. But that's all. Don't think I've changed my mind about living out there."

His hang-dog face disappeared and he flashed his most engaging smile. He was sure once she saw how beautiful the setting was that she wouldn't be able to resist; however, he was wrong. She did resist. Finally when all else failed, he tried bribery. He threatened her resolve with a promise that if she'd move she could build any house she chose with no limits. When he added that the offer would include the fanciest chicken house in the country, that cinched it.

She proceeded to build one of the first red brick houses in the Greenville area where most of the architecture was Victorian and of wood construction. The new house featured all the latest things, even a large indoor bathroom, a rarity for houses at that time. Large white pillars supported a balcony which hung over the wide porch that wrapped around the front of the house. When finished, the house was outstanding. It sat back from the road and was surrounded by trees and flowerbeds where a variety of plants were in bloom most seasons. And out behind the house and beyond the back yard sat the most impressive chicken house to be found anywhere

He sat in his car reminiscing about the times they'd shared here over the past ten years. It made him happy to know that in time she had come to love this place as much as he. Leisurely he opened the door of his parked car and left it with a backward glance for one last admiring look. As he started toward the house he could see in the distance the gleaming tin roof and white wooden sides of his modern dairy barn. "I'm a lucky man," he said to himself, as he took in all he had to be thankful for.

Upon entering the kitchen, he noticed at once that the sounds coming from the little radio that sat on the cabinet were unfamiliar. Instead of the soap opera Dandy usually listened to, anxious voices filled the air.

"Hello, Dandy. What in the world is that you're listening to?" he said as he grabbed her and stopped her trek across the kitchen to give her a hello peck.

Slowing down just long enough to turn her cheek to him, she answered, "I don't know. They interrupted my program. It's something to do with Wall Street and a wreck or a crash or something. Whatever it is, it's happening in New York City."

"Oh," he said, brushing it aside. He'd never been out of the state of Texas, and being a true Texan, had never felt the need. "Well, I never did understand that Wall Street, high finance, New York business," he said. "Let those damnyankees worry about it. Whatever it is, they probably brought it on themselves." A chocolate cake sat on the cabinet nearby and as he walked past he stuck his finger in the icing and licked it off, then grinned when Dandy protested.

"Shoosh! Listen!" Dandy stopped in the middle of the kitchen and turned her attention to the voices on the radio. "Did you hear that, Papa? Did they say something about whatever's going on might cause banks to fail and people to lose their money?"

"I don't know. But as you are aware I never did hold with banks, anyway. That's why I've got all our money right here on this farm." A feeling of self satisfaction swam over him as he thought of the large black metal safe which stood in a dark corner of the closet under the staircase. Also, in the smokehouse in the backyard, fruit jars stuffed with money were hidden on shelves behind jars of peach preserves and green beans. And in a dark corner, a large crock meant for brining cucumber pickles was filled to the top with five, ten, and twenty-dollar bills.

Skirting around Dandy, he ran his finger across the icing once again and then walked toward the kitchen door. "While you finish up supper, I think I'll wander out to the dairy barn and see how the milking went today." By the time he got there, the entire thing had slipped his mind.

The following week, however, when he arrived at his office in the bank building early one morning, he was unable to get through the mass of frightened people pushing impatiently to get in, hoping to withdraw their money before the bank closed its doors.

1932

CHAPTER 2

Four-year-old Betty Lou found it difficult to understand why the laughter so frequently shared between her mother and daddy had slowly disappeared, leaving a void filled with her mother's tears. Or why deep creases in her daddy's forehead replaced the smile to which she had become so accustomed. Though she couldn't understand it, she felt it. Her parent's unhappiness filled the space of their lives like something alive, surrounding them all with its misery.

One hot August morning the sun beamed down without mercy, leeching the last remaining green from the dry grass and wilting the few flowers that had survived the heat of a relentless summer. Betty Lou was relegated to the shade of their covered front porch while her baby sister took her nap. She busied herself with dressing and undressing her doll, Mary.

Their buff brick bungalow sat on a treeless street near the edge of town; a street lined with similar houses. Theirs was among the last built in Lubbock before the Great Depression stopped most construction. A few blocks away, deserted half-finished houses sat in a field covered with weeds and gave evidence of the broken dreams of contractors who had envisioned this place as becoming one of the most desirable new neighborhoods in the city.

The street where they lived was usually quiet, with traffic mostly confined to husbands and fathers leaving their houses in the morning to search for work and returning later in the day without success. So Betty Lou was startled when she heard the roar of a large truck and looked up to see it turning down their street. Her surprise grew even greater when the truck came to a stop in front of their house. Dropping half-dressed Mary to the floor of the porch, she stood and watched while two men got out of the truck and opened the back end. After observing them a few moments more, she spun around and ran in the house, letting the screen door slam as she yelled, "Mama, Mama! Come see!"

Inez stood at the kitchen sink washing diapers on a rub-board. She frowned as she looked over her shoulder and whispered "What is it Betty Lou? I told you to be quiet while the baby's sleeping."

"But Mama, come see. There's a big truck and some men in front of our house."

By this time the two men were on the front porch, knocking on the door.

Inez dried her hands on her apron and pushed back a strand of hair that had fallen into her eyes as she walked to answer the knock. She peered through the screen door and her voice showed her irritation at being interrupted. "Yes?"

she asked, staring at two shabby looking men in coveralls. She waited for them to say something, and when they just stood there looking at their feet, she added, "Can I help you?"

"Well, ma'am," the taller of the men answered, looking up to meet her eyes for a moment, then hurriedly looking down again, "Uh, we're mighty sorry, ma'am." He hesitated and looked over at his partner as if begging him for help. When none was forthcoming, he continued, still avoiding looking at her. "We've been sent here to pick up your refrigerator and cook stove."

Inez stood without moving for a few seconds while she tried to comprehend what he was saying. When she realized their intention, her mouth dropped open and her brown eyes grew large with disbelief. "No! You can't do that. No! No! I won't let you. I'll call my husband," she threatened, forgetting that she didn't know how to reach him, and even if she did, their phone had been disconnected the week before.

The men looked at each other, then shook their heads in agreement, opened the screen door and came in without her invitation. "We're sorry as we can be, ma'am, but no payments have been made for over six months and it's our job to pick them up." The men walked with their heads bent as they tromped through the living room and into the kitchen.

Inez wailed and wrung her hands as she followed them. "You can't do this. What will we do if you take away our cook stove? I beg you, please don't do this."

Both men stopped and looked at her, their eyes showing their discomfort. Once again the tall one spoke. "Look ma'am, this is a lousy job. We hate doing this to you, but we have to. We ain't got no choice."

Inez dropped to her knees and covered her face with her hands. "This can't be happening," she moaned. She couldn't stand to watch so she kept her hands over her face and remained on the floor as they loaded the stove and refrigerator into the back of the truck and drove away.

When Erby came home from another unsuccessful day of job hunting, he was not met with the usual aroma of supper cooking. Inez wasn't waiting for him at the door with her familiar anxious look and the inevitable question. His eyes searched the living room but there was no one in sight. Next he looked in the baby's room and found her asleep, but no one else was there. He checked their bedroom. No one there either. Roaming through the house he called out, "Inez? Betty Lou?" No answer. Fearful now that something awful had happened, he rushed into the kitchen repeating their names and stopped abruptly when he almost tripped on Inez. She lay on the kitchen floor, her body in a fetal position. Betty Lou looked up at him from where she sat in the spot formally occupied by the refrigerator, her thumb in her mouth and her doll clutched tightly to her chest.

* * *

In the week that followed, several other trucks stopped before their house and left with more furniture delinquent in payments. When things seemed so bad they couldn't get worse, the final blow fell. Erby reached in the mailbox and pulled out the inevitable stack of bills. As he went through them he found a letter that grabbed his attention. When he read the address in the top left hand corner his breath caught in his throat. He stood by the mailbox staring at the envelope for a few moments before taking it in the house. Holding it in shaking hands, he read then reread the return address. Reluctantly he tore open the envelope and pulled out the letter. After reading it, he stood as if frozen in place, his eyes fixed on the floor.

When Inez entered the living room holding the baby, he was still standing with his arm by his side, the letter grasped in his closed fist. Alarmed by the look on his face, she stopped suddenly. "What is it, Erby? You look terrible. Are you okay?"

He raised his arm and showed her the crumpled letter in his hand.

"What is it? What does it say?"

He didn't answer her right away and when he raised his eyes, she could see his desperation. In a moment he said in a broken voice, "This house isn't ours anymore, Inez. The bank's foreclosing."

She slumped into one of the few chairs left in the living room and looked up at him silently shaking her head. Lately, it seemed to her, disaster was wrapping around them like a python slowly tightening its grip.

* * *

The next morning Inez arose and left Erby to sleep for a while longer. Neither had fallen to sleep until almost dawn. She dressed quietly and walked from room to room surveying the damage. As she made her way through the empty rooms she recalled how not long ago their lives had been wonderful; their future seemed so secure. Erby had a great job at the Lubbock Cotton Compress, the busiest in the state of Texas. No one could imagine the demand for cotton would ever end. She rubbed the sides of her forehead with her fingers. "What happened? What happened?" she cried aloud.

During the 1920s Lubbock had been a boom town; in fact the entire country was on a boom. The stock market soared, and people they knew were getting rich from investing. Some even called it "A Golden Age, a great time to be alive". Everything anyone could want was available on credit: stocks, cars, houses, furniture, clothes. Making small monthly payments had seemed so easy at the time. According to newspaper and radio advertising it had been almost unpatriotic not to junk your old stuff and buy new. Sighing deeply, she lamented how she and Erby had been only too happy to comply. As she roamed around the house she wondered how much longer before someone else would come to pick up the bedroom suite and what was left of the living room furniture. Feeling as empty as the rooms of her house, she dropped to the floor and sat cross legged, letting her eyes climb the walls. Noting the pictures that still hung there, she wondered if they'd take those too.

Darkness slowly faded into light. Soon the girls would be awake and they'd be hungry for breakfast. Rising from the floor, she walked from the living room to the kitchen and stopped in the doorway staring at the place where the gleaming white refrigerator had stood against the wall a week ago. Then she tried to swallow the lump in her throat when she glanced across the room to where the stove had been. She entered the kitchen, opened a cabinet door and reached for the lone cereal box that stood in the middle of the otherwise empty shelf. Her eyes roamed again to the refrigerator's empty spot. Obviously, they'd have to eat their cereal without milk again.

*   *   *

The next day as Betty Lou stood watching out the front window, she saw another truck stop in front of their house. The men in this truck soon entered and took away what was left of the furniture. The rooms were now empty except for their personal belongings, clothes still hung in the closets but items from drawers were dumped on the floors.

Trying to make light of the seriousness of their situation, Erby retorted, "Makes it easier to pack I guess." Then he cursed as he tripped over a clump of the baby's belongings. Shaking his head as he went to dig suitcases out of the storage closet, he said, "At least they left the baby bed. The funny thing is there's no room for it in the car."

"Yeah -- funny," Inez said as she looked around at the impossible mess. "Real funny."

Betty Lou sat on the floor in the corner of the room and watched the chaos with her thumb in her mouth. She had given up her thumb almost a year ago but the habit returned now with intensity.

* * *

That night, Betty Lou lay on a pallet on the floor near the one occupied by her mother and daddy. Her heart pounded with fear as she listened to them arguing.

"No, Erby. I refuse. I'm not going. I'm absolutely not going."

"Inez, please be reasonable. What else can we do?"

"You go ahead if you must, but I'm staying here with Grace and Mama. I've never been away from them and I'm not leaving them now."

"Honey, how can you not understand? Even though your sister Grace still has her job at the bank, they've cut her salary in half and she told me they'll probably have to cut it even more. And there's always the fear that the bank won't make it; so many have been forced to close. She'll do well to take care of your mother and herself. She can't take care of you and two babies, too."

"Oh, Erby. I just can't go live with those people," Inez cried. "I don't even know them."

"They're my folks, Inez. And they have a place for us. Papa said he'd send the money to get us there." He reached over and put his hand on her cheek. "Listen to me, Inez! We have no choice. We're broke and we have no place to live."

When Betty Lou heard her mother sobbing, she got off her pallet and climbed in between the two of them. Her daddy wrapped his arms around them both, and the three of them clung together through the night.

A day later, the sun was just starting to rise and spread the first rays of light as they climbed into the car parked beside the house, the house which was no longer their home. All they'd been able to save was their car and what few belongings they could cram in around the passengers. Betty Lou sat in a little nest in the back seat among boxes with pots and pans, linens and clothes, a death grip on her doll.

In the front seat, Inez clung to the baby as she looked longingly out the car window at the house she loved. Erby struggled for something comforting to say but could think of nothing that didn't make things worse. He reached over and laid his hand on her shoulder, allowing her a few more minutes for a farewell look before he started the car and turned his eyes to the road ahead.

CHAPTER 3

Erby and his family drove down the narrow ribbon of highway through the parched and barren fields of West Texas. They squinted as strong winds lifted sand from the dry soil and blew it into the cramped car, burning their eyes. Even though they raised the windows, sand still filtered in making it hard to breathe. The heat in the car was almost unbearable and everyone got more and more cross as sweat ran down their necks and backs and dampened their hair. The baby wouldn't stop crying and all the other occupants of the car felt like joining in her chorus with their own screams of protest.

Months had passed since West Texas had been blessed with rain and sandstorms were almost a daily occurrence. On occasion the sand so completely blocked out the sun that it became necessary to turn on electric lights in the middle of the day.

Inez moaned as the wind howled and sand continued to blast their car. "God must really be mad to punish us like this.

It wasn't enough He sent a depression; He had to send the wind and sandstorms, too."

Erby shook his head as he pondered what she'd said. "I don't know whether we can blame God for this depression. I'm afraid men brought that on themselves." Then with a deep frown creasing his forehead he added, "But you could just be right about the sandstorms." Those were the last words they spoke for hours, aware that in this heat tempers could flare over just about anything. There was enough to contend with without that. Erby kept his eyes glued to the road and Inez sat with her back straight, her forehead wrinkled, holding tight to the baby.

After what seemed an eternity, they left the dry flat lands where a barrage of tumbleweeds insistently blew across the road and even the scrubby mesquite seemed to struggle for survival. For hours they had seen no trees, no water, no hills, just mile after mile of flat, colorless land. When the terrain started to roll a little and patches of green began to appear, they felt relief. Clumps of trees could be seen in the distance and the little car crossed an occasional river that still held water, giving them hope that maybe east Texas wasn't going to be so bad after all.

Betty Lou wiggled in her seat and asked for the hundredth time, "How much longer will it be, Daddy?"

The answer always came back the same: "Why don't you take a nap, Betty Lou. We still have a long way to go."

Finally, she did go to sleep, and when she awoke the first signs of sundown were coloring the sky. She glanced out the car window and saw they were passing through a town. "Where are we, Daddy? Are we there yet?"

"Almost. We're in Greenville and in a few more minutes we'll be in Ardis Heights where your grandparents live. So please Honey, just hang on for a few more minutes."

The sun was making its final dip behind the trees in the west when they pulled off the highway on to a gravel road that ran along one side of a large red brick house. The car pulled to a stop before a wire gate that separated the gravel road from the pasture beyond. Erby breathed a deep sigh of relief as he turned off the motor. He had driven more than 400 miles across Texas on narrow, dusty roads and if he'd been merely tired when he left Lubbock, he was beyond exhaustion now.

When she saw the animals on the other side of the gate, Betty Lou seemed to forget how tired she felt. Horses, cows and sheep roamed the pasture, nibbling at the grass. "Daddy, look. Look at all the animals. Let me out. I wont'a see."

"In a minute, Betty Lou. Just let me get my bearings."

He and Inez sat in silence, staring straight ahead. After a few moments he turned to her, reached for her hand and held it in his. "Well, Darlin', here we are, for better or worse." His smile was unconvincing, but at least he was trying. "We better go in before it gets any darker."

She made no attempt to return his smile and he noticed tears starting to roll down her cheeks. Closing her eyes, she whispered, "Erby, I can't move. I feel if I tried to move I would fall into a million pieces."

He realized she was hurting, but he knew of no way to comfort her. Besides, he was too tired to try. He squeezed her hand. "Come on, Inez. We have to go in sometime. We might as well get it over with."

She still didn't move.

Betty Lou's impatient voice came from the back seat again. "Daddy, I want out. Let me out of here." She tried to stand up but was trapped by all the boxes surrounding her.

"Okay. Please wait just one more minute. Then I'll help you out I promise." He removed his hand from Inez's and pleaded once more, "Come on, Inez. Let's go in."

She continued to ignore his plea.

He was trying not to lose his temper, however his patience was growing thin. He opened the car door and got out, reached around the boxes to where Betty Lou struggled and lifted her to the ground.

After all the hours trapped in the car, Betty Lou seemed happy to feel the pleasure of ground beneath her feet. Immediately, she broke loose and ran to peer through the gate, lacing her fingers on the wire as she tried to get a better look at the animals.

Erby walked around to the passenger side of the car, opened the door and took the baby out of Inez's arms. "Please come on, Inez. You've got to get out of the car." This time his voice was more demanding but she continued to sit with her jaws clamped and her hands in tight fists on her lap. Erby's mouth grew tight over his teeth as he fought back anger. To add to his stress, the baby was starting to fret. He stood by the side of the car, holding the fussy baby and staring down at Inez. After a few moments of trying to decide what he should do, he reached in the car and grabbed her arm and pulled. "Come on. Get out."

Tears flowed openly now, as Inez yelled, "No, I'm not getting out. I can't. You don't understand." Then the words he knew she'd been fighting not to say slipped through her lips as she glared at him. "How could you let this happen to us?" As soon as the words escaped, her face turned red. "Oh, Erby, I'm sorry. I didn't mean to say that."

His shoulders sagged under the weight of her accusation. He knew she blamed him. Maybe she was right. Maybe there was something he could have done. He just didn't know what. "Inez, I'm sorry. God knows I'm sorry. I wish I knew what to do, but let's face it, whoever's fault it may be we're trapped. You've got to get out of the car now."

This time she hesitated only a second, then climbed out slowly and searched his eyes. "Erby, I'm so sorry I said that. I didn't mean it."

"That's okay, Inez. I can't blame you for feeling that way."

The sun disappeared rapidly now and darkness was enveloping them. With the baby wiggling in one arm and his other arm around Inez's waist, he started across the gravel road toward the backyard of the house. As he walked, pulling Inez toward an uncertain future, he looked over his shoulder and called to a reluctant Betty Lou who still held tight to the fence that separated her from the animals. "Come on, Honey. It's dark now. You can see horses and cows tomorrow. Tonight you're about to meet our family."

The night air was hot and sticky and mosquitoes swarmed around them as he led the way. Perspiration dripped down his brow and stung his eyes and he thought longingly of how Lubbock's nights cooled off, regardless of how hot it got during the day. Living with Greenville's hot humid nights would be something more for them to try to adjust to.

He kept looking back to make sure Betty Lou was following. In fact, she was running close behind, her eyes searching in all directions. The night was filled with strange, unfamiliar sounds: crickets chirping, locusts buzzing, and somewhere close by an owl hooted.

Light shown through the windows on the back of the house breaking up the darkness enough for them to see their way. Voices could be heard now, coming from inside the house. He stopped walking and looked down at Inez who was still whimpering. "Inez, listen to me. The hardest part is just about over. We've got to put on our brave faces even if we don't feel it."

Wiping her tear-streaked face with the handkerchief he offered, she promised, "I'll try, Erby. I'm sorry I've made everything so hard for you. I know none of this is your fault. I realize you're doing the best you can."

Erby pulled her a little closer. "Things are going to be okay. You'll see." He wished he could believe that was true but he was filled with as much grief and fear as she.

After they climbed the steps to the back stoop they stopped for a few moments, working up their courage before going in. "Let's take deep breaths," Erby suggested and drew the night air deep into his lungs. Then he knocked, opened the door a crack, and stuck his head in before they entered the room.

Surrounding a table on a large enclosed porch, adults and children sat eating their evening meal. Everyone stopped chewing and looked up when Erby and his family came in. Bess Nell, his sister, jumped up from the table and ran to put her arms around him. The other grown-ups rose, one by one, and the next few minutes were filled with hugs and handshakes.

It appeared he and his family weren't the only refugees of this depression. Two of Erby's three brothers and his sister and their families were already living here. The only brother missing was Raymond, a doctor in Amarillo, who was apparently surviving on his own, at least to this point.

Betty Lou tugged at her mother's dress and pointed shyly at the food-laden table. She'd been warned on many occasions it wasn't polite to ask for food at other people's houses, but this was a test she wasn't prepared for. The table was covered with all sorts of wonders: salad, green beans, cornbread, ham and delicious smelling apple pie. All they'd had to eat on the way was peanut butter and jelly sandwiches. In fact, they'd almost lived on peanut butter sandwiches since their stove and refrigerator had been taken away.

Hearing the commotion on the porch, Dandy came out of the kitchen and stood in the doorway wiping beads of perspiration off her forehead with the tail of her apron. "Well, son, you're here." Her voice was flat, without emotion. Her tired blue eyes looked at him through thick frameless glasses. Part of her kinky gray hair was piled up off her neck and secured with hairpins; the rest formed ringlets around her face. She was what one might call of sturdy build, not fat by any means but not thin either. Her posture told a lot about her. Even at almost sixty years of age, and in spite of the heavy load of having all these people to care for, she held herself like a queen, shoulders back, head held high. She had an air about her that suggested nothing would be capable of conquering this woman's spirit. Life's challenges might get her down for a bit, but they would never get her out. She was a force and anyone who'd ever dealt with her could vouch for that.

Erby crossed to where she stood, wrapped his arms around her and kissed her on the cheek. "Hi, Dandy." He took a step back and held her at arms length, studying her for a long moment. "You look hot and tired. Are you still doing all your cooking on that old wood cook stove?" He looked beyond her into the big kitchen, which was just off the sun porch. The fancy electric stove his dad had bought her stood cold and unused against one wall. The same wood cook stove he remembered from his childhood stood on the opposite wall and was fired up, filling the room with unbearable heat.

"As you well know, Erby, I've never been one who likes change," she answered as she looked around the room at the many faces that had invaded her privacy and changed her life.

Obviously Dandy had given up any pretense of hiding her true feelings, if she'd ever been so inclined.

Inez stood nearby holding the baby. After her eyes left Erby, Dandy turned to greet her. Without smiling, she approached her with an outstretched hand. "Hello, Inez. Hope your trip wasn't too uncomfortable." She didn't wait for an answer before turning to kiss the two little girls on their foreheads. She even managed to give them a little smile before she turned back to Erby. "Have ya'll eaten your supper?"

"Afraid not," he answered.

Dandy started issuing orders. "Bess Nell, get some plates and silverware from the kitchen." Then she turned to a little girl who looked about Betty Lou's age. She was sitting at the table with a bite of apple pie half way to her mouth. "Patsy, run upstairs and see if your Papa's home yet. Did anybody see him come in?"

Heads shook around the table.

"Well, I thought I heard his violin playing. Anyway, Patsy, go see if he's here and if so, tell him Erby and his bunch have arrived."

Patsy gave Betty Lou a look out of the corner of her eye as she put down her fork and left her seat at the table. Then she ran out of the room to do as she was told.

"Here, ya'll sit down and have some supper," Bess Nell invited. She motioned for those at the table to move over and make a space. Then she put down plates and silverware and Erby's older brother, Agnew, brought over more chairs.

Once seated, Erby's moral dropped even lower when he took inventory of the large family that crowded around the table. Apparently there wasn't room for them in this house. It was full to overflowing already. He knew the house to have only four bedrooms and apparently they were already occupied. Dandy and Papa would be in their big bedroom at the end of the upstairs hall and Erby assumed that Bess Nell and her family had her old bedroom at the head of the stairs. That left the other bedroom upstairs, the one directly across from the only bathroom in the house, for Agnew and his new wife, Valera. And since his younger brother, Archie, was drunk most of the time, Erby figured that he and his wife, Evelyn, and their little boy would be put in the downstairs bedroom, as far from everyone else as they could get him.

He started to eat but food began to catch in his throat as the reality of the situation hit him and he completely lost his appetite. Obviously, other arrangements would have to be made for his family and he feared they would not be to Inez's liking.

CHAPTER 4

Dr. Swinson was late leaving the office after a particularly trying day. He'd seen too many children dangerously sick because their parents postponed bringing them in for treatment. Emotionally and physically exhausted, he clinched his jaw and gripped the steering wheel of his car tighter. "Damn this depression!" he said aloud as he sped down the highway toward home. As the son of a Baptist mother he wasn't inclined to cuss under ordinary circumstances, but sometimes a person needed strong words to express strong feelings and this was one of those times. This depression was doing more than harming people's spirits. It was ruining their health as well. Most people were too proud to ask for help they couldn't pay for, so day after day, week after week, people who'd waited too long for treatment filled his waiting room. To make matters worse for him, they insisted on paying with jars of homemade jellies and home-canned vegetables, or occasionally a chicken or a pig. He hated taking their food, knowing they needed it much more than he did. But he couldn't refuse. His refusal would do more harm to their already damaged pride. And even though he knew the Bible teaches pride is a sin, he had to wonder if people didn't need to hold on to a little.

When he pulled into his driveway, he turned off the motor but didn't get out of the car right away. Voices traveled out the open windows of his house and he knew the family was gathering on the sun porch for supper. If he entered the house by the back door as he usually did, he'd be expected to visit. He loved his family, but today he just wasn't ready for the transition from "Doctor Swinson" to "Papa". All he wanted was some time alone, to play his fiddle and try to forget about the desperate people who'd filled his day.

After he left the car he strode toward the front porch of the house and up the steps. The front door opened directly into the seldom used living room and Dandy had an unwritten law that no one was to use that door except on special occasions. Rarely did anyone dare to challenge her rules, not even him. But today, he wasn't in any mood to follow anybody's rules, not even Dandy's. Still he was careful to be quiet so he could get in the house undetected. Once inside, he tiptoed up the stairs to his bedroom and quickly closed the door and locked it.

A deep sigh of relief escaped him at having successfully sneaked in and he felt an immediate release of tension as he stripped off his coat and tie and ripped off the stiff celluloid collar that imprisoned his neck. Standing in his shirtsleeves, suspenders holding up his baggy trousers, he stretched his neck and shoulders before crossing to the table where his fiddle lay in its case. He lifted the lid and stood over it, looking down at it admiringly before taking it in his hands. Worries soon slipped away when he picked up his bow and started to play.

So absorbed in his music was he that he wasn't sure he heard the first knock at the door, but there could be no doubt about the second. "God knows, am I never to have any peace in my own home again?" He grumbled as he stomped to answer the knock. Holding his fiddle in one hand and the bow in the other, he stood for a second and pondered whether to open the door at all. But at the sound of another insistent knock he gave up, unlocked the door and opened it a crack. His frown faded when he looked down and saw Patsy. She was standing in the hall, letting her eyes roam and shifting her weight from one foot to the other while she waited.

"Patsy," he said, attempting to turn the corners of his mouth up, "What do you want, Dear?"

"Dandy said to come tell you that Erby and his family are here."

"My Lord!" he said, the frown returning to his face.

"Papa, don't say 'My Lord'. You know Dandy doesn't like it when you take the Lord's name in vain."

"I'm sorry, Patsy. I wasn't taking His name in vain. It was more like a prayer," he said, rolling his eyes to the ceiling. He had forgotten that Erby was due to arrive today. Resigned to his fate, he looked down at her and said, "Okay, Patsy. Go back downstairs and tell Dandy I'll be there in a minute." He closed the door, grumbling to himself and continued to grumble under his breath as he returned his fiddle to its case and slammed the lid closed impatiently.

Patsy turned immediately and raced back down the stairs. "He's coming," she said as she plopped back into her seat at the table, grabbed her fork and crammed a big bite of apple pie into her mouth. She glanced up as she chewed and exchanged looks with Betty Lou, who sat across the table from her now; but both appeared to be more interested in the pie than in each other at the moment.

* * *

When Papa entered the porch a few minutes later he found the family at the supper table sharing some of the experiences that brought them here. Conversation stopped abruptly and all eyes focused on him.

Erby was shocked to see how much his dad had aged since he last saw him. Even though he'd lost most of his hair at an early age, keeping only a fringe encircling the dome of his head, his dad's powerful presence had always made him appear much younger than he actually was. Now, to Erby's dismay, he looked smaller, shrunken. His eyes drooped with weariness behind his wire-framed glasses and his carriage was that of an old man, his shoulders bent forward as if he carried the weight of the world on him. Erby and Inez both rose to their feet and waited and watched as he extended his hand and walked toward them.

"Son," Papa whispered, a smile creasing his face and crinkling his eyes. Erby smiled back and reached out to take his hand, but when they got close enough, they grabbed each other and embraced in a bear hug. They clung together a few moments and when they released their hold their cheeks were moist with tears.

After greeting Inez with a hug, Papa cast his eyes on Betty Lou who stood shyly by her mother's side looking up at him. "Well now, you must be Betty Lou," he said bending down to kiss her on the cheek. He gave her a soft pat on her head then stroked the head of the baby Inez held in her arms before turning back to focus on Erby.

Looking around at all those present, Erby grinned and said, "So -- appears all your chickens have come home to roost, huh?" The room went quiet at this attempt at joviality. Obviously no one here had a sense of humor about their predicament.

Papa wrinkled his forehead and lifted his eyebrows as he looked around the table at his children and grandchildren. "Yeah, it would appear so." Making no further comment, he asked, "Have you finished your supper?"

"Yes sir, I have, thank you."

"Then come with me. We need to talk."

As Erby marched out of the room behind his dad, he glanced back at Inez and threw her a worried look. He followed through the dark hall that housed the staircase leading to the second floor and they were soon in the living room. A large room, it stretched across the entire front of the house. It was formal, but comfortable. On the walls were numerous paintings done by Dandy. They pictured tranquil country settings, farmhouses, ponds, trees and animals grazing in pastures. Her baby-grand piano and a large red brick fireplace occupied one end of the room. Floor to ceiling bookcases that housed Papa's medical books covered the wall at the opposite end and in the center sat large overstuffed furniture with carved woods, elaborate brocades and velvets. Heavy drapes covered the windows on three sides and were always closed except on special occasions, keeping the room in semi-darkness the rest of the time.

"Sit, please," Papa said, waving to a loveseat across the coffee table from the chair and ottoman he chose for himself. After he settled into his chair he rubbed both hands over his bald head as if to straighten hair that was no longer there, a habit the family had learned signaled he was perplexed. As if to delay what he must tell Erby, he removed his handkerchief from his pocket and slowly and deliberately cleaned his eyeglasses before replacing them on his nose. Then he leaned back in his chair and closed his eyes. When he opened them again he looked directly at Erby who sat on the edge of his seat anxiously waiting.

"I'm sorry that you've been forced to ask for help, Erby. No doubt that was hard for you. You were always my most independent son."

Erby shifted his weight trying to find a more comfortable position for his tired body before nodding in agreement. "Yes, it was. Very hard."

"Would you like to tell me what happened to ya'll? You didn't tell me much over the telephone."

Erby dropped his eyes to stare at his hands which lay palms up in his lap. "Where do I start? For a while it seemed

I was one of the lucky ones. My job at the cotton compress lasted longer than most people's; even though I was forced to take several cuts in salary. I watched as my office of six people dwindled until I was the only one left. As I'm sure you know, the demand for cotton around the world just disappeared. Farmers weren't able to sell their cotton crops and many of them around the country, who'd done well in the past, lost their farms. Finally, the compress had to close its doors." A groan escaped him as he thought about it. "When that happened thousands of people were affected. The waves rippled out everywhere, not just in West Texas, you felt it here in Greenville too. The depression was taking its toll on everything. I found myself among the millions of jobless struggling to keep their heads above water. We held on for a while, living on our savings. When those ran out we lost everything. We owed money on too many things we'd bought on credit." Erby shrugged, his eyes revealing his total despair. "That's about it. So here we are. I don't know what we're going to do. Sponge off you I guess until I can find something." When he finished speaking, an uneasy silence fell between them.

Papa twisted in his chair and rubbed his chin. He could delay it no longer. "I didn't want to tell you this on the telephone. I knew you must really need to come home or you wouldn't have asked. But as you can see a lot of the others got here before you."

Erby feared hearing what was to come next.

"There's just no more room in this house. I hate to do this to you, especially to Inez, but there's no place else except the little house I have for farmhands on the other side of the vacant lot next door. It's been empty quiet a while. You gave me such short notice I didn't have a chance to do any fixin' up. I'm afraid it isn't in very good repair but I'll do what I can to make it livable for you." His eyes drifted away from Erby as he continued. "The thing is there's no electricity or plumbing in the house and even the outhouse is pretty crude. I'm sorry, Son," He added shaking his head.

Their eyes locked and Erby manage to say, "Don't worry Papa. We'll be okay." He was determined not to show his disappointment. His dad was doing his best for them. But something caught in his throat and it wouldn't come up or go down. The hardest part was yet to come. How was he going to tell Inez that he'd dragged her away from everything she knew and loved to live in a rundown farmhand's house with kerosene lanterns, no running water and a dilapidated outhouse.

CHAPTER 5

Inez welcomed the sound of roosters crowing, announcing dawn had come at last. No longer would she have to battle the long, hot night and the struggle of trying to sleep on a pallet on the sun porch floor. Erby had opened all the windows trying to coax in a breeze, but none came and they'd continued to sweat as the air hung heavy and wet. Adding to the misery, flies buzzed around their heads, lighting on their eyelids and mouths. She'd spent the night tossing and turning and longing for the soft bed they'd had in Lubbock.

As she and Erby rose and dressed they could hear Dandy already in the kitchen rattling pots and pans. Shortly, the crackling of fire in the wood cook stove could be heard and the wonderful smells of bacon frying and biscuits baking floated throughout the house. As if signaled by the aroma, the family started to appear on the porch and after nodding greetings; they took their places and sat silent at the table.

Inez couldn't understand why no one was in the kitchen helping Dandy and after a few moments she said to no one in particular, "I think I'll go see if Mrs. Swinson needs any help."

Valera, Agnew's wife, grabbed her arm as she passed and shook her head. "Don't go in there while she's fixing breakfast. You'll be sorry." She added in a whisper, "You'll soon learn the rules."

Inez looked puzzled but took a seat at the table and waited with everyone else for the scrambled eggs, grits, and homemade peach preserves that were soon to be served with the bacon and biscuits. She observed that the rules for entering the kitchen must change after breakfast, because when the other women finished eating, they cleared the table, and went to the kitchen for cleanup. Afraid of breaking another unknown rule, Inez glanced at Erby and shook her head, then decided to remain in her seat and wait for further instructions.

Before long Dandy came in from the kitchen untying her apron and laying it across the back of a chair. "Well, Erby, if ya'll have finished your breakfast, I'll take you over to see the little house you're gonna be living in for a while."

They accepted Bess Nell's offer to take care of the baby and holding Betty Lou's hand, they followed Dandy out the back door. As they walked their sweating bodies seemed to issue an invitation to every gnat and mosquito in the area and they swatted at insects as they made their way through the backyard. Dandy charged across the gravel road they'd come in on the night before and they hurried to keep up with her. Soon they found themselves on a narrow dirt path that meandered through knee high weeds and led across the vacant lot that separated the big house from what was to be their new home.

When they'd arrived the night before, it had been too dark for them to take in the surrounding area, but now they could see across the highway to the rutted fields that had once been home to rows of cotton. The naked stalks that remained stood as reminders of the demise of the cotton market. Except for Dandy and Papa's house, all the buildings and houses they could see were in great need of repair. In every direction, signs of economic disaster hung like a storm cloud.

The glint of the morning sun bouncing off the corrugated tin roof of a little box of a house soon caught their eyes. Sitting in the middle of a yard grown high with weeds, it was the picture of neglect. Grayed boards were mostly bare of the white paint that had graced it in some long ago past. Dilapidated steps led up to the front porch where a number of boards were broken and some totally missing.

"Be careful," Erby warned as he took Inez and Betty Lou's hands and guided them across the porch to the front door. "Watch out, Dandy" he said as he turned back to offer his help to her. She shrugged and shook her head and hastened across the porch on her own.

Erby forced open the stuck front door and they entered a small musty-smelling room with two narrow windows and well-worn board floors. Torn paper shades over the windows filtered out sunlight adding to the gloom in the room. Traces of faded flowers and vines were barely visible on the stained and torn wallpaper that attempted to cover the walls. The only object in the room was a blackened potbellied woodstove that occupied one corner.

Inez was determined to keep her composure as she observed all this. Biting her lip, she had managed not to comment up to this point, but she looked up pleadingly at Erby, as if begging him to do something. Anything!

Helpless to know what to do, he masked his feelings with an unconvincing smile and reached for her hand, but she jerked it away and bit her lip harder as the tears behind her eyes pushed relentlessly for release.

The rest of the house consisted of two small bedrooms and a bare kitchen with no cabinets. A single faucet protruded from the wall and connected to a ten-foot tall metal tank that nestled up to the outside of the house and caught rainwater. An enameled tin dishpan replaced a sink and sat on a bare table under the faucet. Inez could see clearly that life here was going to be bare survival. She still had not spoken since entering the house, but now as she looked around this room that was to be her kitchen, her resolve disappeared. Her voice came out high and thin. "There are no cabinets in this kitchen. Where am I supposed to keep the things I need?"

With no further explanation Dandy crossed the kitchen and opened a door that led into a small room. "The pantry," she answered.

Inez was not consoled by the bare bones room where no paint had ever graced the shelves that lined one wall. She felt her face turning red.

Observing Inez's reaction to all this, Erby needed fresh air. He opened the back door and stepped out on a small stoop where an abandoned wooden icebox stood next to a large galvanized washtub hanging on a nail.

Inez followed and when she saw the tub she stopped and stared. She remembered when she was growing up and a tub like this had acted as her family's bathtub. It was at this point that she gave up what little hope she had of a bathroom in this house. She remembered the night before when Dandy appeared on the porch with a chamber pot for their use, she had commented to Erby how inconvenient it must be for eleven people to have to share the one upstairs bathroom. Now when compared to no bathroom at all, it suddenly seemed a luxury. In the blink of an eye, all of the things they'd considered to be necessities were now luxuries.

Inez stood in the middle of the bare room and put her hands to her forehead as the flashing lights that preceded a migraine began to appear. In the past, when she saw the signs that announced these attacks, she would call her mother to come take care of the children. Then she'd go to bed in a darkened room and be alone in her misery. Now she had no place to hide away. No mother to call. At this point, she didn't even have a bed of her own. In the less than twenty-four hours they'd been here, Ardis Heights had become an enemy camp. She felt robbed of all her defenses. Unable to contain herself any longer, she burst into uncontrolled sobbing.

Totally at a loss, Erby went to Inez and tried to embrace her, but she pulled back and snapped at him, "Don't touch me. Please, don't touch me! Just leave me alone!" When Inez rebuked his attempts, he stepped back into the kitchen to try to comfort Dandy. who stood looking through the screen door at Inez with disgust. She too brushed him aside, throwing up her hands and shouting, "What do you expect me to do? I'm too exhausted to deal with all these unhappy, displaced people." She looked skyward and pleaded, "*God, please help me. This is more than I can handle.*" With that she started to cry.

Shaking his head in a gesture of total frustration and impotence, Erby pulled his handkerchief from his pocket, wiped the perspiration off his face and swatted at a fly that buzzed around his nose. Then he looked down at Betty Lou, who stood nearby trying to understand what was happening. He took her hand in his and glanced one more time at Inez, then at his mother. "Don't worry. It'll be okay, Honey. Come on," he said, and the two of them turned and walked out the back door and down the path toward the big house without looking back. As they slowly made their escape, he said under his breath, to himself and not to her, "I've never had such a need for oblivion. I have to find Archie. This is definitely cause for a good stiff drink and he'll know where to get one."

CHAPTER 6

Inez put down the broom she'd been using to sweep the bare floor and dropped into a chair at the kitchen table that filled most of the small square room. Her eyes were fixed on the only window. It framed the barbed wire fence that separated their yard from the yard of the neighbor's next door. The barbed wire heightened her sense of being in a prison. She sat with her hands folded together, her eyes roaming the room, taking in every aspect of her present surroundings. Then she laughed a bitter laugh. The things happening to her life were so ironic. Here she was, back to a place she had fought so hard to escape. In spite of all her promises to herself, all her protests, her life had come full circle.

She had few memories of her father. A conductor on the Santa Fe railroad, he was gone weeks at a time. On many occasions, he would come home from a trip to find an empty house, no note and no one to tell him where his wife and three children were. Tracking them down was not an easy feat as no telephones and few cars existed in west Texas at that time.

Since Inez's mother Eliza was one of eleven children, she had many brothers, sisters, and cousins who welcomed them. In those days, people were accustomed to having relatives come for long visits. They would stay one place for a while and then move on to another. Often when her daddy would find them at last, her mother would refuse to come home with him. In desperation, he'd go to Inez's grandmother. "Please, Mrs. Ezra, make Eliza come home."

Her answer was always the same. "I'm sorry, Mr. Egan. But nobody has ever been able to make Eliza do anything she doesn't want to do. She's always gone her own way."

Proving this to be true, when Inez was six years old, her mother did a scandalous thing. At a time when women didn't consider divorce as an option, her mother divorced her daddy, an act that ostracized them all from "proper society".

Inez still felt a jab in the pit of her stomach when she remembered the day she had gone to visit one of her school friends after the divorce. When her friend's mother saw them playing together, she asked, as if Inez weren't standing right there, "Isn't she one of those Egan girls whose mother is divorced?"

"Yes, Mama, this is Inez Egan. She sits next to me at school."

"Well, you just tell Inez Egan to run along home. She isn't welcome here. I don't want you playing with children whose mothers are divorced."

Besides the pain of being a child of divorce, she only saw her daddy a few more times after the breakup. The last time, when she was visiting him in his new place, a large bowl of apples and oranges sat on his kitchen table. Fruit was a rare delicacy in her life. When her daddy noticed her staring at the fruit bowl he frowned. "Inez, while you're here you can have all the fruit you want, but when you leave you can't take any to your mother." Even now when she thought of him, she could see him standing in the middle of the kitchen, his hands on his hips, saying those words. Strange the things we select to remember from our childhood, she thought. Not long after that he was killed in an accident on the railroad.

The divorce put an end to their many visits to relatives. From that time on her mother bent over a pedal sewing machine from early morning till late at night, sewing clothes for others in order to support her three children. They'd always had a roof over their heads and food to eat, but there was no money for extras. In fact, they'd lived in circumstances very much the same as she found herself in now: a small frame box of a house with kerosene lanterns, a wood stove, an outhouse and a washtub like the one on this back stoop for bathing.

By the time she was 16, and could pass for 18, they'd moved from Big Springs to Lubbock where her mother hoped to have a larger clientele. Inez got a job as a telegraph operator and when she started making her own money, she didn't have to wear her sister's hand-me-down clothes anymore. She delighted in wearing the latest fashions and having her hair hennaed and arranged in the deep waves that were the style of the day. When she had enough money saved, she moved out of her mother's house and into an apartment with an indoor bathroom and electric lights. She'd sworn to herself that she would never again be denied these comforts and before long she forgot the hardships of her youth and took for granted living in a certain style. After she married Erby, life became even better. It never occurred to her that everything would all be ripped away one day.

Her attention returned to her present surroundings and she allowed herself to sink farther into self-pity. Over the last few years she'd become something of an expert at feeling sorry for herself; however when she heard the sound of footsteps approaching, she knew that today there would be little time for it. She looked up to see Erby coming up the steps of the back stoop, carrying an armload of logs for the cook stove. Quickly, before he could see that she had been crying, she tried to wipe away her tears, jumped up, grabbed the broom and started to sweep the floor again.

"Hi, Honey. What have we got to eat? I'm starved." He dropped the logs on the floor by the stove, pushed his shoulder blades together and stretched his back. Then he noticed the tearstains on her face and hurried to her, grabbed the broom and forced her to stop sweeping. His arms encircled her waist, and he nuzzled her neck. "Inez, please don't be so unhappy. This is all temporary. We won't have to live here long, I promise."

Inez pulled away and gave him a woeful glance over her shoulder as she started to sweep again, this time more vigorously. "I know," she lied, fearing that to be untrue.

"I admit this certainly isn't the Ritz, but we are blessed with privacy here. How'd you like to live over in the big house with the rest of the family?"

Inez didn't want to smile but she couldn't help it. "That's true. Guess there's always something to be grateful for if you look hard enough!"

"And you've got to admit, this place is beginning to be more livable every day," he said as he surveyed the progress they'd made. The wooden icebox they'd found on the back porch now stood against one wall of the kitchen. It housed ice in the top section and milk, eggs, and other food, donated by Dandy, were in the lower section. He had cleaned up the old rusted wood cook stove and made it useable again, and a freshly painted cupboard that Dandy found in her storage shed gave Inez a place to keep her dishes.

She was sorry but she couldn't get excited by these crude replacements for her beautiful kitchen in Lubbock and her smile quickly disappeared. She continued to sweep while Erby watched for a moment. He reached out and took her broom again. "Inez, please stop and look at me. We have each other, we have our girls and we still have things to be thankful for."

Inez managed a half smile. "Okay. You're right, Erby." Then in a moment of self awareness she said, "I'll try not to be such a spoiled brat."

They both laughed at her confession and he pulled her to him.

Hearing a noise coming from the back steps, she looked over his shoulder to see Dandy coming through the back door carrying a small table she'd found somewhere. She'd been dragging in miscellaneous pieces of furniture all week -- some of it wanted, some not. She never knocked, just barged through the door without warning.

Without so much as a hello, she marched through the kitchen, "Thought ya'll might have a place for this," she said as she headed toward the living room and set it down next to an old wooden rocking-chair she'd hauled in the day before.

Inez looked at Erby, rolled her eyes and whispered, "Did you say, 'we're blessed with privacy here?'"

He raised his eyebrows and looked at her with wide eyes but made no comment.

Returning to the kitchen where Inez and Erby stood unmoving, giving each other a "what's next?" look, Dandy stopped and took in the room. "Well now, looks like things are beginning to take shape around here. I think by next week you'll be ready to start helping in the garden, Inez. There's always so much to do there, and then of course there's the canning." She looked at Erby and continued. "And I'm sure your brothers will be glad to have another helping hand with the farm chores. Why don't ya'll plan on starting right after breakfast Monday? Just be over at the big house no later than seven." She hesitated while she considered. "Or maybe you better make it a little earlier, Erby. There's the milking to be done and Preacher has a hard time handling it."

She looked at Betty Lou, who sat on the floor with crayolas and a coloring book and then at baby Gloria, who sat nearby in her highchair. She smiled at them, then turned and left without another word.

After she'd gone, Inez turned to Erby, her hands stretched in front of her palms up. In a voice filled with apprehension she said, "I don't know anything about working in a garden, and I know less about canning."

Erby's look of concern equaled hers. "And we lived in town when I was growing up. I've never milked a cow in my life."

*   *   *

Betty Lou sat on the floor of the kitchen, trying hard to stay in the lines of her coloring book, as she'd been instructed. At the same time she eavesdropped on her parents. She could tell that they didn't like this house; however she didn't mind it. It was nice to have a bed again and not to have to sleep on the floor at Dandy's.

There were lots of new things to get used to. She'd never lived in a house without electricity before and she was constantly being warned about the danger of getting burned by, or knocking over, the kerosene lanterns. Without electricity, she couldn't listen to the radio and she knew her mother missed the soap operas she used to listen to everyday.

Not having a bathroom was a mixed blessing. The good part was she only had to take a bath and get her hair washed on Saturdays. The bad part was the dreaded outhouse that sat in a grove of trees at the end of the long dirt path. It was a scary place. She hated sitting on the dark hole with her bare bottom exposed to all the possible terrible things that could be hiding in the black pit below. Yes, she thought, some things about the new house and most of her new life she didn't mind so much; some things she even liked --like the chinaberry tree in the back yard she could climb, and having cousins to play with was nice, but the outhouse -- that would take a lot of getting use to.

CHAPTER 7

"Inez. Open the door. Hurry!" Erby urged as he carried the large block of dripping ice up the back steps.

She ran to comply and stood out of the way as he rushed into the kitchen to deliver his heavy load into the top of the icebox. "Man, I don't look forward to having to do this every few days. I remember when I was a kid and we lived in town, our ice was delivered. I used to watch the iceman drive up to our house in his horse drawn wagon. He'd park in front, pick up a big block of ice with his tongs and throw it on his shoulder. Then he'd bring it right into the house and deposit it in the icebox. I guess people who live in town and don't have refrigerators still get that service, but living out here, looks like one of my new titles is going to be 'iceman', as well as 'cowmilker' -- and who knows what else." He dried his cold wet hands on a cup towel lying nearby and sat down at the kitchen table. "Any coffee left?"

Inez picked up the percolator sitting on the back of the wood stove and shook it. "A little. Might be pretty strong. It's been sitting a while." She poured coffee into a cup then joined him at the table. "How'd you find things in town? Lots of changes since you were here last?"

"God, Inez. You wouldn't believe how different Greenville is from Lubbock. I've rarely been back here since I ran away and joined the navy when I was sixteen." He shook his head and looked into the black liquid in his coffee cup as he reflected. "Talk about a dumb thing to do. Did it to get even I guess. I thought my mother didn't care anything about us boys once my sister was born. I was jealous. A trait that seems to run in this family. Not an admirable one, I might add."

"Is that why you moved to Lubbock instead of coming back here after the war? Because you were angry at your mother?"

"I don't know. Don't think so. I'd grown up. Lubbock was more of an adventure. It was on the move, newer, more progressive. I was anxious to embrace new things. Greenville's stuck in another time."

"How so?"

"To this day, people in Greenville have never conceded that the South lost the Civil War. When I was a kid I was taught that anyone who fought for the 'North' was a 'damnyankee'. I get the feeling that even today, if a 'damnyankee' is in these parts, he better work on his southern drawl and learn to say 'much obliged' instead of 'thank you', or else you can be assured once recognized he'll be ostracized."

"That's probably true of most of Texas." she said.

"Yeah, but more so here. I learned in high school that before the Civil War the population in Greenville was a little over six thousand whites and there were almost an equal number of slaves. I sense that a lot of the people around here still think of coloreds as slaves. This town is clinging to the past. As I drove through town this morning, reminders were everywhere that the Civil War is still very much alive here."

"Like what for instance?"

"For one thing, most of the streets are named after southern heroes of the War. And that sign is still hanging over Lee Street as you come into town: GREENVILLE, TEXAS, THE BLACKEST LAND AND THE WHITEST PEOPLE. That sign was there the whole time I was growing up. I guess I can't argue that the land is black, but as I drove through town I saw more black faces than white ones."

"There's actually a sign saying that?"

"Sure is. Guess I shouldn't be surprised it's still hanging there. Don't know why it hit me like that. Maybe because in Lubbock there aren't many black people. Never thought about it till this morning but the population there is mostly white. Just a smattering of Mexicans who come in to pick cotton and help with the harvest but most don't stay. The Civil War was long past when Lubbock was founded, so since slavery never existed there it wasn't ever an issue. People there focused on wheat and cotton, land and cattle, and didn't think much about blacks and whites."

He didn't say anything more for a few minutes as he sipped his coffee and was obviously lost in thought. "And there were plenty of reminders of what the depression has done here, too. On my way into town I passed the cotton compress. Used to be a busy place. Now it's closed down and I could see equipment rusting in the side yard.

When I drove pass the First National Bank Building, a bunch of white men were lined up against the railing that faces Lee Street. They looked so forlorn, smoking hand rolled cigarettes, chewing tobacco, and just standing there, spitting on the sidewalk. Brings the reality of this depression home when you see so many men idle, with no jobs and no place to go. Reminded me that although my life seems pretty rough right now, at least I don't have to stand on a street corner all day. Farm work doesn't seem so bad after that. At least it's something to do."

"What's happened to this world?" Inez said as she let out a breath and got up from the table. Still shaking her head in dismay, she crossed the room to start dinner.

He looked down at his folded hands and continued in a low voice, "Then there were the colored men standing around the courthouse lawn across the street from the men at the bank. The Courthouse seems a likely place for them to gather as it's one of the few places in town that offers a drinking fountain and a restroom marked 'Coloreds'. These stand next to a drinking fountain and restrooms marked "Whites only", and they mean exactly that. Even as a kid I wondered how black people managed when they weren't near the courthouse or the bus or train station, the only other places in town with facilities for coloreds. I recall that once when I asked my mother what they did when they needed to go to the bathroom and couldn't use the 'Whites only', her answer was 'Never thought about it.' Then she'd gone on with her needle work, the question immediately forgotten. That was probably pretty typical."

He continued thoughtfully, "Certain things are still obvious. Most white people around here are only concerned that the niggers know their place. And the niggers understand what 'staying in their place' requires. Black men are never to look directly at a white woman and coloreds of both sexes know to always address anyone with white skin as Mr. or Miss, regardless of age. And unless they're there to serve, they are not to enter white schools, restaurants or hotels. Seventy something years since the Civil War and slave mentality is still very much alive here."

Inez glanced at him from across the room where she stood rolling out biscuit dough. "You're really upset aren't you, Erby? You should see the look on your face. I don't understand. This isn't something new. You grew up here and it's been going on for a very long time. Why is it affecting you so much now?"

"I don't know. Maybe because of what's happened to us." He frowned and scratched his head. "I think what got to me the most was the incident I witnessed at the ice house."

"What was that?"

"When I drove up, there was a young white guy standing on the sidewalk below the dock watching this elderly gray haired colored man creep down the steps balancing a large block of ice on his shoulder. The guy was yelling at the old man, 'Hurry up there, boy. I don't have all day.' The old black man apologized and stumbled when he tried to hurry. I wanted to hit that white guy. I know now how it feels to be the underdog."

CHAPTER 8

The shabbily dressed men loitering around the parking lot of Watson's grocery store watched with hollow eyes as Erby turned the crank on the front of his Model T Ford. He could feel those eyes watching his every move and for some inexplicable reason he felt embarrassed -- or guilty -- he didn't know which. When he heard the motor catch he raced around the fender of the car and hopped into the driver's seat, pulled out the choke on the dashboard, pumping the foot feed until the motor coughed and then whirred. Pressing his left foot on the clutch, he put the car into gear and it slowly jerked out of the parking place. As he pulled away he raised his hand and gave the men a slight wave, touching the tip of his hat. Smiles were not exchanged, just slight nods of their heads. Erby felt sick. These men were the boys he'd grown up with, gone to school with, played games with. Some of them had owned successful businesses, others had been on the ladder to promising careers, all had had jobs.

As he drove down Lee Street he turned to look at Dandy who sat in the passenger's seat, her eyes fixed, staring neither right nor left. Her jaws were locked with tension and her body was upright and stiff. She was obviously very upset but there was nothing he could say. What her eyes had seen said it all. Erby allowed the silence between them to continue on the drive back to Ardis Heights.

Besides milking cows and carrying ice, another job Erby had acquired since arriving in Ardis Heights was driving to town for necessities not produced on the farm: flour, baking powder, cornmeal and things such as soap, toilet paper, toothbrushes and sometimes a coloring book for the children. Also there was usually a long list of farm needs. He welcomed this excuse to get away from the farm chores which he hated with a passion.

Since Dandy hadn't been into town in quite a long time except to go to church on Sundays, she decided to accompany him today. There were a few personal things she needed to purchase herself. Their errands took them on some of the back streets she hadn't frequented in a long time and she was not prepared for what she saw.

When the car returned to the farm and pulled into the driveway it was late morning. The singing of locusts greeted them, indicating all was well in the locust's world, and the picture of tranquility painted by the sights and sounds that surrounded the farmhouse gave the false impression that all was well in the human world as well. If only that were so, Erby thought as he unloaded the purchases from the car and began to carry them toward the house.

Dandy remained seated in the car, her jaws still clinched. After several minutes lost in thought, she climbed out and slowly walked toward the back door, watching her feet move one in front of the other as if she had never seen them before.

Bess Nell had just left the children in the back yard to play and returned to the kitchen to have a glass of iced tea and wait for instructions before starting the noon meal. When she saw Dandy walk through the door, she was immediately alerted. "Dandy, what's wrong? You're white as a sheet. Are you sick?" When she saw the distress in her eyes, she became more alarmed. "What's wrong? What's happened?"

"Oh Sister, you won't believe what we saw in town. There was a long line of people outside the Salvation Army and it wasn't just colored people, most were white. All those people were waiting in line just to get soup and bread."

"Dandy, where have you been? That's been happening for a long time now."

"Well it's the first time I've seen it. I knew things were bad in other places but I never thought I'd see such a thing in Greenville. I saw people I've known all their lives in that line. Whole families. People from good families. I couldn't believe it when I saw Mr. Thomas and his family. He was the manager at the cotton compress for years. Mrs. Butler whose father owned the insurance office and old Mrs. Curtis who was in my china painting class were all standing in that line waiting for food. I tell you it was a shock. And they wouldn't look at me.

They pretended not to see me. It was as if they were ashamed. I felt so embarrassed for them I had to look away."

Bess Nell looked at her mother with disbelief. "Haven't you been listening to us? What do you think we're all doing here? If we hadn't come here we'd be standing in one of those lines ourselves, living in our car or who knows what. In fact before we came here we *were* standing in one of those lines." Exasperated, Bess Nell dropped into a nearby kitchen chair, suddenly too exhausted to stand another minute. She stared at the kitchen table and said, "Every week at least one young man is knocking on this back door asking for food. And you feed them. Where do you think they come from? There are literally millions of young men, boys really, as young as 16, who are roaming the country, riding box cars and living in hobo jungles, looking for work and food, just trying to stay alive. How can you *not* be aware of the suffering that's going on around us?"

Dandy stood motionless. She was so taken back by this outburst from Bess Nell that she could think of nothing to say to defend herself. It was asking too much for her to apologize and admit she'd been guilty of thinking only about what this depression was doing to her life; however, she silently vowed that from now on she would be nicer, more considerate of the terrible experiences that had brought all her children here.

*   *   *

Erby spent the rest of the afternoon unloading and storing away the farm supplies he'd purchased in town. He was in the backyard of the big house getting ready to go home when the rest of the men came in from the fields. Even before they arrived at the back door they were greeted with the nauseating aroma of mutton cooking. They looked at each other and made faces. Try as they may they'd never been able to develop a taste for sheep, but one had recently been slaughtered and now – unfortunately -- must be eaten. Erby grinned at them as he waved goodbye and walked down the dirt path that led to his own back porch. The smell of mutton cooking made him grateful that Inez did most of the cooking for his little family.

"Hi, Hon," he said as he entered the kitchen and as was his habit, gave her a pinch on the bottom and a kiss on the neck. He had learned not to ask what kind of day she'd had but she didn't wait to be asked.

"What in the world's gotten into your mother?"

"I don't know. What do you mean?"

"It was 'honey, please do this' and 'honey, would you mind doing that?' all afternoon. In all the time we've been here 'honey' and 'please' are not words she's often spoken to me. And I didn't have to go begging for milk. She actually brought milk over here, 'in case we might be out', she said. She even knocked at the back door and called my name before she came in. It's almost scary she's being so nice."

"Hmmm. That is interesting. I think maybe it has something to do with what Sister said to her when we came in from town today. When Dandy told her how upset she was by the soup line she saw in town, I overheard Bess Nell's reply. She couldn't believe Dandy had so little understanding of how desperate we all had to be to come back here to live off them."

"Good for Bess Nell. Let's pray the 'good Dandy' sticks around for awhile."

Erby took off his hat and laid it on the kitchen table. As he washed his hands under the faucet across the room, he thought back on the trip to town this morning. "You know Inez, it is upsetting to go into town and see what's happening to all the people we've grown up with."

"Oh Erby, will this nightmare ever end? Will people ever get their lives back?"

Not wanting to worry her with all the bad things he'd been hearing lately, he remained quiet. Their two little girls were playing on the kitchen floor and as he looked down at them he wondered if there would even be any schools left by the time they were ready to start. People couldn't pay taxes so there wasn't any revenue for schools. He'd read in the Greenville Herald that some places had shortened school terms to five months and others had cut back to three days a week. Teacher's salaries had been cut to the point that some didn't have enough to eat and were fainting in class because they were malnourished. *"When will this nightmare end?"* Inez's question was one everyone was asking.

Her voice interrupted his thoughts and brought him back to the kitchen. "Erby, this is the third time I've said it. Supper's ready."

"Sorry," he said and reached down and removed his hat from the kitchen table and hung it on the hook by the back door. He didn't want to share all his concerns with Inez. He'd said too much already and her life was challenged enough. Smelling the good aroma of beef stew as he headed for the table, he smiled and said, "Well, there are a couple of bright spots in our lives at the moment. Dandy's on her best behavior and we don't have to eat mutton for supper."

1933

CHAPTER 9

Today it seemed everyone in Hunt County was sick. Finally, Papa saw the last patient, said goodnight to Mildred and slipped out the back door, exhausted. His steps were slow as he forced his tired body down the darkening hall to the elevators, pushed the down button and fought impatience as he waited.

When the door opened, Joe, the elevator operator, moved back to allow him to enter.

"Hello, Joe," he greeted him as he stepped inside.

Joe nodded, but kept his gaze lowered.

Concerned, he looked Joe over, then asked, "What's going on, Joe? You don't seem your usual cheery self today."

"Well, now that yo' ask, I'ze worried today. My grandson that live with us is bad sick and my wife and I ain't had no sleep for several nights."

"What seems to be his trouble?"

"He awful hot and he jest cries all a time and holds on to his ear."

"Sounds like he must have an ear infection. You can't let that go on. You have your wife bring him to see me first thing in the morning. I'll be here by eight." Then he stopped to think of the consequences. "Uhhh, now Joe, you know how things are around here. I'm sorry but I can't have you bring him into the reception room with the white patients. I'll leave the back door unlocked and you tell your wife to just come on into my back room and wait."

Joe's eyes lit up. "Oh, thank yo', Doctor. Yo' sure it be okay?"

"Yes, Joe. It'll be fine." The elevator bell rang indicating they had reached the street floor and as Papa left the elevator, without thinking he extended his hand to the black man.

Joe stood immobilized for a moment when he saw the outstretched hand. He raised his head and looked directly into the doctor's face and saw a smile there. Suddenly white teeth gleamed in Joe's black face as he slowly and cautiously extended his hand.

As Papa left the lobby of the building and walked down the street to his car he had a nagging feeling in the pit of his stomach. It didn't feel right that he had to sneak this little sick boy in the back door just because he was black. But he shrugged and said to himself, "Nothing I can do about that. Some things a person just can't change."

As he passed the men lined up against the bank building they all yelled greetings to him and watched as he jumped in his car and roared away. Then one of the men commented with a grin, "Well, there goes Doc in that fancy car of his. Everybody better get out of the way."

"Ain't it the truth," another one agreed as he spit tobacco out the side of his mouth and watched it splatter on the sidewalk.

Papa proved them right as he sped through town, past Palmers Drug Store, Perkins Department Store and Tom's Café. Soon he was flying by the town square where the farmers brought their produce to sell on weekends. Suddenly he remembered he didn't have a treat to take home to the grandkids. He slammed to a stop at one of the open air grocery stalls that lined the street across from the town square. These stalls all shared a common roof. Two sides and the back were enclosed, but the fronts were open to the street. Noticing a stalk of bananas hanging from the ceiling of one of the stalls, he decided to take the entire stalk home.

He paid the grocer and while he waited for his change, his eyes traveled across the street. A chill ran down his back when he saw the oak tree that stood in the center of the square. Visions of that awful day recreated themselves in his mind. Over twenty-five years had passed but he could still hear the noise of the crowd and the screaming of the colored man as a horse came galloping up, dragging him behind it. Three blocks away, a group of men had torn him from the sheriff who had been taking him to jail. While they tied him to the horse, another man who'd stayed behind in the square strung a rope over a limb of the big oak tree. These men proceeded to hang the colored man right there in the middle of the day, in front of the crowd of people who'd gathered to gawk. To this day he regretted it, but he had been one of the gawkers. Some people in the crowd were horrified, others just curious, but no one made a move to try to stop the lynching. He would never forgive himself that he, too, had made no effort to stop them.

None of the men involved were ever prosecuted. In fact he'd heard that the mayor condoned the lynching. To add to the disgrace, later the sheriff confided to a friend that he didn't t think "that nigger ever raped that white woman." He had done nothing even though he believed they'd hung an innocent man.

Papa jumped when he felt someone touching his arm and turned to see the grocer standing next to him.

"You okay, Doc?"

"Yes, sure." He shook himself back to the present.

"I've been standing here trying to tell you, here's your change."

"Oh, sorry. I was just thinking about something." He took his change, mumbled "Thanks" and grabbed the stalk of bananas. Back in his car, the memory still gripped him. All these years he'd been trying to come to some understanding. He could never make sense of it. The people involved in the lynching, those watching and those doing the hanging weren't normally bad people. They were people he'd known all his life, Christian people he saw in church every Sunday morning. He knew they thought of niggers as something less than human. Did that make their action okay to them? He was aware that way of thinking had been handed down from generation to generation. He'd been told as long as he could remember that niggers were dishonest, unreliable, lazy, shiftless and dumb. But somehow he was having trouble believing that anymore. He knew Joe wasn't like that at all, and somewhere deep inside him a little voice kept saying it just wasn't right.

Deep in thought, he turned the key in the ignition and started the car. With the bananas on the seat beside him, he headed for Ardis Heights. The wheels of the car screeched to a stop when he pulled into his driveway but he sat for a few minutes while he continued to think about the things that had confronted him today. Finally, he convinced himself he better let go of worrying about solving the problems of the world when he couldn't even solve his own.

Once out of the car, he stood with his hand on the hood, admiring it again. This car seemed to be the last remnant left of his dreams. His dairy barn had been destroyed by fire five years after it was built. He could see what was left of it as he looked across the pasture to where it once stood. A bare cement floor covered the ground and the iron frames where the cow's heads had been secured while being milked jutted skyward in the open air as rusting reminders of how the best laid plans can go astray. No shortage of those reminders he thought as he gazed at the house where he and Dandy had planned to grow old together, just the two of them. Just then four of his grandchildren came out of the house, screaming his name and running to meet him and he thought how that dream too, had been destroyed, or at least interrupted for heaven knew how long.

"What did you bring us today, Papa?" they cried in unison as they surrounded him.

He reached in the car, held up the stalk of bananas and smiled at their squeals of delight. He tore off a banana for each of them and then made his way for the back door of the house. When he entered the kitchen he found Dandy stacking kindling in the wood cook stove. Even after all these years, it still warmed his heart to lay eyes on her. He put the bananas on the kitchen table, then grabbed her and gave her a kiss. "Hello Dandy. What's going on?"

"What's usually going on around here. I'm getting ready to cook."

"Well you look mighty good." He stood back from her to get a better look. "Isn't that a new dress you have on?"

"Bess Nell made me go shopping. She insisted I buy a couple of new dresses. She said I looked dowdy."

"The dress is awful pretty," he said, hesitating, "but don't you think it's way too short? What are you trying to do -- attract some other man?"

"Oh for goodness sakes, Papa. Don't start that foolishness tonight. I'm too tired to deal with it."

"It's just that I can't think of any other reason for a woman to show so much of her legs."

"I don't know when you think I'd find time for another man, even if I wanted to. Besides, this dress is plenty long.

Now go on upstairs and read your paper or play your violin or whatever. I've got to get supper started for this bunch."

He took one last look at the curve of her well-shaped calves and sucked in his breath. By the time he reached the stairs that would take him to the sanctity of his bedroom, his body was beginning to shake. "Maybe I'll play a couple of little tunes on my fiddle before supper," he said to himself, hoping that would calm the storm brewing inside him. The very thought of any other man ogling those beautiful legs made him physically ill. If she was going to insist on wearing those short dresses, he'd have to do something about it.

CHAPTER 10

After breakfast, Dandy sent the other women off to the garden while she finished the breakfast cleanup. She looked out the kitchen window to check on the weather and was pleased to see no clouds obstructing the blue sky above. Looks like it's going to be a beautiful day, Dandy thought. Today was Friday; the day for her weekly fried chicken supper. A lot of extra work, but she didn't mind because she'd get to spend the morning alone with her favorite granddaughter. Of course, she'd deny with her last breath that she had favorites. It would never do to let on to anyone she felt that way about Betty Lou. But it should be obvious to anyone that this granddaughter was like her in so many ways. And though she wasn't a superstitious person, she did feel it was bound to have some special significance that Betty Lou had been born on her birthday. Besides, just look at that child. No one could deny that girl looked like the Swinson family through and through with her fair hair and blue green eyes.

Dandy screwed up her face as she thought about Betty Lou's little sister, Gloria Nell. She didn't look or act anything like a Swinson. Fact was, she was the image of Inez, with her dark hair and dark brown eyes. She knew that shouldn't make a difference, but it did and she just couldn't help the way she felt. "Yes sir-re, that Betty Lou's a chip off our block," Dandy said out loud. She was having this conversation with herself while she finished drying the breakfast dishes when she heard the back door slam.

Betty Lou walked into the kitchen earlier than expected with the basket full of eggs she had gathered from the chicken house. She put them on the cabinet with care and stood quietly with her hands folded in front of her stomach, waiting to be acknowledged.

Dandy glanced at her out of the corner of her eye and smiled to herself as she pretended not to see her granddaughter until she had dried the last dish and put it away. After hanging the dishtowel on the arm of the cook stove to dry, she turned to face Betty Lou. "Well," Dandy said, reaching out her hand, "are you ready to do it?"

"Yes ma'am," Betty Lou answered with enthusiasm. She had been taught, like all good Southern children, to say "ma'am" and "sir" when addressing her elders, and she was a child anxious to please.

The sun smiled down on them as they left the house holding hands. They walked together along the path across the back yard and through the gate that led to the pasture beyond. A few dozen yards away, the white walls of the chicken house gleamed in the sun and they could hear the clucking of chickens in the large screened area adjacent to the chicken house. After they arrived they stood and watched Dandy's prized White Leghorns run around the yard, pecking at the ground incessantly for any leavings of chicken feed, or anything else they could find. Dandy's chickens were her pride and joy and she never tired of watching them.

After a few moments, she dropped Betty Lou's hand and looked down at her. "Okay, Dear, I'll wait out here while you go in and bring me out four pullets -- not hens mind you -- not the big fat chickens. Be sure they're pullets, those are the young ones. Understand?"

Betty Lou shook her head, confirming she understood.

Dandy sighed. "I'm afraid I've gotten too old to chase chickens anymore, so I'm counting on you."

This brought a bright smile to Betty Lou's face. "Yes ma'am," she said, then ran to make her way through the door of the chicken house to do battle with four condemned pullets. The chickens seemed to sense the reason for her presence. They flew around frantically, feathers flying as they tried to escape her; but she didn't give up until she gripped a chicken in her small hands.

As she brought out each pullet, clawing and scratching and flapping its wings, Dandy took it from her and put it into a big burlap sack. When they had four, they carried them to the backyard. Once there, Dandy reached into the tow sack, grabbed a chicken by its head and whirled it around in the air, wringing its neck until she was holding nothing but a white and red chicken's head, its round open eyes staring into space while its headless body ran helter-skelter around the yard. They watched while each finally surrendered to its fate and flopped over on the ground.

Dandy chuckled to herself when she glanced up and saw the look on Betty Lou's face. It showed both horror and fascination. Her back was pressed hard against the wall of the brick smokehouse and she appeared to be holding her breath. Dandy remembered last week when she'd let Betty Lou try to wring a chicken's neck. When the head refused to detach from the body after a couple of twirls, she'd thrown up her breakfast. Dandy had to hide a smile but after that she decided to excuse her from that part of the process.

When four chicken's heads lay at Dandy's feet, she announced, "Well, you can relax now, Honey. That's done. It's time to pluck feathers." This was the signal for Betty Lou to run around the yard and gather up the dead chickens and bring them one by one to Dandy. An hour or so later, their ritual completed, the naked chicken bodies lay before them on the table in the back yard. Feathers covered the ground and each of them.

"Job well done." Dandy said, picking a feather out of Betty Lou's hair. "Run on home now and get yourself cleaned up and I'll do the same. See ya'll tonight at supper."

Dandy always invited Erby's family to supper on the evenings she fried chicken. Everyone enjoyed the occasion, and secretly, she loved cooking for her family. If anyone knew how much pleasure she got from it, she could no longer play the martyr and she knew herself well enough to realize she didn't want to give up that role. As she climbed the stairs to bathe and dress she congratulated herself that one of her saving graces was her ability to see her own faults clearly.

After her bath, she wrapped herself in her robe and returned to the bedroom. As this was sort of a special occasion, at least as much of a special occasion as ever happened around this place anymore, she decided to wear one of the new dresses that Bess Nell had talked her into buying. She'd worn the navy blue already, so she thought she'd wear the floral print tonight. Her husband might think it was too short but Bess Nell would be pleased. Her daughter had been right to insist she buy new dresses. She had let herself go and needed to update her wardrobe a little.

As she searched through her closet, she wasn't too concerned at first when she couldn't find the dress. She'd seen it just the other day. It must be hidden behind something else hanging in the closet. When she still couldn't find it after shuffling through all the clothes, she decided not to waste anymore time looking. If she couldn't find the floral print, she'd just wear the navy blue checked dress again. However, she couldn't find it either. One by one, she looked through all the clothes that hung in the closet. Then, almost frantically, she went through again. Nowhere. The new dresses were definitely not there.

She stood with her arms crossed, staring into the closet and shaking her head in disbelief. Someone must have taken those dresses. She couldn't imagine anyone in this family would do such a thing. But what other explanation was there?

Well, if that was the case, then *who*? She knew Bess Nell was above suspicion, so that only left one of her daughters-in-law.

She considered the possibilities. It wouldn't be Evelyn. She wouldn't have the courage to steal anything. Valera? It certainly wasn't beneath her. She had a real sneaky way about her. Dandy picked that up the first time she laid eyes on her. However, her clothes would never fit Valera. Besides which, they were much too conservative for Valera's vulgar taste.

So, that just left Inez? She stood quietly, biting her bottom lip and continuing to shake her head as she thought about it. Finally, she said out loud, "Well, that's who it's got to be. Now that I think about it, I'm sure of it."

*   *   *

Usually when the family got together on fried chicken night, even in such trying times as these, there was an exchange of teasing and laughter. However, tonight at the supper table a heaviness in the air seemed to be a weight on everyone. Even Preacher, Bess Nell's husband, who was always the loud mouth and the jokester of the group, ate his fried chicken and mashed potatoes in silence, with only an occasional attempt at conversation. No one knew why exactly, but all felt strangely uncomfortable. And most uncomfortable of all was Inez. Every time she looked in her direction, she found Dandy staring at her with a sinister look in her eyes.

*   *   *

After supper, Papa followed Dandy up the stairs to their bedroom. With each step he could hear her mumbling to herself, but he couldn't understand what she was saying. He didn't interrupt her. He didn't want to open Pandora's Box.

After they walked into their bedroom, she slammed the door as hard as she could. He pretended to ignore it and crossed the room in silence. Sitting down on the bed, he started removing his shoes and socks and tried to disregard the tension in the room. But the pounding in his heart finally reached a point of such discomfort that he could no longer remain quiet. Bracing himself, he asked "Okay, Mother. Want to tell me what you are so upset about?"

She didn't look at him. "I don't think so. You'll just tell me how ridiculous I am."

Relieved by this answer, he thought better than to push it any further. He was afraid he knew what she was upset about, and his guilt made him wish he could sink into the floor and disappear. He finished getting ready for bed, then lay down and buried his head in his pillow, hoping she wouldn't change her mind and force him to defend himself with a lie.

Dandy continued to mumble under her breath as she slammed around the room and when she got into bed he could tell she didn't fall asleep right away. However, after a time she'd drifted off. He wasn't so lucky. He lay sleepless, staring into the dark with eyes wide open. Lost in deep distress, he wondered if he would ever be able to sleep again.

CHAPTER 11

Dandy's mind was still in turmoil about her missing dresses the next day when she joined the other women in the garden. How was she going to get a confession out of Inez? Totally obsessed with this, she found it impossible to settle down to harvesting vegetables or doing anything else in the garden. Finally, she gave up trying. She had to be alone to think. As her excuse for leaving the garden, she announced to her daughters-in-law that she had to make a pie for the noon meal.

The big grandfather clock that sat against the dining room wall was just striking ten when she stomped into the kitchen. It was as if by bringing her feet down with force she could expel some of her boiling emotions. Wadding up paper, she stuffed it hard into the wood cook stove, then jammed in the kindling before striking the match to start the fire. When she pulled an apron out of a bottom cabinet drawer and slipped it over her old dress, it triggered her frustration over her missing dresses and her anger flared anew. She slammed around the kitchen, banging everything she picked up.

Though lost in her turbulence, she managed to get an apple pie in the oven and pots and pans of food cooking on the stove. When she lifted the lid off the pot of boiling potatoes, steam rose and formed a layer of moisture on her glasses, blinding her. She grabbed the glasses off her nose and cleaned them on the tail of her apron, grumbling as she did so. She had a habit of talking aloud to herself and now she gave way to it. "What can happen next?" she sputtered. Then she raised her eyes and prayed, *"Lord, show me a little mercy will you, please."* Her head throbbed and beads of perspiration ran down the back of her neck as she bent over the wood stove. "I swear, life seems determined to make it just as tough on a body as it possibly can," she cried, convinced she was the world's most put upon victim.

Pork chops sizzled and popped in two cast iron skillets on the burners next to the potatoes and about that time hot grease from one of the frying pans popped out and landed on her arm. "See what I mean?" she bellowed to the empty room. Exasperated, she glanced down at the red spot where the grease had landed and saw a blister already starting to form. Sighing deeply, she crossed to the cabinet where she kept the baking soda and dabbed a little on the burn, then slammed the cabinet door so hard it made the kitchen rattle. Slamming doors and breathing deep sighs seemed to be the only acceptable avenues available to her for letting off steam. What she would really like to do is scream and yell and kick things, but most times she had too large an audience for such displays.

As she walked back to the stove, she heard a small but demanding voice calling her name and turned to see Patsy standing in the doorway of the kitchen. Golden ringlets surrounded the pretty little face now screwed up in a pout.

"What is it, child?" Dandy tried not to sound as impatient as she felt.

"Betty Lou stole my coloring book. I can't find it anywhere," she cried. "I'm sure it was her that took it."

Dandy rolled her eyes and looked up at the ceiling before answering. She could no longer pretend patience. "Well, don't tell me. Tell your mother. I can't take care of everything that happens around here!"

"Tell your mother what?" Bess Nell asked as she entered the kitchen holding her young son in her arms. Just a little over five feet tall, she was a tiny woman and Johnny was a plump child almost as large as she. Her petite size and a scattering of freckles that danced across her small, turned-up nose, gave her the look of someone far younger than her twenty-six years.

When Dandy looked up to see her in the door, she felt embarrassed to think her daughter had witnessed her impatience with Patsy. Bess Nell was the last person on earth that Dandy wanted to make feel uncomfortable about living here. In fact, her being here was the one good thing about having all the others move into her house.

Patsy saw her mother enter the room and it seemed her signal to surrender to full blown wailing. "Oh, Mommy, Betty

Lou stole my coloring book," she cried, grabbing Bess Nell around her legs and almost throwing her down.

"All right now, Patsy. Just simmer down and tell me what makes you think Betty Lou took your book."

"We were playing on the front porch and I shared my book and colors with Betty Lou, just like you told me to. But after a while we got tired of coloring. I left my things on the porch and we went to the backyard to play. Later when I went back to get my book and colors they were gone and so was Betty Lou."

"Well now, Patsy," Bess Nell replied, her voice calm, "You can't be sure she took them if you didn't see her doing it. If you left them unattended on the front porch anyone could have taken them." Putting her hands on Patsy's shoulders and turning her to face her, Bess Nell looked deep into her eyes. "Look at me, Patsy. It's not nice to accuse people of something if you aren't absolutely positive they did it."

Apparently, this bit of advice failed to console Patsy because she cried with added gusto.

Johnny was getting restless in Bess Nell's arms and his squirming combined with the heat in the kitchen made it urgent to get this situation resolved as quickly as possible. Her normally placid expression was replaced by a look of confusion. She turned to her mother who had been watching this scene without comment. "Dandy, I want to be fair, but there is constant turmoil between the children and I hate to say it but Betty Lou is at the center of most of it. Just yesterday she bit Patsy on the arm until blood ran because Patsy had put some of her chinaberries on the wrong mud pie. She's becoming a real problem. What do you think? Do you think she would steal Patsy's things?"

Dandy pulled her handkerchief from her apron pocket and wiped the perspiration out of her eyes, stalling for time as she mulled over the wisdom of speaking what was on her mind. Finally she could hold her tongue no longer. "I wasn't going to say anything but since you asked me, Sister, I'm going to tell you. I always say, 'like mother, like daughter'. You can't blame Betty Lou. What can you expect of a child whose own mother is a thief?"

"Dandy! What in the world are you talking about? You can't be serious." Her eyes never left her mother's face as she put Johnny down to scamper across the kitchen floor.

"Well, I am. You know those dresses you and I bought?"

"Yes, of course I do."

Dandy lifted her nose in the air, "They've disappeared from my closet."

"What? How could they?" Bess Nell asked. "Are you sure you looked everywhere?"

Dandy bobbed her head up and down and shook her index finger in the air. "Of course I'm sure. Now I've given this a lot of thought; in fact I've thought of little else so don't think I'm going off half-cocked. I'd bet my life on it. Inez stole those dresses."

"How can you think such a thing? Inez wouldn't do a thing like that." Then Bess Nell laughed at the idea. "That's absolutely ridiculous. Where do you think she'd wear them? Where does she ever go besides here?"

Dandy looked at her with her eyes bugging and her jaw set firm. Wisps of her curly gray hair escaped their pins and darted out in all directions giving her the look of someone deranged. "Well, Sister, you can just think what you want, but I know what I know." She stopped speaking and breathed one of her deepest sighs, then turned her eyes toward heaven. *"I swear, Dear Lord, why did every single one of my children show such bad judgment in choosing their mates?"*

Bess Nell's face turned white and she recoiled as if she had been slapped. There it was again. Another not so subtle attack on her husband. She bristled and gave her mother a hard look. "Why don't you just come out and say it. You hate Preacher. You hate anything you didn't choose, anything you can't control."

Dandy was taken back by Bess Nell's outraged reaction. It was so out of character. Her better judgment told her not to respond. She'd said too much already. She turned her back and pretended to focus on her cooking, in spite of the fact that at the moment she could care less if all the food burned. Even with her back turned, Dandy could feel Bess Nell's penetrating stare and her heart ached. Now she'd made Bess Nell mad at her. When would she ever learn to keep her mouth shut?

For a few moments Bess Nell stood paralyzed by anger. Then she grabbed Johnny up in her arms and ignoring Patsy's continuing fit, she turned and ran out of the kitchen.

Stumbling as she went, she raced through the hall and up the stairs to her room, tears burning her eyes.

Once inside her bedroom, she put Johnny down and stood with her back pressed against the door as she looked around her. This room was unchanged since she had lived here as a girl. The same brass bed and the same quilted bedspread Dandy had made for her, using scraps left from the dresses she'd sewn for her. The walls were covered with the same wallpaper, large pink flowers; more yellowed now, her mother's choice again. She'd hated this room then and she hated it even more now. This was the place where her mother had kept her supposedly protected from the "evils of the world".

There were voices hidden in the walls of this room. She could hear them now. They kept coming back to taunt her. "Bess Nell, I saw you out in the yard playing with Mary Jones from down the road. I've told you before; I don't want you playing with her. Her people are just plain riff-raff and you could only learn bad things from her. I want you to grow up to be a lady." And "Bess Nell I don't want to have to tell you again, when Lena Mae brings her little girl with her when she comes to clean, I want you to stay in your room. What will people say if they see you playing with a little nigger girl? Why even the Bible warns that whites and darks aren't supposed to mix. White people with any respect don't have anything to do with coloreds. Now you remember that!"

And so it went with anyone Bess Nell played with. She remembered a childhood alone and lonely. The animals on the farm were her only acceptable playmates, with one exception:

Charlotte. Her father was a doctor and Papa's partner in his medical practice. That made Charlotte okay by Dandy's standards. The irony was that it was Charlotte who helped arrange her secret meetings with Preacher; Charlotte who helped her escape.

Preacher was not only her escape from this prison but her revenge as well. She could never have found a boy with more crude habits. It seemed every time he opened his mouth, something profane popped out. And to make it even sweeter, he was from a lower class family, people on the fringes of what Dandy considered "white trash", "riff-raff", "low class", all her mother's favorite labels for the unacceptable.

As Bess Nell thought about it now, a twisted smile replaced the tears of a moment before. Although she hadn't been conscious of it at the time, these qualities that Dandy had tried so hard to keep her away from were the very things that attracted her to Preacher. And now Dandy was forced to live under the same roof with him. The perfect irony, the absolutely perfect comeuppance for her ruined childhood. This realization suddenly made her misery easier to bear.

CHAPTER 12

Papa cursed under his breath as the windshield wipers whished back and forth. He squinted and leaned forward as he strained to see through the driving rain, his body tense as he tried to keep his car from going off the narrow asphalt highway. He remembered a time when he'd blessed the rain, when he'd thought of it as a welcome bath that washed everything clean and new. He'd delighted in watching his thirsty plants perk up and thrive with new life. However, today he looked at the world through different eyes and the gloomy gray skies and the rain seemed only to increase the weight of his burdens.

At last he pulled into his driveway and got out of the car. As he walked from the driveway to the backyard the pelting downpour soaked him to the bone. Half blinded by the deluge, he waded through puddles then labored up the steps to the porch. He grasped his medical bag in one hand and a brown paper bag in the other, the wet sack which held fruit for his grandchildren threatening to disintegrate at any moment.

Hoping to shed any rain that hadn't soaked through, he shook his hat and stomped his feet before entering the big enclosed porch. Just inside the door, hooks hung to accommodate hats and coats, and after depositing his still dripping things, he became aware of the sounds of music and laughter and his eyes searched the room to find its source.

An oak cabinet at the far end of the porch housed a Victrola and a large collection of records. A crank on one side of the Victrola started the turntable and his grandchildren loved to wind it up, put on one of the large black records and dance to the music. Papa couldn't help but smile as he watched his five grandchildren giggling and moving their bodies in swinging circles. He only stood there a short time before they discovered him. Immediately they stopped dancing and ran to gather around him.

"What did you bring us today, Papa?" they asked, looking up at him with the large innocent eyes that always gripped his heart.

As he handed them the wet sack the bottom collapsed, scattering apples in every direction. Small hands and feet were immediately in pursuit, and the room was again filled with giggles as they chased down the apples.

He watched them with amusement for a moment, but his pleasure was short lived. Feelings of guilt allowed him little time for enjoyment before consuming him again. His smile from a moment ago disappeared completely as he headed for the kitchen where he knew he'd find Dandy. Instead he found Evelyn, Valera, and Bess Nell cleaning turnip greens and getting ready to fry okra for supper. The aroma of cornbread baking filled the kitchen. Usually the smell of cornbread made his mouth water, but even that wasn't enough to distract him today.

Puzzled, he looked around the kitchen. "Where's Dandy?" he asked, alarmed she wasn't in her usual spot.

"Oh, hello, Daddy," Bess Nell looked over her shoulder at him. "She has one of her headaches -- must really be a bad one when she lets anyone else take over her kitchen. She's up in the bedroom and said to send you right up with her headache medicine. She seems to have run out."

Papa shook his head and grunted as he left the kitchen and started for the stairs with his medical satchel in his hand. He knew Dandy wasn't just *out* of her headache medicine. Lately, he'd been forced, for her own good, not to leave it where she had easy access to it.

Slowly he opened the door to a dark bedroom. All the window shades had been pulled and Dandy lay stretched out on the four-poster bed. He walked quietly across the room and bent to kiss her lightly on the forehead. She flinched and moaned but kept her eyes closed.

"Hello, Dandy," he whispered. "Did you have a bad day, Sweetheart"?

She looked at him through squinted eyelids, then opened her bloodshot eyes wider. "Did I have a bad day? Hrump!" She paused a second. "Did I have a bad day you ask?" Her voice dripped with sarcasm. "My day was just *wonderful*---as usual," she said, looking at him with disgust. "Let me tell you how every day in my life is. I'm almost sixty years old and I work like a dog taking care of all you people. And how am I repaid? My husband accuses me of being a shameless hussy. He thinks I'm trying to get the attention of every man in town just because he doesn't like the length of my dress." She glared at him but didn't wait for his response before she continued. "And there's Erby who brings a den of thieves into our lives and then disappears to heaven know where most of the time. And if that's not enough to get a body down, Agnew brings me his second wife, who is as common as a sow's ear." She was gathering steam now as she continued. "Oh, and don't forget Archie, who not only stays drunk most of the time, but also moves in a wife who doesn't have the personality or pluck of one of my chickens." She paused to catch her breath. "Then to top it all off, there's Preacher." Her voice broke and she hesitated, choking back the tears that she had controlled up to now. "To top things off," she repeated, "my daughter is angry with me because I don't just love all the riff-raff my children have dragged home to live with us." She looked as if she thought the world was coming to an end as she cried, "And I think Bess Nell hates me!"

She closed her eyes and a moan accompanied a burst of pain that exploded in her head. When the pain subsided, she opened them and glared at him accusingly. "You hid my medicine again! How could you? My head is about to burst."

Ignoring the accusation, he said, "Dandy, please calm down. You've worked yourself into a real tizzy. Be still now and I'll take care of you."

He went to the bathroom and got a glass of water, returned to the bedroom, took a bottle of pills from his bag and gave her two of them. While waiting for the pills to take effect he sat on the edge of the bed thinking about what she'd said. Lord knows, he thought, some of it had merit. It was the part about Bess Nell that stung him though, reopening an old wound. He felt relief she hadn't mentioned her missing dresses but perplexed that out of all those grievances, Bess Nell's anger was what upset her the most. Her precious Bess Nell was angry with her, and that was enough to put her in bed with one of her headaches. At times it seemed to him that no one else had mattered to Dandy since the day her daughter was born. It was and had always been about Bess Nell first and foremost.

At last the pills took effect and she was calm. He rose and stood by the bed, quietly looking down at her. Even old and sick, and sometimes annoying -- very annoying -- she was still the most fetching woman he'd ever known, the only woman in the world for him. As he watched her breasts rise and fall with each breath, he felt his body respond with desire. He found it amazing that he still longed to be inside her, even after all these years.

He ran his hand over his bald dome in exasperation. Everything and everybody around him seemed be out of control. The incident with the dresses had convinced him that he was out of control. Crossing the room to his favorite chair, he collapsed and closed his eyes. He wished he didn't still harbor resentment toward Bess Nell. After all, she hadn't been the one who made the decision. He'd tried to keep it out of his mind. Now the wound Dandy just reopened triggered memories that came flooding back as if a dam had broken and he found himself back twenty six years to the night it happened.

Month-old Bess Nell lay in her basket near their bed, sleeping soundly. Papa felt he had waited more than the appropriate time since the birth, but when he reached for Dandy to pull her to him, her body was stiff and unyielding. Lying rigid in his arms, her voice came back cold through the darkness. "John, we need to talk."

He felt an electric current pass through his body. She never called him "John" except on the direst occasions. His breathing grew shallow as he waited for her to continue. A long minute passed and she still said nothing more. Finally, he cleared his throat and forced out, "Okay, Dandy, what do you want to talk about?"

"Well," she hesitated again as she struggled to find the right words. "After a lot of thought, I've made a decision you're not going to like." She avoided looking in his direction as she continued. "I've given you four sons and now a beautiful daughter. I don't want to have nine or ten children like our mothers. Five are quite enough for me, thank you! And there's only one sure way to avoid more children and I don't have to tell you what that is." She paused and waited for a comment from him, but none came. "John, I've made myself available to you whenever you've wanted for all these years, and now I feel I've fulfilled my wifely obligation. I don't want to do *that* anymore."

Slowly, he removed his arms from her and pulled away. He lay on his side of the bed, staring into the darkness while his mind begged to refuse what his ears had just heard. His voice cracked when he spoke, "Lula, I can't believe you're saying these things. You must be joking. And it's not a funny joke."

"I'm not joking, John. I've never been more serious in my life. I'll still sleep in your bed, but my obligation to you about that particular thing is done."

This was just too crazy. He wouldn't lie here and listen to this another minute. He tossed back the covers, got out of bed and threw on his clothes. Without another word, he stormed out of their bedroom, slamming the bedroom door behind him.

As if in a trance, he walked down the stairs, through the house and the yard and soon found himself out in the street. A full moon lit up the sky and threw dark shadows across his path. In the bright moonlight, the world seemed eerie, unreal, dreamlike. His mind whirled as he wandered aimlessly around the neighborhood. Surely he would wake up soon and find this was all a bad dream. But her words kept repeating themselves. He couldn't shut them out. "I've fulfilled my obligation" -- her obligation? *Obligation?* That word buzzed over and over in his head, making his insides churn.

He wandered for hours, trying hard to understand how she felt. He wanted to be fair. He knew all too well that abstinence was the only reliable birth control, and who could blame her for not wanting more children. Their boys were a handful--always in trouble it seemed. But reason as he may, what he could never understand, and what hurt the most, was how a woman could pull away so completely from a man she supposedly loved, and deny him something he wanted and needed so much, something until now he'd believed they shared.

As the night wore on, anger replaced his feelings of hurt, and early the next morning, his eyes rimmed in red, his face puffy, and his body exhausted, he returned to their bedroom and approached the bed where Dandy lay sleeping. He grabbed her shoulders and shook her roughly.

"Wake up, Lula," he insisted, his voice shaking. "I have something to say to you, and I want you to listen to me! I've tried to be a sensitive husband. I've always tried to be gentle and unselfish, concerned that you have pleasure, too. But now that I think back, I realize in all honesty I've been a blind fool. You've never really been responsive to my caresses. Could it be that in all these years, you've never loved me?"

Raising herself up on her elbows, her eyes wide as she looked at him, she responded, "Oh no. I love you, and I've been glad to be a source of pleasure to you and to give you children. But surely you know as well as I do that women don't expect to get pleasure from *that sort of thing*. *That's* for men's pleasure. And it has nothing to do with whether I love you or not. I know I've hurt you deeply and I'm sorry about that." She reached for his hand. "I don't mean that you can't touch me or kiss me or hold me. I just mean I don't want to do that other thing anymore."

He had been so lost in his reverie that it took him a few seconds to return to the present when a soft tapping at the door was followed by Bess Nell's voice.

"Papa. Papa, are you all right?"

"I'm okay, Sister."

"Don't you want to come down and eat your supper?"

"Ya'll go ahead and eat. We'll get something later." Then he added as if trying to convince himself, "Don't worry about us. We're gonna to be okay."

CHAPTER 13

Dandy didn't need to speak a word in order for everyone at the supper table to know she was still in a black mood. They were beginning to wonder if this mood was going to be permanent. They exchanged glances, wordlessly suggesting the potential for danger. The sum total of conversation this evening was: "Please pass the potatoes" and that was mumbled softly.

Later when they were in the bedroom, again Papa avoided questioning the source of her bad mood. He'd been fortunate so far. The reckoning for what he'd done was sure to come eventually, but he wanted to avoid it as long as he could. Heaven only knew what she would do when she found out.

He watched out of the corner of his eye as Dandy started to prepare for bed. Slowly she took off her old housedress, threw it on the floor, then with great drama, kicked it into the closet. Grabbing her gown off the hook where it hung, she held it in front of her and stood in her slip, her eyes roaming the room as if she were looking for something hidden in the walls.

Her silence had the feeling of a firecracker, lit and ready to explode at any moment. The tension it produced could be seen, heard, and felt. Papa tried to ignore it but, finally, he could stand it no longer. He gathered his courage. Might as well get it over with, he decided. He drew in a deep breath. "Okay, Dandy. I know you've made peace with Bess Nell, so you might as well get it out. Let's hear what's bothering you."

This time that invitation was all she needed. She dropped her gown and snorted, waving her arms in the air. "I didn't want to tell you this. But now that you insist, I'm upset because my two new dresses are missing from my closet and I know who took them."

Panic gripped him, froze him to where he was standing. He felt his face burning red hot.

"I know you're not going to believe this, but I'm sure it was Inez." Then lifting her eyebrows and opening her eyes wide, she added with great emphasis on each word, "Inez has stolen my new dresses."

Oh my God, he thought, not sure whether to be relieved or sick at his stomach. "What?" he asked, incredulous at this turn of events. "Lula, are you crazy?"

She answered with assurance, "I've gone through every possibility in my mind, and the only conclusion I can come to is that Inez was the only one who would take them. No one who lives in this house would dare. And I remember now, the other day when Inez was over here helping to can peaches, she went upstairs, pretending to go to the bathroom. That must have been when she slipped into my closet and took those dresses." She put her hands on her hips and her eyebrows came together in a frown as she added with conviction, "I know that as sure as I'm standing here." Having said this, the expression on her face suddenly changed, and looking very vulnerable, she slumped into a nearby chair. "I know Inez hates me. Not just her, but everyone in this house hates me." Noticing his expression of protest, she added, "With the possible exception of you -- and sometimes I'm not too sure about you." She looked up at him, her eyes appealing, "Oh, Papa, why is God punishing me like this? I'm not a bad person. I don't want to be mean, but trying to get along with this bunch is just too much for me."

He stood by helplessly watching her despair and as he did, her face seemed to age before his eyes. He hadn't noticed before that the smooth clear skin of her face was no longer wrinkle free. Deep lines formed around her mouth, lines that turned down and pulled the skin of her face with them. The thick, lustrous, copper colored curls that surrounded her face not so terribly long ago had turned dull gray almost overnight. But what he found most upsetting was that all the sparkle was gone from her pale blue eyes.

His torment was almost unbearable. He still couldn't believe he'd done such a thing. And now Dandy was blaming Inez. At this point, he wasn't sure whether he should comfort Dandy, defend Inez, or confess. His body sagged with exhaustion and he could hardly maneuver himself across the room to where she sat slumped in the chair. Dropping to his knees in front of her, he put his head in her lap and encircled her legs in his arms. "Oh, Sweetheart, none of that's true. Nobody hates you. You're the glue that keeps this whole thing together." He lifted his head, reached up and wiped the tears from her cheeks with the tips of his fingers. Then he fell silent while he thought about what a coward he was. He'd evaded the issue of Inez and now he had to add that to his guilt.

CHAPTER 14

The only light in the upstairs hall came from a large window over the stairwell. Bess Nell stood in its filtered glow and leaned her head against the locked door of the bedroom as she knocked softly and whispered, "Dandy, are you okay?"

Dandy's thin voice could barely be heard through the door. "Yes, I'm okay, Sister. I just have a headache. I'll be fine in a while. Please, just let me be."

A few minutes later, Papa arrived home from the office and when no one was in the kitchen, he raced up the stairs to find Bess Nell standing outside his bedroom door. "What's going on?" he asked.

"Papa, I'm glad you're home. I'm worried about Dandy. She's locked herself in her bedroom and I can tell by her voice she's taken those pills again. Do you think it's safe for her to keep taking so many of those strong pain killers?"

Oh Lord, he thought, as he remembered that he had forgotten to hide the pills. However, he didn't want to share his concern with anyone else, even Bess Nell. He answered defensively, "Sister, her headaches are terrible. Do you suggest I don't give her any more painkillers? I can't just let her suffer."

"Well, okay. But are you aware she's taking those pills more and more frequently? I just want you to know that it worries me."

You're not the only one, he thought, but didn't say so out loud. The last thing he wanted was to take on one more problem right now. Of course she was right. Dandy was taking too many pills, but he couldn't address that at present. This thing with Inez and the dresses was much more pressing.

He watched Bess Nell walk back down the stairs and was about to knock on the door when he caught himself. In spite of being worried about Dandy, he just wasn't up to dealing with her right now. He'd lived in a constant state of nausea ever since he'd taken those damn dresses. Having Dandy accuse Inez for what he had done was the final blow to his ravaged mind. Rather than face her right now he decided to take a walk, hoping that might clear his head, help him to think of some way out of the mess he'd created. He climbed back down the stairs, left his suit coat and the stiff white celluloid collar from his shirt in the downstairs hall closet and started for the back door. As he passed the kitchen he saw that Bess Nell and his daughters-in-law were there, beginning preparations for supper. He waved to them as he passed but didn't slow his pace. He was in no mood to make conversation.

His entire body felt heavy as he trudged down the steps to the back yard. He had no destination in mind as he walked, just allowed his legs to take him anywhere they wanted. However, after he'd wandered through the open fields for an hour or more, he was still in a state of agitation. Daylight was fading fast when he looked up to find his undirected legs had taken him out behind one of the barns to the place where the trash was burned. Unconsciously, he had returned to the scene of his crime. He stood staring blankly at the remains of charred tin cans and ashes when suddenly, to his horror, a button from one of Dandy's dresses jumped out at him. Quickly he reached down and grabbed it. The button burned hot in his hand, as if it had just now escaped the fire that had tried to destroy it. Clasping it tightly while praying for God's help, he was startled by a voice from behind him.

"Hi, Papa."

He jumped and jerked around to see Erby standing nearby. "Why Erby. Where did you come from? What are you doing here?" He felt trapped, exposed, as if he'd been caught naked.

"I came to burn some trash. How about you?" Erby said, looking into his Papa's eyes accusingly as he dropped his sack of trash on top of the ashes.

"Oh, I was just taking a walk and stopped to watch the sunset," he lied.

"Really?" Erby replied, making no effort to hide his sarcasm.

"What do you mean by that tone of voice?"

"Well, I thought maybe you might be burning some more of Dandy's dresses," Erby said with a knowing look.

"What-what are you talking about?" Papa asked indignantly, trying to control his shaking voice. The palms of his hands were wet and he knew his face failed in its attempt to look innocent. He'd never been a very good liar, never had much need to be before.

"Aw, come on Papa, goddammit. You know what I'm talking about. I was out for a walk the other night when I couldn't sleep and I saw a fire burning over here. I could see that someone was standing by the fire and I was on my way over to check it out when I saw it was you. I stopped when I saw you reach into a sack and pull out some things and throw them on the fire. I stood in the darkness while you watched them burn." Erby studied his dad's face in the dwindling light. "Papa, I have to ask. What on earth is going on with you that you'd do such a thing?"

Papa stared at the ground, then at the sky, waiting for, praying for, some revelation to hit him, some way to explain an unexplainable act, an unforgivable act. After a miserable silence, he looked down at the button he still clutched in his hand. His face was distorted with anguish as he tried to explain. "Son, all I know is that the old green monster has such a hold on me that at times I feel as if a giant sword has come down and severed the cord that holds me to rational behavior." He stopped and looked up at Erby. "Let this be a lesson to you about what jealousy can do. My jealousy of your mother drives me to do unforgivable things. When I see her showing off her legs for every man in town to see, I'm filled with…I don't know what," he choked. "I just feel like worms are eating away at my gut and I can't stop myself. I've got to take some kind of action." He let the button fall to the ground and they both stood staring at it as it rolled a few inches on its edge, then fell over.

"You aren't going to tell your mother what I've done are you? She'll never forgive me. She hates it when I'm jealous. And this! How could she ever understand this? How can anyone? I can't."

"Goddammit, Papa." Erby shrugged and looked away. It was his time to stand silent and be miserable. He stared at the sunset for a few moments without really seeing it. Then he spoke, "After the other night I'd decided not to say anything to anyone about what I'd seen. I felt it was your business, no matter how strange. But that was before Bess Nell told me that Dandy's dresses were missing and she was blaming Inez. Now you surely understand I can't let Inez take the blame for this."

Papa hung his head and covered his face with his hands. "Son, you'll never know how much I suffered when your mother told me she believed Inez took her dresses." He hesitated and when he looked up at Erby, he looked as if he'd aged ten years. He drew out the words through his pain as he confessed, "And I'm such a coward that I just couldn't bring myself to tell her what an old fool I am."

Seeing how distressed he was, Erby felt both annoyance and pity at the same time. "Okay, Papa. I won't say anything -- that is if you can come up with a way to clear Inez from blame.

But you've got to promise me you'll do something, I don't care what, to convince Dandy that Inez is innocent."

"I will. I promise. I'll do something," he said, nodding solemnly. But he was thinking, *Good Lord, something -- but what?* His felt as if his heart was in a vise and someone was screwing it tighter and tighter.

*   *   *

"Is that it, Mildred?" Papa asked as he stuck his head through the door to the waiting room. It was almost six P.M., the day after his encounter with Erby.

Mildred stopped shuffling through papers on her desk and looked around the empty reception room. "Yes, Doctor, that's the last of the patients today."

"Okay then, I'll be leaving shortly. I'll see you tomorrow."

Mildred had worked for Dr Swinson so long that she felt entitled to speak her mind. "I hope you'll forgive me for saying this, but after all these years I think I know your moods inside and out, and frankly I'm growing concerned about you. You look awful. Get some rest, won't you please?"

He didn't respond, just stared blankly around the room with haggard eyes, then slowly he nodded and closed the door. An ironic smile turned the corners of his mouth up slightly as he walked through the examining room and into the small windowless room that was his office. "Yeah, get some rest," he mumbled to himself. "That's a joke." His Stetson hat and navy blue suit coat hung on two hooks of the walnut coat rack that stood in one corner of the room. A white dress uniform with gold epaulets and brass buttons from his days as a Mason hung on another hook of the same coat rack. Although he never wore it anymore, he liked having it where he could see it. It reminded him of parades and happier days.

He walked over to the small sink that hung on one wall and as he was washing his hands, he glanced up and caught sight of himself in the mirror that hung over it. A long time had passed since he'd really looked at himself. He turned the water off slowly and stood transfixed as he stared at his reflection. Looking back at him was an old man, bald except for a fringe of reddish hair that surrounded the large bare dome of his head. He reached up and ran the palm of his hand across the smooth hairless skin, recalling the thick auburn hair that had once covered it. Gold-framed glasses rested on a nose that he thought a bit too long and his once bright eyes, now faded, looked out through thick lenses. This was not a handsome face and it showed the wear and tear of all his sixty-one years. He lifted his body and held his shoulders back. The six-foot frame of his younger years now stood at only about five feet ten and his once flat stomach now tended to hang over his belt. As he assessed himself, what he saw was certainly reason enough for his wife to no longer find him attractive.

His eyes left the mirror and searched across the room for the picture of Dandy he kept on top of his roll-top desk. He walked over, picked it up and studied it. Pain was present in every part of his body as he addressed the picture, "You'd be married again in six months if something happened to me.

And when you find out what I've done, maybe you won't even wait for that. You'll probably tell me to leave."

Today had seemed an eternity, treating his patients while his insides gnawed at him. He had to face it. There was no way to convince Dandy that Inez was innocent without admitting what he'd done. He must confess and accept the consequences. Before replacing Dandy's picture, he took one last look, then slipped through the back door of his office into the deserted hallway. He walked to the elevator like a man on his way to the gallows, resigned to meet his fate.

A smile broke across the Joe's face when the elevator door slid open and he saw who was waiting. "Hi there, Doc."

Papa tried to smile, but his mouth refused to cooperate, so he nodded his head and touched the brim of his hat, hoping his silent response would discourage any further conversation.

Joe apparently got the message and said no more for the rest of the trip down to the lobby.

Once Papa was out on the street, he passed the unemployed men who propped their bodies along the side of the bank building each day. They stopped their chewing and complaining when they saw him approaching and yelled, "Hi, Doc. How's it going?"

The usual smile and greeting they'd come to expect was replaced with a simple nod. He found it impossible to pretend. Even seeing his treasured car, which was parked a few dozen feet away, didn't give rise to his usual feelings of pleasure.

Before getting into the car, he paused and looked back at the men he had just walked past. His predicament would seem small when compared to the plight of these poor men standing idle. However, although he felt deep compassion for them, his own dilemma had too firm a grip on him and refused to be set aside.

Lost in a fog on the drive home, he was almost surprised when he pulled into his drive. The trip from town seemed much too fast. But there was no more time for pondering because almost before he could get out of the car, laughing grandchildren were upon him.

"What did you bring us, Papa?"

There was that familiar question and today he'd come home empty handed. As he towered above them looking down into their expectant faces, his heart overcame his troubled mind and at last he was able to produce a genuine smile. He turned and opened the car door. "Okay children, pile in the car. We're heading for the grocery store and we're going to buy ya'll something extra special."

CHAPTER 15

Inez awoke this morning with a feeling of foreboding, one of those strange, indefinable feelings that tend to interfere with breathing. Since the other night at supper when Dandy glared at her across the table, she'd felt as if something heavy were sitting on her chest. There was no doubt about it. Something was wrong. She'd searched her behavior for the past several days to see if she'd done anything that could have displeased Dandy, but she could think of nothing. She'd always shown up at the right time and place as required, and never questioned when she was told to do something. had always complied. In fact, she was surprised at how compliant she'd become since coming to live here. All her spunk had disappeared, and she didn't like that in herself one bit.

She lay with her eyes closed and when she became aware that light was breaking through the window shades, she held them shut tight. With her eyes open she would have to face the reality of another day. With them closed, she could pretend she was waking up in her beautiful bedroom in Lubbock, big red roses covering the walls and lace curtains floating over the windows. She could imagine that when she got out of bed she could walk into her bathroom with the porcelain bathtub and use the porcelain toilet. Erby would be shaving at the bathroom sink, getting ready to put on his starched shirt and necktie. He'd then dress in a nice suit and prepare for another day at the office. And the two of them would be laughing about something. There was a time they were always laughing together.

If she kept her eyes closed, she could pretend the other side of the bed wasn't empty. If she opened them, she'd have to face the fact that he hadn't come home for several nights. She didn't know which she dreaded more: another day of not knowing where he was, or his coming home with alcohol on his breath and the fight that would inevitably follow.

When she first met Erby he was immaculate, dapper. All the girls who worked with her at the telegraph office were jealous when he'd pick her up in his new black Ford. He had a wonderful dry wit and clean-cut good looks, well-groomed hair and turquoise eyes. She'd never seen eyes that color before. Over the past few years, she'd watched while the mischievousness that was always twinkling behind those eyes was replaced by a look of despair. Now when she looked at him she saw a stranger, unkempt, faded shirts, and baggy pants that hung on his thin body. He had turned into a person who ceased to care about appearance, or anything else it seemed.

Well, she told herself, forcing her eyes open and throwing back the covers, she couldn't afford the luxury of dreaming or longing for the past. The reality was that she must get up and dress, feed her girls their oatmeal, and report to Dandy, ("the warden", she now called her) for the orders of the day. She was convinced the only difference in being here and being in a real prison was that there were no walls here and all the inmates were members of the Swinson family.

Later when she joined the other women who gathered in the garden to weed, it was still early morning and dew was clinging to leaves. Vegetables grew in abundance here, but unfortunately, so did weeds, and Dandy wouldn't tolerate weeds in her garden. As everyone else exchanged greetings, Dandy noticeably refused to speak or make eye contact with Inez. Being ignored and the icy silence that followed convinced her beyond the shadow of a doubt that Dandy's coldness was not her imagination. The atmosphere between them sent a chill through her as both crouched on the ground and pretended to concentrate on their weeding.

However, after only a few minutes, without any warning Dandy sat bolt upright, raised her head and looked directly at Inez. As if she had swallowed a time bomb and it had reached the correct time, the words exploded. She framed them distinctly, never taking her eyes off Inez. "A certain party has stolen my two new dresses, and I know who that party is." After making this declaration, she continued to stare at Inez, her eyes aflame with indignation.

Valera and Evelyn, who were weeding a few rows away, stopped what they were doing and looked up with wide eyes to make sure she wasn't talking to them. Relieved when they saw Inez was the victim of Dandy's wrath, they returned to their weeding, keeping their heads lowered, embarrassed to be witnesses.

Inez's face flushed hot while anger followed disbelief. She wanted to scream out in her own defense but she knew she'd cry if she did and she wouldn't give Dandy that satisfaction. Instead, she bit her lip, got up from her perch on the ground, and ran out the garden gate. She raced down the dirt path that led from the garden to her house, hot tears released to stream down her face now that Dandy could no longer see them. The anger she felt was not only directed toward Dandy, she was angry with God, as well. As she ran she cried aloud, *"God, what have I done to deserve that woman in my life?"* In spite of Erby's opinion that this wasn't all God's doing, Inez tended to blame Him for everything that was happening. She must have committed some terrible sin, she thought. The Bible says that when people are sinning too much, God punishes them by sending a flood, a famine, a drought or some sort of disaster. Inez was convinced that in her case He doubled up and also sent Dandy.

As the dilapidated house she was forced to live in appeared at the end of the path, her running slowed to a walk and she struggled to put one foot in front of the other. When she reached the back porch of her house, she dropped on the steps and buried her head in her hands. After she had a good cry, she lifted her head and looked around her with unfocused eyes. Finally, she forced herself up the back steps and across the porch. When she entered the kitchen she stopped and looked around the bare room. "Even this I could stand if it weren't for her," she yelled aloud as she crossed the room to splash cold water on her face. While drying her hands and face, she glanced out the kitchen window that was directly above the faucet. Her eyes fell on the house that stood on the other side of the barbed-wire fence that separated her yard from her neighbor's.

As she watched, her neighbor, Mrs. Leggett, came struggling out her back door, balancing a baby on her hip. No one seemed to know, or to care what her first name was. She was always just Mrs. Leggett, poor, unfortunate Mrs. Leggett, the mother of eleven children. Rumor had it that when she was pregnant with her eleventh, Mr. Leggett went to the store one day and never came back. He hadn't been seen or heard from since, and because everyone knew the circumstances of his life; no one even considered the need to call the police or look for a dead body. In fact, people imagined that Mrs. Leggett must surely have wished many times that she had been the one with the idea of disappearing. Her husband left her with no money, no skills, and the total responsibility of giving birth to a new baby and feeding and clothing it and the eight children still living at home. And, as if all that weren't enough, she had a grown son who was incontinent and confined to a wheel chair after an automobile accident. When his wife tired of caring for him, he was forced to return to live with her and the other children.

Inez imagined Mrs. Leggett must be only a few years older than she, somewhere in her late twenties or early thirties.

Her age was difficult to guess, so hidden was she in her three hundred pound body of flesh and fat. She'd probably married at fifteen or sixteen, not unusual in large poor families. Girls married young hoping they had found a way out, and parents gave their permission, relieved to have one less mouth to feed. Sadly, all too often, it wasn't a way out of anything for the girls, only a doorway into even deeper misery.

Home for the Leggetts was a decaying three-room shack that sat in the middle of a dirt yard. Inez had been inside the house once and remembered that wall-to-wall beds sat on the sagging floors of the front two rooms, leaving just enough space for Rayford to get through in his wheelchair. In contrast to the two front rooms, the kitchen was bare. A small free standing cupboard and a large distressed wooden table with an assortment of unmatched chairs and a long bench were the only furnishings. A big iron wood cook-stove showing signs of rust, stood against one wall and doubled as the only heat in the house. Newspapers had been pasted on the bare walls in hopes of keeping cold air from coming in between the cracks. The two narrow windows were covered with pull down paper shades, so tattered they did little to provide any privacy or relief from hot sun or cold air. The kitchen had no sink, no running water. All of their water must be carried from a well about a quarter of a mile away. Daily, the Leggett children could be seen struggling down the highway, carrying heavy tin buckets filled with water they'd drawn from the well. This might have been just an inconvenience except the only way Mrs. Leggett found she could try to support her family was to do other people's laundry, and this required lots of water.

Inez knew the routine. She'd watched numerous times before. Mrs. Leggett would gather wood with her free arm and place it under the big black iron kettle that sat in the middle of the back yard. Next she'd build a fire and after the water heated, she'd add a bar of the lye soap that she made herself. After it melted, the dirty clothes would go in and she'd stir them around in the kettle with the end of a broomstick. Since she had no clothesline, the barbed wire fence that stretched across the back of her yard was always covered with clothes hung there to dry.

As Inez observed all this again, she felt a tug at her heart and was embarrassed by her own self-pity. A curtain suddenly lifted and an awareness of how much she still had to be thankful for flooded over her. Silently, she thanked her neighbor. Mrs. Leggett would never know, but it was watching her life through the kitchen window that gave Inez the strength to endure and suddenly even be grateful for her own. As of this moment Inez vowed she was going to try to concentrate on only the good things in her life. Even though Erby certainly fell far short of a model husband, she never doubted that he loved her and the children, and even when he disappeared for a few days, she always knew he'd return. Her children were clean and adequately clothed and had never gone hungry. The Leggett children sometimes had to walk to school with no coats to keep them warm. Their toes were exposed in their worn out shoes and they survived on little more than dried beans and biscuits made of flour, water and baking powder.

When the Swinson family got together for a meal, the table was always covered with an abundance of food. Sometimes after they ate, they played card games and ended the evening by gathering around the old upright piano on the porch. Some of the adults would join the children singing Baptist hymns at the tops of their lungs as Dandy banged out "Onward Christian Soldiers" and "Bringing in the Sheaves". Sure, there were conflicts at times, but there was also a comforting feeling of family that assured them that in spite of their problems they weren't alone. Mrs. Leggett didn't have any of that. She was one of the many unfortunates who had no place to run, no one to turn to or to care, and no hope it would ever be any different.

Inez continued to stare at Mrs. Leggett out the kitchen window as she thought about what had upset her so much this morning in the garden. In fact, the words still rang in her ears. She'd been falsely accused and that was hard to swallow. Very hard. She didn't even know what dresses Dandy was talking about. But, she reasoned, Dandy was a given in her life for now and though it was a bitter pill, she was going to have to try to make the best of it. Giving Dandy the benefit of the doubt, Inez conceded that she was under a lot of stress, and apparently it had affected her mind.

CHAPTER 16

The silence in the garden was deafening after Inez left. Dandy could feel Evelyn and Valera stealing glances in her direction but she couldn't bring herself to look up. She was so embarrassed by her outburst at Inez that remaining in the garden was agony for her. She should never have accused her in front of Evelyn and Valera. Absolutely nothing she could think of was more humiliating than making a fool of herself in front of her daughters-in-law.

She hated to admit it, but after seeing Inez's response to her accusation, she suffered serious doubts about her guilt. She'd been so positive it was Inez. Now she was bothered by the look of surprise on Inez's face, and the fact she didn't even try to defend herself. But if Inez didn't do it, who did? This whole thing had gotten way out of proportion. The fact was she didn't even care that much about the darn ole dresses, and now she was letting them drive her to act like a crazy person.

Pretending that she didn't notice the stolen stares from Evelyn and Valera, she forced herself to finish weeding the rows of beans she'd started. After what seemed the longest morning she'd ever lived, she found a legitimate excuse to leave the garden. The sun was almost directly overhead, signaling it was time to fix the noon meal. She rose from the ground and headed for the house. Since she had no intention of defending her behavior to the other women, she left the garden without a word or even a glance in their direction.

After lunch, Dandy left the others to clean up the kitchen while she made a hasty retreat to hide in her bedroom. Once there, she locked the door. She couldn't remember when she had ever felt so miserable and confused. She searched the room for something to divert her attention. An unfinished landscape painting still sat on the easel in a corner of the room, gathering dust. Months had passed since she touched her paintbrushes. She crossed the room and made a feeble attempt to distract herself with her paints; however, it didn't take long for her to find she wasn't able to settle down to painting. Shortly after picking up her brushes she jammed them into a jar of turpentine and roamed the room, restlessly searching for something – anything -- to settle her nerves and take her mind off her embarrassing behavior.

After trying in vain to read, then to crochet, she finally just gave up. At her wit's end, she dropped down on her bed and tried to relax. From her bed she could see out a window and a flock of geese caught her eye. She rose and made her way to the window in time to see them flying overhead in perfect formation. How free they looked--flying away to find a better place to be. She wished she could sprout wings and fly away with them. Any place would be better than this. Then as suddenly as they'd appeared they were gone and she was left staring at an empty sky, stuck where she was.

She was still standing at the window, looking aimlessly at the sky when she felt the first pain. The headaches were coming more frequently now. Thank goodness for her pills, she thought. She felt anger sweep through her when she thought about Papa no longer allowing her to have her own bottle of headache pills. He'd taken to rationing them out to her two at a time, as if she were a child. Well, she'd taken care of that. One night when he was in the bathroom, she'd stolen into his medicine bag, helped herself to a supply and now they lay hidden, wrapped in a handkerchief in the back of her sewing table drawer.

When the pain started to envelop her, she retrieved the handkerchief and gulped down a couple. Then she walked around the room pulling down all the window shades before the light became unbearable. She lowered herself on to the bed and before closing her eyes, she took off her glasses and laid them on the bedside table. With her hands folded across her chest and her head resting on her pillow, she waited for the pills to take effect. Before long, she began to drift into the misty world of liberation to which the pills transported her. She had no idea how much time passed before she became aware of a banging on the bedroom door. Startled back to reality through her fog, she blurted out "Go away! Leave me alone."

"Lula, it's me," Papa answered. "Are you okay? I've been knocking on this door for five minutes. Unlock it and let me in. I have something important I need to talk to you about and it won't wait."

CHAPTER 17

A brilliant sun shown unobstructed in a cloudless blue sky as the two men sat patiently watching their red and white corks ride the ripples of the water. Their small fishing boat was anchored in the middle of the lake and rocked gently with the soft breeze. Every now and then a flock of birds sailed overhead and the men turned their attention skyward to watch for a few moments.

Erby put down his fishing pole, reached in his shirt pocket for a cigarette and pulled out an empty package. With a look of disgust, he crumpled it and threw it into the lake. Then he said, "Tom."

"Yeah?"

"Got any cigarettes?"

Tom, who sat in the back of the boat, reached into his shirt pocket and pulled out half a pack of Camels and threw it at him.

Erby shook one out, stuck it in the corner of his mouth, searched his pockets for matches and finding none said, "Got any matches?"

"Jesus. You want me to smoke it for you, too?" Tom put down his fishing pole, found matches and threw them hard at Erby.

"No," Erby answered with a grin, "I think I can manage that." He lit the cigarette, took a couple of slow deep drags, and watched the smoke as he exhaled before picking up his pole and returning his attention to the cork. He finished his smoke, then put his pole aside, stretched out his legs and rolled his shoulders a couple of times. After sitting in the same position for hours his body was beginning to talk to him. Turning back to his friend he asked. "Anything left in that bottle?"

Tom picked up the whisky bottle from the bottom of the boat with his free hand, held it up and took a look, then tossed it to him without a word. Erby drained the last of the clear brown liquid, threw the empty bottle in the lake and watched as it floated a while, then filled with water and disappeared. As he listened to the sound of the waves lapping against the sides of the little boat, he surrendered to the effects of the alcohol. He was addicted to this feeling: a feeling of numbness to a world that didn't play fair.

"Fish aren't biting today," Tom offered.

"Nope, no fish for supper tonight."

"Want'a go in?"

"What for? I've got no place to go -- except back to a wife who cries and complains all the time, a mother whose delusional, and a dad whose gone half nuts, not to mention farm work, which I hate."

Tom grunted, shook his head.

After a few moments of reflection, Erby added, "Although, God knows, Inez has every right to tears and complaints. She has to live in that hovel of a house and has to put up with the demands of my mother everyday. To top it off, Dandy's on the warpath with Inez for something she didn't even do."

Another grunt from Tom. "That's tough."

They watched their corks ride the gentle waves in silence for a while before Erby continued. "You know, when the war was on and I was in the navy on that destroyer, there were lots of times when I was scared to death. Out there in the Atlantic Ocean, we were always hoping we'd get a German submarine before it got us. However, there was never a time I just gave up. But, damnit, this depression is worse. We were heroes when we went to war and we knew there would be an end to it. But now, no end is in sight."

Tom stared ahead, listening without comment.

"Now I'm where no man's supposed to be." Erby continued. "I can feel the women beginning to get doubts about me as a person, as a man. They don't say it, but every time they look at me I can hear them silently asking if I'm not smart enough or if I'm not trying hard enough to get a job." He sat barely breathing as he reflected on what his life had become. "This depression doesn't seem to have hit everyone the way it has my family. It's like, we've got food and a place to live but we're all falling apart. Let's face it--I depend on alcohol to get me through the day. My dad's burning my mother's dresses, and she's turned into a tyrant." He reached up and pulled the brim of his old gray felt hat down further over his eyes. Picking up his pole again, he lifted his line out of the water to make sure he still had a worm on his hook. When he saw it was there, still wiggling, he lowered it back in the water and was quiet for a few minutes while his mind searched for answers to questions that had no answers.

After a few minutes, he spoke again. "You know, when I started out in this life, it seemed I had everything going for me. I thought I was going to be one of the winners. I was smart enough, had some talents, wasn't bad looking. I had a good home, a prosperous father and a talented mother who loved us in their own way. Shit, I just can't stop wondering -- what was the misstep in my life that marked me as a loser?"

Tom looked up at him, his forehead wrinkled into a frown. "Stop it, Erby. You're not a loser. You're just down on your luck. Lots of people are right now."

"Hell, Tom. I'm thirty-six years old, living off my dad, not able to give my family a decent life. Every day it becomes harder for me to face Inez." He shifted in his seat and got out another of Tom's cigarettes and held it between his fingers as he stared off in the distance. "The thing I used to like most about Inez was the way she loved havin' a good time. She was the most fun-loving person I'd ever met." A half smile turned up one side of his mouth. "We used to do really crazy things together. There was a time, when we hadn't been married long, and we were in our bedroom in Lubbock getting ready for a party. She had this cockamamie idea. I remember asking her, 'You really think we ought to do this, Inez?' She just giggled as she tried to help me button the party dress I was putting on. Then she handed me a big flower covered hat she'd picked out for me to wear. She was already dressed in one of my suits, her hands completely hidden in the sleeves and the hem of my pants dragging the floor around her feet. When we looked at each other dressed in our ridiculous garbs, we laughed until tears were rolling down our cheeks." He paused for a second and took a deep drag of the cigarette and watched the smoke float away in the breeze. "Now, I don't even remember the last time we laughed together." He took one last drag and snuffed out the cigarette.

"The other morning when I woke up, the first thing I saw was the picture of her that sits on our dresser. She was wearing a fancy dress, a black one covered with shiny things. Her hair was set in those deep waves she used to wear and she had some fancy comb stuck on the back of her head. In this picture she was holding a rose and was posed on this love seat, draped over it like some movie star. She never was what you'd call beautiful. Glamorous. Yeah, that's what she was: glamorous." He sat, bent over at the waist, appearing to examine the floor of the boat. "As I lay there, I turned my head and looked over at her lying on the pillow next to me. Hell, even asleep she looks unhappy, and down right dowdy, no trace of what she used to be. All gone. Everything that drew us together smashed out of us by this goddamned depression. Now, even when she doesn't say anything, she looks at me with those accusing eyes. She's mad at me most of the time. Who could blame her? I do awful things. Why wouldn't she be mad when I haven't been home for the last two nights?

"I have to admit no woman would like that." Tom said.

Erby pulled out another cigarette, lit it and watched as the tobacco glowed red. "It's not a good excuse, I know -- guess I don't really need a good excuse to get drunk any more, but after my confrontation with my dad, when I saw how miserable he felt about burning my mother's dresses, I was really upset. I needed a drink bad. And as you know I can't drink at home."

Erby studied Tom who was bobbing his head up and down as he listened. He was a tall lanky man. His long legs were folded up in front of him as he patiently watched his cork and listened to Erby talk. A well-trimmed mustache covered his upper lip and an abundance of dark brown hair fell over one side of his forehead. The face beneath was a nice face, not handsome, but good and kind. Deep creases in the corners of his soft brown eyes gave evidence that this was a face that smiled a lot.

Looking at Tom gave Erby a warm feeling. "Tom, sure good to have a friend like you, one who doesn't judge you, who'll put you up overnight when you can't go home and who'll have a drink with you and listen to your whining. No one else, not even my own family, seems to understand. I know that behind our backs they call Archie and me the black sheep of the family because we drink." Then he added after a moment of thought, "and I guess they're right. Yeah, they are."

Tom continued to shake his head as he listened, aware there were no words that could console. Occasionally he'd say "I know."

After a few more minutes of just watching their corks bob up and down on the water, Tom said, "Erby."

"Yeah?"

"It's getting late. I gotta go to work. We'd better go in."

"Okay," Erby agreed but didn't make a move to get ready to leave. "You know, you're pretty lucky. At least you have your café, Tom, and a place to go everyday that belongs to you."

"I guess. I've managed to hang on by the skin of my teeth, but it's been awfully close, I can tell you for sure. Every month I think I can't possibly make another one, but by some miracle I manage to scrape by. Guess I'm lucky that people still have to eat, even in this depression, and seems they can manage to rake up a dime for a hamburger. But how long can that last?" Tom smiled and sat up straighter and put his fishing pole aside. "Hey, goddamnit. Enough of this. It's a beautiful day, even without fish. We've had a nice time and we're here for each other." With a halfhearted laugh, he looked at Erby and asked, "You wanta feel better? Have you heard the latest Will Rogers joke?"

Erby shook his head and pulled another of Tom's cigarettes out of the pack and lit it with Tom's matches. He really didn't feel too receptive to a joke right now but he appreciated his friend's attempt to lift the mood.

"Well," Tom continued with a silly grin, "Will Rogers said the situation is so bad in New York City that the clerks at hotels ask the incoming guests if they want a room for sleeping or for jumping? And, Will adds, you have to stand in line to get a window to jump out of."

"Not funny, Tom, for God's sake," Erby frowned.

"Yeah, guess you're right, but Christ, you've gotta try to keep your sense of humor or you'll go under. At least you have a place to live. Remember my cousin Ralph who worked for Bethlehem Steel in Chicago? Not only did they sack him and six thousand others, they evicted them from company housing so they could tear down the houses and save the property taxes. And my cousin Bobby, who still has his job at the newspaper, for now anyhow, told me the other day that things are so bad there that not only did the paper cut everyone's salary, they unplugged all the electric clocks to save money on electricity. So Erby, when you look around you -- guess we could be worse off."

"Glad you didn't say we're lucky. But true, guess they're right when they say, 'things are never so bad they couldn't be worse.'" He smiled at Tom. "You always were one to look at the bright side. Guess that's why I chose you to be my best friend in first grade. In spite of the fact you were ugly as hell." he added with a smirk.

"Go to hell, Erby." Tom responded laughing. "But for sure we've been through a lot together, and we'll see this one through, too."

"Yeah, hope your right."

"Well," Tom said starting to pull in his line, "Guess it was too much to wish for, to have a beautiful day like this and to catch fish, too." He looked at Erby and motioned. "You might not care to go home but I've gotta get back to the café. This is the second day this week I've left Maggie to run the café with only Abner to help and she's gettin' a mite edgy about it. Can you believe that? Some women just don't understand about fishing."

Just as Erby was pulling his line in and getting ready to leave, he was jerked to full attention as his cork jumped a couple of times and then disappeared under the water pulling his line taut. With a quick yank, he hooked a big bass. "All right!" he cheered as he pulled it out of the lake and into the boat. A big smile spread across his face. "Well now, does look like fish for supper, after all." He worked to remove the hook from the fish's mouth and secure it on the otherwise empty line while Tom pulled up the anchor and started to row toward shore.

* * *

It was nearing supper time when Tom's car stopped on the road in front of the little cube of a house where Erby's family lived. With effort, Erby climbed out of the car onto the gravel shoulder of the highway, turned and stuck his head in the car window. "Thanks, Buddy. See ya' later," he said, his fish secure in the bucket he held in his right hand.

"Okay, sure thing, Erby. Good luck with Inez." Tom waved as he drove away down the highway toward town.

Narrow planks formed a bridge across the ditch that separated the highway from Erby's weed covered yard. After two days of imbibing, he still felt a little tipsy and had difficulty keeping his balance while holding on to his fish bucket and treading the narrow bridge.

Betty Lou sat under the big shade tree on the side of the house making mud pies to feed her doll. She looked up and saw him coming across the yard. Immediately, she left Mary to wait while she ran to meet him. "Hi, Daddy. Did you catch a fish? Can I see it?" she said, looking at the fishing bucket he clutched in his hand.

"A big one," he answered. "Here, Betty Lou. Why don't you take it around to the back porch so we can clean it for supper? Where's your mother?

"She's in the house and she's mad at you."

He wanted to say, "So what's new?" but didn't. Instead he said, "You take the fish and run on now. I'll be there in a minute."

She grabbed the bucket in both hands and he watched as she struggled to carry it toward the back yard. Then he tried to straighten himself up, making an effort to appear sober. It wasn't easy. He tripped going up the steps that led to the front porch. Several of the boards had broken loose again and presented a challenge he wasn't up to in his present state.

He found Inez standing at the stove cooking supper. If she'd heard him come in the front screen door, she didn't show it. She continued to ignore his entry into the kitchen until she felt him pinch her gently on the bottom, then put his arms around her from behind and bury his head in her neck. Only then did she acknowledge his presence.

"Don't you dare touch me, Erby Swinson," she whispered, her jaw clamped with anger, her brown eyes shooting sparks.

He pulled his arms away and backed off a step. "Oh, Inez, please don't be mad. I'm sorry. You just don't understand what happened. You know I love you, Honey."

"Don't you *honey* me! Where have you been for two days? You -- you son of a bitch. While you were out getting drunk, I've gone through hell. Your mother accused me of stealing her *damned* old dresses and…" She caught herself and stopped in mid sentence -- she'd never cussed before moving here. Realizing this made her even angrier. "I needed your support and you let me down again." She reached out and pushed him as hard as she could.

He fell back, then somehow managed to regain his balance. "Oh god, Inez. I'm so sorry." He looked as if he could cry.

"You're always sorry. But that doesn't seem to change anything, does it? Frankly, I don't want to hear it anymore until you show you really mean it." Filled with fury, she pushed him again, harder this time, and he fell back against the wall. He was struggling to regain his balance when he saw her coming toward him again, and before he even had time to think, he reached out and slapped her across the face.

Immediately, he sunk to the floor on his knees, hiding his head in his arms, horrified at what he'd just done.

Two-year-old Gloria was sitting on the kitchen floor where she'd been playing with her wooden blocks but was now watching them. When she saw her father hit her mother, she screamed and put her tiny hands over her face and peeped out through her fingers. Then she sat, surrounded by her blocks, and cried inconsolably.

Inez gasped and stepped back startled. Turning, she staggered across the kitchen, her hand caressing her cheek where the blow had fallen. She braced herself on the table and looked over at Erby who was huddled on the kitchen floor. She could hear him sobbing now and she couldn't decide whether to hate him or pity him.

After the shock wore off, she turned to rinse her face from the water faucet that jutted from the kitchen wall. When she raised her head, she caught sight of Mrs. Leggett out the window. It was almost dark and she still stood in the middle of her yard, stirring her wash. Inez was reminded of her resolve to be grateful for the good in her life and to be forgiving of what wasn't. After the scene in the garden this morning, she had stayed away from everyone and Dandy had left her alone. Good thoughts and resolutions had been easy when she wasn't challenged. But now she found at the very first test her resolutions dissolved. The bad in her life was just too overwhelming.

CHAPTER 18

Papa continued to knock on the bedroom door, growing more insistent as he waited for a reply.

Finally, Dandy could ignore the banging no more. She forced her body out of bed and crept across the room to unlock the door. When she saw him standing in the doorway, all her composure vanished. Grabbing him, she wrapped her arms around him and buried her head in his shoulder. Every emotion she'd held at bay for so long surfaced and her body shook with sobs as she clung to him.

Slowly her sobs became whimpers and when her body stopped shaking, he said, "Lula, Lula, Lula. What in the world brought this on?" Rarely did he or anyone see Dandy totally lose her composure like this.

She looked up at him, her eyes filled with despair. "I'm so confused. I'm feeling…" she paused and shook her head, "I don't know what . . . awful, just awful . . . like I'm a horrible person in a terrible world."

"What are you talking about? You're not a horrible person. What have you done to make you say such a thing?"

"So many things." she cried. "For one, this morning in the garden, not only did I come right out and accuse Inez of stealing my dresses, I did it in front of Valera and Evelyn. I totally made a fool of myself. I could feel them giving me dirty looks for the rest of the morning. They think I'm not only mean, but crazy as well. And no telling what Inez thinks. What makes it even worse: they're probably right. I think I am mean and crazy. And now to make matters worse, I have my doubts about Inez being the thief."

Dandy didn't notice he was visibly relieved at this decision about Inez. She was too caught up in her own predicament. "I was downright nasty to Inez, I'm ashamed to say. When I accused her, she looked genuinely shocked and without a word in her own defense, she jumped up and ran out of the garden." Dandy pulled back from him and searched his face. "Papa, do you think I could have been wrong about Inez?"

"Yes, you are. That's what . . ."

She cut him off and continued, "But if it wasn't Inez who took my dresses, then who was it? They're gone. That's for sure." She dropped her eyes as she mumbled, "Sometimes I really do think I'm losing my mind." She buried her head in his shoulder again.

He pushed her back, turned her chin up and forced her to look up at him. Her face, which was usually composed or at least controlled, looked like it was made of hot wax, melting, without structure. "Lula, please listen to me for a minute. I have something important I've got to tell you."

"And there's more," she said, continuing to ignore his attempt to speak. "Now don't you laugh because I'm dead serious about this. I know what I'm gonna tell you has got to sound crazy to you. It sounds crazy to me. But I just can't stop thinking about heaven and hell."

"Heaven and hell? What in the world are you talking about?"

Shaking her head vigorously, she insisted, "Just let me finish. I've been thinking about this. There was a time when I was a fairly nice person, but now I'm too mean and far-gone for even Jesus to forgive. And if Jesus can't forgive me, then you and all my loved ones will go to heaven and I won't be there. And you know what bothers me the most? I'll go straight to hell and have to spend eternity with Preacher. That'll be my punishment."

She was too distraught to notice a smile that threatened to cross his face for an instant. He looked at her lovingly, put his arm around her waist, led her across the room and helped her to sit down in the rocking chair. When she was settled, he pulled a chair in front of her and looked directly in her eyes. Leaning his face close to hers, he said softly, "Lula, please, be still and listen to me. You're not mean. You're not going to hell with Preacher. And you're not losing your mind. I came up here to make a confession to you." He looked away for a second. "Lord knows how I'd love to get out of telling you this, but the fact is, this whole, entire painful thing you've been going through is my fault."

"What are you talking about? How could it be your fault?"

"Just listen to me now, *please.* I could make a lot of excuses and I swear some of them would be valid considering all that goes on around here." He paused a second. "However; there's no good excuse for what I've done." He rose from his chair, roamed across the room and stood looking out the window. In the distance, the barn behind which the trash was burned came into view and was a hurtful reminder of what he had done.

Dandy pulled her handkerchief out of her pocket and blew her nose while she sat anxiously looking at his back. "Papa, what are you talking about? What have you done?"

"You'll never forgive me, and I can't blame you. But the awful truth is, Lula," he dragged out the words, "it was me . . . I took your dresses, or at least some jealous green monster that lives inside me did." He kept his back to her as he finished his confession. "Then I burned them, down there behind the barn."

Her voice came back weak and shaky. "No! No! I can't believe this. Why? Why would you do such a thing?"

"I'm ashamed to tell it, but you might as well know the whole thing. Because those dresses were too short. I just couldn't stand to think of some strange man seeing your beautiful legs."

A silence fell on the room like some ominous black spell. He continued to stare out the window. When the explosion he'd expected from Dandy failed to happen, he turned slightly and looked at her. "I'm so sorry. The last thing I wanted was to cause you pain. I haven't drawn a peaceful breath since I did it." His eyes pleaded as he looked at her. "I know it's a lot to ask, but can you ever forgive this jealous old man who loves you too much?"

Her only response was to look at him with hurt in her eyes, then she raised her index fingers to hold each side of her forehead as the pounding started again. It was as if she could hear the fragments of her mind breaking into little pieces, like glass splintering. Finally, she said in a thin dry voice, "So. It appears I'm not the only one who's crazy. You're crazy, too." Then she added with a laugh filled with bitterness, "We've both lost our minds."

Her body seemed to fold in on itself and she felt very old and tired as she slowly rose from her chair and made her way across the room to lie down on the bed. Once there, she raised her arms to cover her face in an attempt to shut out everything around her. She didn't want to look at him, or to think, or to hear anymore. All she wanted was to just disappear, to become like smoke and drift away.

* * *

For three days Dandy stayed in her bed, refusing to eat or to speak to anyone. When different family members brought food to her room, she hid her head in her pillow. Hours later when they returned to pick up the food tray, they found it untouched.

Papa seemed beside himself, wandering aimlessly around the house like a lost lamb. The family was more worried about him than about Dandy. However the cause of their parents' strange behavior remained a mystery. They could only speculate among themselves about what might have brought all this on.

In the beginning, although no one said so out loud, everyone on the farm enjoyed Dandy's seclusion and the peace they felt without her driving them. However, before too much time passed, they began to realize that not one of them knew which pasture the sheep should go in or what vegetables needed to be harvested and canned on any given day. There wasn't one farmer among them. Agnew was an optometrist, Erby a bookkeeper, Preacher a flooring salesman and Archie had done a little of everything except farm work. Their wives were equally ignorant of what needed to be done to keep the farm going. Although Evelyn had grown up on a farm, she'd never had responsibilities other than cooking and house work. So after a couple of days on their own, they came to the sad but true conclusion that without Dandy's supervision, the farm was like a rudderless ship.

On the fourth morning of Dandy's withdrawal, everyone in the house was surprised and delighted to awaken to the aroma of bacon frying and biscuits baking. It was with unexpected relief that they welcomed Dandy's return. But although she cooked and served the family meals, she still refused to look at or to speak to anyone, even Bess Nell.

For the next week, mealtime remained quiet and uneasy. People spoke only when absolutely necessary, and for reasons they didn't understand themselves, when they did speak they felt they should whisper. The strain from Dandy's behavior was getting under everyone's skin. As soon as the dishes were done and the kitchen was in order, they all escaped to their bedrooms early, even the men, foregoing their usual games or listening to the radio together.

After several days of this, Dandy was secretly beginning to see that she couldn't keep this up much longer. There were too many things around the farm that were being neglected. In spite of her resolve not to give a hoot about any of it ever again, she was beginning to care.

* * *

A few nights later, Bess Nell and Preacher were in their room preparing for bed. Patsy and Johnny were already asleep in the single bed that stood against one wall of the bedroom. As Preacher unbuttoned his shirt, he looked over at Bess Nell and said, "Looks like your mother is finally returning to her old sweet self. I knew her silence was too good to last."

Bess Nell stopped brushing her hair and looked back at him over her shoulder. "Preacher. That's not nice." Although she chided him, a smile was beyond her control. "What do you mean she's *returning*?"

"She was barking at me again today."

"Really? What did she say?"

"When I came in from feeding and watering the horses, she was in the kitchen trying to churn butter. She was sitting there with that churning crock between her knees, giving the churn handle hell. She had that expression on her face. You know the one she gets when she's really pissed about something: her lips pursed and her eyes bugging out. I expected her to give me that blank stare and then just ignore me like she's been doing all week. But instead, she jumped all over me."

"What about?"

"She said I'd left too much milk in the cream when I'd separated it this morning. It was all my fault because it was taking her so long to get the butter to churn." He stopped unbuttoning his shirt and frowned. "Goddammit! I never milked a cow before in my life until we came to live here. And I'd never planned to either. How the hell does she think I'm supposed to know how to separate cream from milk? I do good to get the goddamned milk out of the cow."

"Preacher, I hate it that Dandy treats you so badly but you know it's a losing battle for me to try to get between you and her. And I'm sorry to remind you again, but there's just no way that she's ever going to forgive you for stealing her 'precious daughter'." She turned her attention back to the dressing table mirror and started to brush her hair again. With an ironic smile on her face she raised her eyebrows and said under her breath, "Welcome back, Dandy."

CHAPTER 19

Preacher listened to the steady breathing that told him Bess Nell was asleep. Sleep hadn't come easily for him for a very long time; not since he'd been forced to move his family in with Dandy and Papa. As he did most nights for the years they had been here he tossed and turned and pounded his pillow into different shapes but there was no position he could find that would turn off his mind. Bess Nell was right. Her mother would never forgive him no matter how hard he tried to please her. She was unwilling to even give him a chance. As usual, he lay in the dark, eyes wide open, unable to stop scenes from his past life from replaying.

In his mind's eye, he was back at the Dallas train station, having spent some of the money he'd saved on a shoeshine and haircut. The barber had parted his straight brown hair in the middle and slicked it back with good smelling hair tonic. He was dressed to the teeth: suit, white shirt, tie. He'd gotten a job at Big D Carpet and Flooring Co. when he was still in high school, and his Aunt Martha had given him one of her husband's old suits. Except for sleeves and pants legs which were just a bit too short, it fit him pretty well. He looked good, smelled good, and in his big hands he clutched a bouquet of white daisies, Bess Nell's favorites. She would surely be impressed.

He paced back and forth on the platform of the depot, his eyes pinned to the tracks on which the train from Greenville was scheduled to arrive. His thoughts tortured him and a gnawing grew in the pit of his stomach. *What if she isn't on the train? What if she changed her mind?*

At long last he heard the train's whistle and looked to see it round the bend and come down the tracks toward him. Almost before it slowed he started running down the platform. When it came to a stop a short distance away, the porter stepped down from a car and began to help passengers off. Holding his breath, he watched person after person take the porter's hand and step down and sighed with relief when he saw the porter hold out his hand to Bess Nell.

Her eyes searched for him as she got off the train, then her face broke into the sweetest smile he'd ever seen when they found him. Preacher was sure his heart must have stopped beating for an entire minute.

Her eyes were large and shining and the auburn hair that peeked out beneath her funny little hat glowed red in the sunlight. She looked much younger than her eighteen years and it had always amazed him how tiny she was, how fragile she looked. It never failed to arouse in him the need to take care of her.

His smile stretched from one side of his face to the other as he looked down at her and even though public displays of affection were not thought proper, he couldn't help but wrap her in his arms. She grabbed her little hat and blushed as he squeezed her to him. Then without a word between them, he took the small suitcase that held her few belongings. She looked up at him with such love in her eyes he felt he would surely melt. Then hand in hand they walked the two blocks to catch the streetcar that would take them to a Justice of the Peace to be married.

There was no money for a honeymoon but they happily settled down to married life in the tiny two room apartment he'd rented for them. Preacher was now a full time employee at Big D Carpet and Flooring Co. His outgoing personality made him popular with his customers and his co-workers. They overlooked his profane language because they appreciated his good humor and he kept them entertained with his seemingly endless supply of jokes.

One day after they'd been married a couple of weeks, Preacher came home from work to find Bess Nell making a special meal: chicken fried steak and potatoes fried with onions, things she knew to be his favorites. Their small kitchen table was covered with a tablecloth and set with a candle and flowers.

"Hummm! Smells good in here. And look at all this! What's the occasion?"

She sparkled with excitement. "Guess what? I got my first job today. I am now an employee of Montgomery Wards, Co."

He lifted her up in his arms and kissed her. "That's great, Darlin'. I'm so proud of you."

"I've got it all figured out. You're doing so well that I believe we can live on your salary and save most of mine and in a year or so, we'll have a nice little nest egg and can think about buying a house."

One evening, a little more than a year later, as Bess Nell was starting to prepare dinner, she heard Preacher racing up the stairs to their second floor apartment. Flinging open the door, he ran into the living room, a huge smile plastered across his flushed face. He crossed the room and caught her up in a hug and gave her a big kiss.

She pushed him back and batted her eyes. "Wow, Preacher, what's going on?"

"Guess what, Babe? We're going to be rich!" With that announcement, he did a little dance, then grabbed her off the floor and whirled her around the room.

"Hey, wait a minute!" she said, struggling to get down and trying to catch her breath. "What in the world are you talking about?"

"You know Larry Bishop that works with me? Today he was telling all of us at work that six months ago he invested in the stock market. For only $300 down he was able to buy

$3000. worth of stock and already it's worth $5600. What do ya think of that?"

"I don't understand. Sounds too good to be true. There must be a catch."

"No, just listen. Larry told me that all you've gotta do is give 10% down to the broker and then the broker borrows the rest from a bank. Then all we have to do is make small monthly payments. It's called 'buying on margin'. All the guys at work are going to do it, even if they have to borrow the 10% down. But, we're lucky. We have money in our savings." With that he yelped and reached his arms skyward as he danced around the room again. "I tell you, everyone is going to get rich. It's guaranteed. This is a goddamn golden opportunity." Then seeing the look on her face, he stopped and said, "What?"

"Well, I don't know, Preacher. We've worked awfully hard to save that money and we have enough to start thinking about a house. This apartment is awfully small and someday we'll have a baby and need more space."

"That's the whole point, Darlin'. We'll be able to buy a much better house when we make all this money. Why, before long, the way the stock market is climbing, we'll be able to pay cash for our dream house." He paused, then added, "Think about it, Bess Nell. Think what your mother will say when she sees us in a big fine house? Then she'll know she was wrong to get so upset about you marrying me."

Bess Nell smiled at this. She knew how important it was for him to prove himself to her mother. Knowing this, she relented, but it was still with some reservation on her part that in January of 1928, they withdrew most of their savings and took the money to Mr. Lowe, the broker Larry recommended.

"Congratulations, Mr. and Mrs. Rowan. The smartest people in the country are putting their money in the stock market. Count yourselves farsighted to be among them. I promise you, you won't be sorry. Just stand back now, and watch your money grow."

Hearing this, Preacher and Bess Nell exchanged smiles and felt assured. If the smartest people were doing it, it must be the right thing to do. At first, Mr. Lowe proved to be correct. In just three months time their account showed big gains -- on paper. Bess Nell had insisted, and Preacher agreed, that they would purchase stock in Montgomery Wards, Co. since it was one of, if not *the* most promising department store. Electricity was available to most everyone now and people were starting to buy electrical appliances. Bess Nell reasoned that Montgomery Wards seemed a likely place for people to buy them. Her theory proved correct and Montgomery Wards stock soared.

With their future assured, it was time to start their family. In March of 1929, Bess Nell happily confirmed that a baby was on the way and they started looking for a house to buy in an upscale neighborhood of Dallas. However in late October of 1929, the bottom dropped out. In a single day, many very rich people became poor, and average investors like them were wiped out. Their own private investment in Montgomery

Wards stock dropped to $33 a share less than they'd paid for it.

Preacher wasn't immediately sure what the stock market crash meant to them since all their gains had been on paper. He only knew the situation was bad. One evening shortly after the stock market crash, he found how desperate it was. He and Bess Nell were having dinner when the phone rang. They exchanged glances and he got up to answer.

"Hello," Preacher said.

"Mr. Rowan?"

"Yes, this is Mr. Rowan."

"This is Mr. Lowe, your broker." He cleared his throat. "I'm sure you're aware of what's happened to the stock market. I'm afraid I'm forced to ask you if you want me to sell your stock at the present market value or if you want to put up the margin?"

"Put up the margin? God," Preacher gasped into the phone." Goddamn, how much is that?"

"Well, Mr. Rowan. You still owe $3900 on what you borrowed on your stock."

"Lord God! How much is it worth if you sell it?" Preacher asked, panic beginning to take hold.

"If I sell it at market value, I'd say, oh, probably in the neighborhood of maybe two or three hundred dollars.

"Mr. Lowe, how could this happen? How could we still owe that much?"

"Since you bought the stock on margin, Mr. Rowan, you've just been paying interest on a loan for the stock; the stock itself was being used as collateral."

This was all too complicated for Preacher to understand. Suddenly, he felt sure his dinner was going to come up. "Please, Mr. Lowe. Would you hold on just a minute?" He held the phone to his chest while he tried to catch his breath. When he felt capable of speaking again, his voice choked as he asked, "What if we can't come up the money? Jesus Christ, Mr. Lowe, that's a lot of money!"

"Well, Mr. Rowan, I'm afraid if you can't come up with the cash to cover the loss, the bank will take your stock and pursue you for the rest of the money you owe."

Bess Nell sat nearby trying to figure out what was happening. When he hung up the phone she responded to the look on his face. "Preacher. What's going on?"

He pushed his plate aside and let his head drop on the kitchen table, his face burrowed into in his arms. In all his life he had only cried a few times, even as a child. However, now he could taste the salt from the tears that broke free.

At work the next day, he was surrounded by others who'd joined in the same race to get rich in the stock market. Some had invested their life savings; some mortgaged their homes, while others cashed in safer investments. They were all ruined. And when he thought things couldn't get any worse, his bank couldn't meet the withdrawals caused by the panic. The attempted withdrawals came at a time when banks were unable to collect on loans and almost 10,000 banks in the United

States failed, wiping out the savings of millions of people, including the little left of his and Bess Nell's.

"At least I still have a job," he said to a worried Bess Nell; however, soon his hours and wages were cut because people had no money to buy carpet. And after a while, even his job was gone.

By now they had a beautiful little girl, and Bess Nell was expecting again. Even though they'd been able to remain in their apartment, only because of the generosity of their landlord, money for food and other necessities was gone. Reluctantly they joined other jobless and homeless people who were forced to stand in line at soup kitchens and to depend on food from welfare agencies and religious groups. Soup kitchen meals consisted of beans, stew thinned with so much water that they had little nourishment, and of course soup. Clothing became equally hard to come by. It made Preacher sick to see his precious Bess Nell in her threadbare clothes and his baby girl in used things passed on to them by people whose own children had worn them out. Now they had to worry about food and clothing for another baby.

One morning, after he'd been out of work for months, and the cabinets and icebox had been bare of food for days, he and Bess Nell sat in their little kitchen, hands folded on the table, with the last of their coffee growing cold in cups before them. The silence between them hung heavy as they stared at the dreaded eviction notice that lay open on the table between them. It was not the first notice -- several others had preceded it and they'd implored the landlord's mercy --

however, they knew this was to be the final one. Their landlord had sadly informed them that he could no longer afford to pay the utilities on their building.

Preacher raised his head and locked eyes with Bess Nell and they sat staring at each other for a long moment. "Well, Honey, I'm afraid this is it." He twisted his hands together and tried to suppress the hopelessness that was eating away at him.

Her small voice came back just above a whisper, "What are we going to do, Preacher?"

"I just don't know," he answered honestly. His heart ached when he saw the look in her eyes. "Not that we're going to do this, but some of the people I used to work with who've been thrown out of their homes, have been forced to move over to Hooversville."

"Where's that?"

"It's that part of town where folks are building shacks from everything they can find -- even flattened tin cans and old crates, I'm told. I've heard some families are even living in old rusted out car bodies. Albert told me the other day he saw one family living in a piano box." His eyes glazed over as he sat pondering their predicament.

Bess Nell was determined to hold back the tears that burned behind her eyes. "How awful. How can all this be happening? Why doesn't the president or the government do something?"

"I don't know. People say President Hoover won't do anything to help because he doesn't believe it's the federal government's responsibility to take care of people. He thinks private business and religious organizations should do it. But it's too much for them to handle -- too many people are in need." He looked across the room to where their little girl slept in her baby bed and his despair grew even deeper.

Bess Nell shook her head and bit her lip, then looked away.

Preacher knew she was trying not to show him how desperate she felt. He also knew Hooversville was out of the question as long as there was any other way. He had to face it. His worst nightmare was coming true. Instead of proving to Dandy that he was worthwhile by becoming rich, he was now forced to throw his family on her mercy. He reached across the table and put his hand over Bess Nell's and squeezed.

She looked up at him and tried to smile but her eyes betrayed her.

All the love he felt for her welled up in him. "Darlin', don't worry. I'd never ask you to live in Hooversville. I'm sorry I even mentioned it. But I can think of only one alternative. You know how I feel about asking for help from your parents. And you've been so good about not pushing me to do it, but I'm afraid the time has come when I've gotta swallow what little pride I have left. Your parents will take you and Patsy in and I'll stay here and keep trying to find something."

"No! No, Preacher. There's no way I'll leave you behind. If I go, you go, too."

She sat for a few minutes longer, then with resolve she pushed herself up from the table, put her hand on Preacher's shoulder and patted it as she walked by him. Slowly, she opened the door of their apartment and stood looking back at him for a moment before turning to walk down the hall. One of their neighbors still had a telephone and she needed to place the collect call.

Three long years had passed since he'd come to Ardis Heights dragging his tail between his legs. If he'd been alone he would have chosen Hooversville over living with his mother-in-law. But he was here, still stuck in Ardis Heights, and Dandy was getting her revenge. But even though life here was almost unbearable for him, he'd never had a single moment of regret he'd married Bess Nell. She had been the first thing in his life that had been absolutely right. She'd given him unconditional love and that was something he'd never had before he met her.

His childhood had been starved of any kind of security. His mother, Sara, was one of two Butler sisters from a prominent and highly religious family in Commerce, Texas. Mrs. Butler, Sara and Martha's mother, was the president of the local DAR and the Commerce garden club. Their father, a successful lawyer, was a deacon in the First Baptist Church and an important member of many civic organizations. Mr. and Mrs. Butler had ostracized Sara when she became pregnant. In their religious community, pregnancy out of wedlock was not something that could be accepted or forgiven, not even when followed by marriage, and certainly not to the man Sara married.

The Butlers had good reason to disapprove of Preacher's daddy, the Reverend Jim Rowan, an itinerant preacher from a poor family. The Reverend's family had no money and no education, owned nothing but the clothes on their backs, and were not inclined to want to work. The Rowans contributed nothing to society and were considered by the Butlers to be no more than "white trash".

Kicked out of the house by his family for various reasons too numerous to mention, Reverend Jim had discovered preaching to be a lesser evil than a real job. Since he was a handsome young man, tall and muscular with wavy black hair, expressive blue eyes, and blessed with charm that seemed to ooze from him, he found himself well equipped to take to the road with his Bible.

While in Commerce to preach at a tent revival, he captured Sara's heart, and unfortunately, also her body. When Sara discovered she was "in a family way", and the Butlers disowned her, she tracked Reverend Jim down and threw herself on his mercy. When he found out Sara came from money, not being one to pass up any possible opportunity, the Reverend agreed to make the baby legitimate and they were married.

The marriage was a disaster for Sara from the start. They were constantly on the move and managed to live just above the poverty level. Reverend Jim would occasionally manage to get a church of his own but he was never welcome for very long, always asked to leave because he became involved with the female choir director, the church secretary or sometimes a member of the congregation. Seemed he couldn't leave women alone -- not a good trait for a preacher. He traveled a lot, doing his "hell fire and brimstone" preaching mostly at tent revivals around the state, leaving Sara and their son alone with little money or food, in the one room they usually lived in.

Reverend Jim came to believe that God spoke to him and had given him a scale by which to measure sin. Convinced that adultery, wife beating, and stealing were minor sins in God's eyes, there was one sin that Reverend Jim knew to be absolutely, positively unforgivable and that was "taking the Lord's name in vain."

Little Jimmy, Jr., being a bright boy, realized at an early age that one sure way to get attention was to use blasphemous words. And since any attention is better than no attention at all, he developed quite a profane vocabulary. Not only did it get him in trouble at home, but also at school with his teachers. At the same time, it made him a celebrity of sorts with the other boys who thought him courageous to be doing something so forbidden. And so little Jimmy became known as "Preacher", a nickname he was never to live down, and though he had tried in later life to clean up his bad mouth, it had proved to be a losing battle. The Lord's names just seemed to slip out of his mouth uninvited.

Despite Mr. and Mrs. Butler's decision to have nothing more to do with their daughter Sara, Martha loved her sister and refused to give up until she found out where Sara was living -- not an easy feat because they moved around so frequently. By the time she tracked her down, Sara was in such a deep depression that no matter how hard Martha tried, she couldn't pull her out of it. Finally, Martha accepted that she couldn't save her sister; however something had to be done about her child. Martha had married and was living in Greenville now and she started bringing Preacher to visit as frequently as she could. Years later, on one of his weekend visits, Preacher met Bess Nell, and from the first minute he laid eyes on her she'd never left his thoughts or his heart.

Daylight was beginning to creep into the bedroom now and Preacher heard the first crow of the roosters. Still lying with his eyes open and exhausted by the memories that had filled his night, he started out the day with the same prayer he prayed every day: *Please God, let this be the day that brings me hope that things will soon return to normal and my family and I can escape this hell.*

1934

CHAPTER 20

Perspiration rolled down Valera's forehead and stung her eyes. The smell of rain in the air gave her hope of some relief from this unbearable heat. What a day to be stuck in the kitchen with Dandy. Inez and Evelyn were at the big table out on the sun porch peeling and slicing peaches. She'd like to know why she had been the one chosen to help Dandy in the kitchen. Just her bad luck -- as if she ever had any other kind. Dandy probably chose her so she'd have more opportunity to pick on her, she thought.

"Valera, did you boil those fruit jars out good?" Dandy asked.

"Yes ma'am, I did, Mrs. Swinson." Valera picked the pan of hot paraffin off the stove and started to pour it into the tops of the fruit jars that sat in a line along the long linoleum topped cabinet.

"Make sure you seal those good," Dandy said, lining up another row of peach filled jars as she removed them from the canner. "They'll spoil if you don't seal them good."

"Yes, Mrs. Swinson, I know," Valera said through clinched teeth.

It seemed Dandy was more determined than ever to make all those present sorry they were here. Valera was convinced Dandy was taking out her frustrations more and more on her daughters-in-law, and on her in particular.

She not only felt sorry for herself but for Dr. Swinson as well. The reason for Dandy's strange behavior last fall was no longer a mystery. The family now knew that he was the one who had taken Dandy's new dresses. An old army cot that had been stored in the garage was in their bedroom for a while. No one dared to ask, but it was assumed it was for him. Valera's heart had gone out to him as he moped around the house like a convict under a death sentence.

"Poor Dr. Swinson," Valera muttered under her breath.

"What was that?" Dandy asked, not able to make out what Valera was mumbling.

"Nothing," Valera answered, wearily. "Nothing at all."

* * *

Exhausted after her trying day in the kitchen with Dandy, Valera wiped perspiration off her brow as she pulled herself up the stairs and down the hall to her bedroom. When she pushed open the door she found Agnew already there, lying on the bed in his underwear, reading. He'd opened the windows on both sides of the room as wide as possible, wishing for a breeze that refused to come. The small electric fan that sat on their dresser whirred away, but offered little relief.

As Valera entered the room they looked at each other but didn't exchange a word or a smile. She stopped and stood observing him. Seeing him now she wondered how she could ever have thought he was distinguished looking. His curly hair, which had always been in tight controlled waves when she first met him, now formed a rust-colored bush around his head. His once thin, well-groomed mustache was now a wild and wooly thing that totally hid the space between his nose and top lip. He'd never been a heavy man but lying there in his underwear, he looked downright skinny, even scrawny she thought. Farm work had definitely done nothing for his looks.

Dripping with sweat, wet down to her skin, Valera striped off her soaked dress and let it drop to the floor. She purposely stepped on it as she crossed the room, opened the bedroom door a crack and peeked to see if the bathroom was available. It wasn't. The bathroom door was closed. "That damned bathroom's never available when I need it," she complained, stomping her foot. Then she picked up the hairbrush that sat on her dresser and threw it across the room. It hit the wall with a loud thud.

Agnew jerked and glanced up at her over the top of his glasses, said nothing, and returned to his book.

She gave him a dirty look. He should be glad I didn't throw it at him, she thought. After a day of biting her tongue and holding in her frustration, she had to explode. A tirade of words streamed from her mouth. "That old bitch. I don't know who she thinks she is. She thinks she's sooo perfect and above everyone else. Does she really think she has us all fooled? That we're all so dumb that we don't know that she dips snuff and that she goes to her room and knocks herself out with those pain pills. Well, when she gets hers, and I've gotta believe someday she will, I'm going to laugh like hell." Valera screwed up her face and in her most sarcastic voice she mimicked her mother-in-law. "'Valera, did you do this? Valera, did you do that?' She treats me like she thinks I'm an idiot. She hates me, can't tolerate me."

As if he'd said something, she stopped and looked at Agnew, a scowl distorting her pretty face. It enraged her that he just continued to read his book and ignore her. Waving her arms in the air she raved on, "Well, I tell you for sure, the feeling's mutual."

She shook her head, and let her arms flop to her sides in a sign of surrender, and added wearily, "But hell, we're stuck with each other, like it or not." She didn't come right out and say, "and it's your fault for bringing me here," but she hoped he got that message.

Depleted after her hard day and her tantrum, she dropped down on the side of the bed and slipped off her shoes. Lost in thought for a few moments, she stared blankly at the wall. Then she moaned and without looking at him, said in a listless voice, "You know, Agnew, I thought when you married me that you was going to save me from my awful life. You looked so good to me then. You was an educated man. 'Doctor Swinson'. You lived in that big house in the best part of town. People in Nacogdoches respected you. Fool that I was, I thought if I was your wife I'd be accepted by people who seem to matter in this world, that I could have a decent life. But who was I kiddin'?"

She rose from the bed and paced the room as she continued. "Of course everyone was shocked that you would marry me. Let's face it, I was a 'lady of the evening', to put it in a nice way." Then she shot him a knowing look and added with a bitter smile, "But as you and I both know, I was just plain and simple a whore. And who's ever going to forgive that?"

She wasn't surprised when there was still no response from Agnew. She seemed to be talking to herself as much as to him anyway. Wringing her hands together and turning to look at him with a smirk, she stopped pacing and continued, "You think I didn't know why you married me? Of course, I knew. You married me just to get even with your first wife for leaving you." The more she talked, the angrier she became and her voice grew louder. "I might be ignorant but I ain't stupid -- although some people around here seem to think otherwise."

Her eyes cut over to where he still lay on the bed, apparently unmoved by her outbreak. *Look at him lying there ignoring me. He never pays attention to me. I know I ain't no prize but it hurts that he's ashamed of me. But then, he is his mother's son. What can I expect?*

She couldn't keep the hurt from rising up in her. Fighting tears, she said under her breath, "Well Agnew, old boy, you just go ahead and ignore me. There's someone in this family that's going to pay me attention and I know just what to do to get that program going. As the saying goes, 'If you're gonna have the name, you might as well have the game.'"

Just then she heard the bathroom door open and close. Without another word she grabbed her robe from the hook in the closet and abruptly left the room.

* * *

Agnew looked up from his book and breathed a sigh of relief when he saw Valera leave, grateful to be free of her terrible tantrum. He had refused to be pulled into an argument he knew he couldn't win, so he'd remained silent, pretending to read; however his eyes had followed her as she'd paced the room, ranting and raving. He was glad to hear that she knew why he'd married her. He couldn't remember why. He must have been out of his mind. Hard for him to believe how little her murder of the English language had bothered him before they came to live here. Now he could feel himself cringe when he'd hear her say, "ain't" or some other abuse of the English language. He couldn't help but notice Dandy cringe too. How embarrassing!

As he'd secretly watched her storm around the room in nothing but her underwear, he did have to admit that she was an amazingly beautiful woman. Even though he'd lost all desire for her now, he couldn't help but admire her perfect body. There was not an ounce of fat on her and everything was well shaped and in exactly the right proportion. Even her foul mood couldn't hide her natural beauty. Taffy colored curls framed a perfectly shaped face with flawless skin and her long black lashes surrounded enormous green eyes that seemed to occupy more than their fair share of her face. Yes, no denying she was a beauty, but as his mother always said: "Pretty is as pretty does". In the past, he'd always made fun of his mother's sayings, but he was coming to appreciate the wisdom in some of them. Closing his eyes, he turned his thoughts back, trying to remember how he could have been so desperate and vulnerable as to allow Valera to become his wife.

His heart throbbed in his chest as if a knife had just pierced it as he allowed himself to relive the day he'd come home from the office to find suitcases in the entry hall. Helen Lee, his wife of almost fifteen years, whom he loved with all his heart, stood beside the bags. She was dressed in her hat and coat, as were his two young sons. She told him she was leaving -- just like that -- no notice, no explanation. She refused to even discuss why. He was in total shock. It had never even occurred to him that she wasn't happy with him. Later, he realized there had been clues which he had subconsciously chosen to ignore.

After Helen Lee left, a deep depression swallowed him and he went even farther down when he learned she'd left him for another man, a supposed friend of his. After that, nothing seemed to matter to him anymore. He let himself go completely. For days he didn't shave and slept in his clothes. He ate out of cans and his house was a complete wreck, dirty clothes and newspapers dropped and left where they fell. It wasn't long before the maid threw up her hands and refused to come back. On the occasion he would go to work, he was late and missed appointments. His practice declined rapidly and his receptionist became so frustrated with his behavior that she quit. Friends were all terribly concerned about him and tried to help, but he refused their invitations for dinners and golf games, pulling away from everybody and everything.

After several months of this behavior, his best friend, George Thompson, decided something had to be done. He stopped by Agnew's house one evening and rang the doorbell. There was no response although he was almost certain Agnew was home. He could see a light was on in the back of the house. Refusing to give up, he continued to ring the bell until finally the front door opened a crack and Agnew peeked out. George could see he was still in his pajamas although it was almost 6 P.M.

"What do you want, George?" Agnew's voice was rude.

"Open the door, Agnew."

He tried to slam the door in George's face but he pushed past Agnew and forced his way into the house. "Enough is enough. You're my friend and I'm not letting you destroy yourself. I'm not asking you. This time I'm telling you. Get dressed! You're going out. I've got a surprise for you and I'm not taking no for an answer. I know what you need to pull you out of this."

Agnew argued and refused in the beginning but his friend finally wore him down and he dressed and got into George's car, grumbling as he did. When the car pulled up and stopped in front of a house that was known to be a 'house of ill repute',

Agnew was indignant. "I'm not going in there, if that's your plan."

"Get out of the car. I've already paid. A good toss in the hay is exactly what you need." With that, George opened his car door, walked around and physically pulled Agnew out. Then he returned to the driver's side, got back in the car and drove off, leaving Agnew standing on the curb with his mouth open. A few feet down the street he slowed the car and yelled out the open window, "Her name is Valera." With that, he sped away.

Agnew stood on the curb a few minutes, cursing George and wondering what he should do. He looked up and down the treeless street. There was no transportation and it was getting darker by the minute in this not the greatest of neighborhoods. Finally, he shook his head and said to himself, "Oh, what the hell." Then he turned with a shrug and walked up the steps of the house and knocked on the door.

Agnew had only had sex with one woman besides Helen Lee in his entire life, and that had been a one-night stand when he was in the army stationed in Germany. So when Valera introduced him to pleasures he'd never known existed, it opened up a whole new world for him. He realized now Helen Lee had never enjoyed sex. She had yielded her body but sent her mind off in other directions when he made love to her. It was clear to him that with her, sex had been a matter of endurance, not enjoyment. Valera enjoyed what she did, or else she was the world's greatest actress.

His life began to take shape again and Valera's bedroom soon became a place where he could forget the pain of his broken marriage and the loss of his daily life with his boys. And before long it became more than just sex. Valera would let him stay the night if she had no one else coming. He felt so comfortable with her. Always a very private person, he'd never been able to share his innermost feelings with anyone, not even his wife. He realized now he hadn't even shared them with himself. To his surprise, he found that he could tell Valera anything without hesitation, and she was always understanding and sympathetic, never judgmental. It was a time when he craved this kind of attention and he began to confuse pleasure and comfort with what he thought was love.

One night while they were lying in her bed, her head on his shoulder and his arms wrapped around her, a feeling of closeness to her enveloped him. He reached over and turned her face toward him. "Valera, we've been seeing each other for how long now? Almost six months? And I've honored your rule about never asking you about yourself, not because I didn't care, but because you asked me not to. And I've shared everything with you, all my most secret thoughts." He picked up her hand and kissed it. "You must know I have feelings for you. It's too much to expect me not to ask how a beautiful, intelligent girl like you came to this profession. Why this? Why are you doing this?

"You really want to know?" she asked.

"Yes, I really do," he answered and kissed her hand again.

"I guess you deserve that." She hesitated for a moment, sighed and began, "Okay, then. My life's story coming up. Not pretty I warn you."

He nodded his head and smiled at her, encouraging her to continue.

She looked at the ceiling as she gathered her thoughts. "Well, no place like the beginning, I guess. I was born in a little town no one ever heard of just outside Henderson, Texas. We lived on what people called the wrong side of the tracks. Believe me, even in our little town, there was a wrong side. My mother cleaned houses for the few people who had money for such a luxury. My daddy worked on traveling construction crews and we wouldn't see him very much. It seemed that he only come home to get my mother pregnant, and then he left again. He didn't shoot any blanks, either. My four brothers were born less than a year apart and I come along not quite a year later. Then my daddy must have skipped some time coming home because there was two years between me and my little sister, and another two years before my baby sister. Then he didn't come home at all no more. No word. He just never showed. He never did send much money home so it didn't make a lot of difference. We'd mostly lived off what my mother made and what my brothers was able to pick up doing odd jobs." She stopped talking and looked at him. "You sure you want to hear all this?"

"I told you, yes!" he said. He was touched by a sudden understanding of a life he could hardly have imagined.

"Okay then." She sat up in the bed, pulled her knees to her chest and glanced down at him to make sure he was serious. "This isn't easy to talk about." she said, but in a moment she continued. "In the days when my mother was expecting all the time, she'd clean houses until she got too big and then she would take in ironing. We didn't have electricity in our house so she had to heat an old iron on the woodstove. She'd stand over the ironing board for hours until her feet swole up so big she couldn't stand no more. Then she'd cry from the pain. My mother was a good woman, bless her heart. She deserved a better life."

She hesitated and seemed to be thinking about something for a few seconds. "I think that's when I started to hate men, because of what my daddy done to her. Anyhow, with my daddy gone and mama working so hard, we kids got used to rooting for ourselves at a very young age. We learned that you do whatever it is you need to do to survive."

"I wasn't very old when I first found out what most men and boys have on their minds. I was an early bloomer and already had big tits. Males started to swim around me like fish after a worm. Out of the blue one day, the fourteen year old boy who lived next door, who had ignored me up to this point in my life, suddenly wanted to play 'hide and go seek' with us younger kids. All of a sudden he was my big buddy and he whispered to me, 'Come on, Valera. I'll show you a really good place to hide.' I was eleven years old. What did I know?

So I let him take my hand and lead me into the cotton patch that bordered our yard. 'Get down in the cotton stalks,' he said as he pulled me to the ground. 'Tommy will never find us here.' Next thing I knew his hands were all over my body and his mouth was smothering me. That was the first of a never-ending battle with every man and boy who passed my way.

Finally, I got smart and decided that there was a good living to be made in this and if they wanted it, they was going to have to pay for it." She didn't say anything for a moment and then she shrugged, "So here I am, whether I like it or not." She gave him a weak smile, "Now I'm trapped. Just like my mother was trapped -- except if I wasn't here, I'd never have met you."

Agnew had closed his eyes as he reminisced. Suddenly he could feel Valera's presence near him. He lifted his eyelids to find her standing directly over him, looking down at him accusingly.

After a long moment of no response from him, she left his side, dropped in the room's only chair and sat picking at a tear in the upholstery. The room was quiet now. Not peaceful, but silent. And though Valera had seemingly spent her venom, he sensed her mind was still raging.

His eyes open now, he watched her for a short time and then drifted away. He felt as if the walls were closing in on him. How had things come to this? he wondered. His whole life seemed to have erupted into nothing but a war filled with daily battles.

CHAPTER 21

The first time it happened Archie thought it was accidental. When it happened again the next day, he convinced himself it was just coincidence. After all, the table where everyone shared meals was so crowded it was impossible not to brush up against someone's leg now and then. However, the third time he felt her leg pressed against his under the table, he knew it was intentional. He began to notice that no matter what seat he took at the table, Valera made it a point to take one next to him whenever possible. Today when he felt her hand rest on his thigh, he could no longer ignore it. This was positively not accidental. Glancing at her out of the corner of his eye, he was surprised to see her staring straight-ahead, grinning like a Cheshire cat.

Feeling embarrassed and confused, he was sure his face was beet red and he quickly looked around the table, checking to make sure no one was looking at them. Oh good God, he thought. What have I done to bring this on? He couldn't deny that he, like the rest of the men in the family, was aware of Valera's sexiness. What red-blooded man could ignore her voluptuous body and the way she swung her hips when she walked. Even the shapeless housedresses she wore to work in couldn't hide her perfect curves. And though it was never talked about, Valera's past history was no secret. In fact, if he was perfectly truthful, Archie had to admit that he had fantasized about her on occasion. But how could she know that? Besides, she was his brother's wife, for God's sake, and even though he'd done some despicable things in his life, even he wouldn't sink that low.

It took all his will power to reach below the table, take her hand, move it from his thigh and place it on her own. When he stole another look in her direction, she was for all appearances, engrossed in a conversation going on across the table between Agnew and Preacher.

Several days passed without another incident and Archie breathed a sigh of relief. However, about the time he decided he was safe and she'd given up on him, he found her sitting next to him again at the supper table. When he felt her hand traveling up his thigh and stopping on his crotch, his breath caught in his throat and he was overwhelmed with mixed emotions. Oh, Lord, he thought, when he felt his body responding to her touch. He hated his own weakness, but he couldn't deny what he felt. It seemed no matter how hard he tried to do the right thing, trouble tracked him down and hogtied him at every turn. His entire life reminded him of the man in the comic strip who had a little black cloud over his head that followed him no matter where he went.

It took all his will power to once again remove Valera's hand and give it back to her. Her response was to glance over at him with an innocent smile. He lost interest in his supper and the minute he could do so without drawing attention, he escaped. His heart was beating like a drum as he ran down the path that led to the hay barn where he'd carved out a secret spot in a dark corner of the loft. This was a place he could drink, free from interruptions and prying eyes. And oh, how he needed a good stiff drink!

When the barn came into sight his feet ran faster and his heart didn't stop thumping until he closed the barn door. Racing for the ladder that led to the security of the hayloft, he climbed the rungs two at a time and after pulling his body through the opening, he rushed to his hiding spot and collapsed on the floor with his back against the wall. Still breathing heavily, he felt as if he'd been chased by a bear and narrowly escaped.

When his breathing returned to normal, he reached under the hay to the place where he hid his bottle. There was only time for one big swig before his body tensed again. He heard the barn door creak open. Someone had just entered. The arm holding the bottle froze in midair and he held his breath listening for the next sound. After a few moments he heard a whispered voice. "Archie? Archie, are you here?"

Oh God, No! he thought as he slowly put his bottle down, drew his knees up to his chest and covered his ears with his hands, trying to remain as quiet as possible. He didn't move a muscle, afraid even to breath. Obviously his resistance to her advances hadn't discouraged her. *Had she felt his weakening resolve? Didn't she feel guilty for tempting him like this? She must know he wasn't a strong person.*

Valera waited a few more moments giving him time to answer, then called his name again. "Archie, please answer me. I know you're here."

His body stiffened but he was determined to ignore her. He scrunched up tighter against the wall and repeated over and over, "She's my brother's wife, my brother's wife. God help me! This is my brother's wife." He wanted to yell out, "Why me, Valera? Why not anybody instead of me?" However, as he thought about it, he understood why him. Of course, if Valera was going to make moves on someone it would have to be him. After all, who were the two big losers in this lovely little Ardis Heights zoo? The two outcasts? He thought about what his mother's reaction would be to this. Knowing how she had a saying to cover every situation, he could imagine her response would be, "Birds of a feather flock together".

After a few more minutes when he didn't response to her calls, he heard the barn door creak again, then slam shut. His body went limp with relief... He feared he couldn't have resisted much longer. The memory of how good it felt to have her hand on him made him shudder. In spite of himself, he fantasized about what it would be like to feel her perfect naked body next to his. He didn't want to want her but she'd set him on fire. He moaned and tried to relax, but he felt as if he were caught in quick sand and the harder he struggled the deeper he sank.

* * *

Archie took his time about getting dressed the next morning and purposely came late to breakfast, hoping to avoid sitting next to Valera. But it was just his luck that the only chair left was the one next to hers. This time when he felt her hand crawling up his thigh, he just couldn't make himself remove it. He didn't do anything to encourage her, but he didn't discourage her either. He tried to keep a straight face as he watched closely to make sure others at the table weren't aware of what was going on. Much to his relief he found everyone so involved in their own conversations that they paid no attention to him and Valera at all.

In the days that followed, Valera became more aggressive and in spite of all his good intentions, he surrendered and soon started taking an active part. Every time they passed each other in the hall or on the stairs they would manage to brush up against each other, their eyes would meet and knowing looks would flicker between them for an instant.

Following a week of exchanged glances and stolen touches, Archie was hiding in his secret place in the hayloft after supper one evening when he heard the barn door creak open again. Shortly, he heard Valera's soft voice calling his name. His will defeated, he heard a voice that seemed to have come from him answer, "Up here."

She made her way to the ladder and cautiously climbed the rungs to the floor of the hayloft. Once there she stopped and stood waiting for her eyes to adjust to the dark. As she waited, she began to slowly unbutton her blouse.

Archie didn't move for a moment, giving his better nature an opportunity to swoop in and rescue him; however it ignored him, as it usually did. He moaned, accepting that his good intentions were defeated. He couldn't fight it any longer. His chest heaving, he rose from the loft floor where he'd been sitting and took slow steps until he stopped directly in front of her. Neither of them moved nor spoke, taking a moment to enjoy feeling their nearness to each other. Then he reached out for her and she stepped into his arms.

They were not under the illusion that what happened next was making love. Love had nothing to do with it. It was pure unbridled passion and it was beyond anything he'd ever experienced with any of the other women he'd known.

* * *

The next morning Archie awoke with a throbbing head, worse than his usual hangover. His mouth was dry and the first thing he thought of was a drink. Maybe a drink would obliterate the guilt he felt about the night before. Even though the whole episode was Valera's fault, he realized he'd sunk to a new low. As he turned his head on the pillow, his eyes spotted some bits of hay on his pillowcase and he quickly grabbed them and hid them in his hand. Although he frequently had hay on him from the loft where he spent most of his evenings, his guilt made this particular hay look like a smoking gun.

His tormented eyes rested on Evelyn sleeping next to him. Evelyn who had always been there for him, no matter what, who had forgiven him so much until he had finally pushed her past the point that even she could forgive. When he'd married her he'd hoped that her love for him would change him. He'd never known a woman like her, so shy, so sweet and innocent, loving and forgiving. He'd hoped some of her goodness would rub off on him. Instead, he'd used it as a license to cheat and carouse.

He flopped over on his back and stared at the ceiling, wishing he could pull the covers over his head and never have to look anyone in the eyes again. He couldn't believe the things he'd done. Sometimes he felt as if he were outside himself watching this strange person occupying his body do things that totally disgusted him. That's how alcohol had gotten such a hold on him; an attempt to numb the devil side of him. The irony was alcohol just gave the devil more control.

His mind turned to Valera. What was he to do about her? How was he to free himself of her? Trapped. He felt trapped -- a feeling with which he was all too familiar. He'd never confessed it to anyone, but his entire life had been spent trapped in feelings of helplessness and fear. He wondered if he'd been born this way or if it was that terrible event in his childhood that had warped him.

One of those born with an inexplicable fear of snakes and spiders, as a child Archie had been convinced they were all poisonous, didn't matter whether they actually were or not. These fears made the family outhouse a chamber of horrors for him. The shadowy corners in the outhouse were an open invitation to spiders and snakes. And as fate would have it, one day he almost stepped on a large snake that was coiled on the floor of the outhouse. After that, he became hysterical with fright each time he was forced to go there. For a while Dandy had to accompany him to make him go in He would stand outside, his eyes large and body quivering while she opened the door wide and stood aside so he could make sure all was well. Then she'd carefully inspect every nook and cranny before giving him a little nudge. "Okay, Archie. It's safe. See?"

For weeks, he'd taken reluctant steps, looking back over his shoulder and balking before he'd step inside. Finally, Dandy decided this had gone on long enough and insisted he start going alone.

Agnew and Erby had loved playing tricks on their younger brother. They thought it disgusting that he was such a "Mama's boy". One day they were climbing in a mulberry tree nearby when they looked down and saw Archie slowly open the door to the outhouse. As usual, he stood outside for a long time looking in before he cautiously entered. As had become his habit since the snake incident, he left the door partly open in case he needed to make a hasty retreat; privacy being of far less importance.

The outhouse door had slide bolts on the outside as well as the inside, to make sure that the door would stay closed when unoccupied. The two older brothers watched and when assured Archie was well inside, they'd climbed down from the nearby tree, careful not to be heard. They tiptoed over to the half open door, slammed it shut and quickly threw the outside bolt.

Archie would never forget his feelings of horror as he stared at the closed door. He jumped down from his perch and started pounding and screaming at the top of his lungs, his pants still around his ankles. He could hear his brothers outside laughing. "Okay, you little sissy. Your mama can't save you now."

The outhouse stood far enough from the house to be out of earshot, so cry and scream as he might, no one could hear him. After almost an hour, Archie was too exhausted to cry or bang on the door any more. Alone, helpless, frightened, he curled up in a ball, whimpering. He remained there until Dandy finally came out and found him, but the damage was done.

As Archie relived this, he broke out in a cold sweat. Those same feelings overwhelmed him now, an inability to save himself, a feeling of being trapped in a place he couldn't get out of.

After a few more minutes, he roused his aching body from the bed and relieved himself in the chamber pot that was standard equipment in every bedroom of the house. Being careful not to awaken Evelyn or his young son, he made his way over to the marble topped walnut dresser that held a washbasin and pitcher. Water in the pitcher was cold but he was accustomed to that. He poured a little into the shaving mug that held his soap and swished it around with his shaving brush until he worked up a lather, then slid his straight-edged razor back and forth on the razor strop that hung nearby. When he was sure it was sharp enough, he picked up the brush and was about to apply lather to his face when he looked in the mirror that hung over the dresser. His reflection sickened him. Unable to meet his own eyes, he looked away and vowed that tomorrow when he looked in this mirror, a different man would look back at him.

He finished shaving, got dressed in his work clothes, and as he was getting a clean handkerchief from his dresser drawer he found the little pint bottle he had hidden there. He stole a glance across the room to make sure Evelyn and Sonny were still asleep. He just needed one last little drink to help him face the day ahead. Then he swore there would be no more alcohol and no more Valera. Checking once again to make sure they weren't watching, he turned the bottle up and drained it.

CHAPTER 22

The breakfast table quickly filled with the family getting ready for another work day. When Archie entered the sun porch and joined the rest he was fortified with new resolve. Today he would turn over a new leaf. No more drink. No more Valera. However, all his good intentions lasted just until his eyes caught sight of Valera sitting at the breakfast table, looking unusually beautiful. Memories of their evening together flooded over him and rendered him helpless. The seat next to her was empty, and he tried to make himself take the one on the other side of the table. However, as if someone else was in control of his mind and body, he found himself sitting down next to her. He had hardly taken his first bite of hot biscuit when he felt her foot resting on his. Then slowly she pressed her thigh against him. That's all it took for his body to respond to her with an urgent need.

A few minutes later, Evelyn and their little boy came into breakfast and took the seats on the opposite side of the table. Archie's conscience pierced him. He was ashamed to look his wife in the eye but he forced himself to greet her with a shake of his head and a smile.

What am I doing? I've got to end this thing with Valera. Oh God, please help me. But even as he prayed, he didn't really expect God to answer his prayer. In his heart of hearts, even as he swore to end it, he knew it was just one more vow that he would break.

* * *

Often the men in the family would stay on the porch after supper, playing dominos or checkers and listening to Amos and Andy, Will Rogers, or Fibber McGee and Molly on the radio. The women usually chose to go to their rooms, eager to spend time alone or with their children.

Since Valera had no children, she was free to do as she pleased and the last thing she wanted was to spend more time with Agnew's family than she absolutely must. In the past, before she decided to get even with Agnew by seducing Archie, she'd gone to her room alone and listened to her little radio or read romance magazines. Or sometimes she would just sit staring at the walls or looking out the window, her mind filled with concerns about what was to become of her. And on many occasions, she sat wondering if this was truly a better life than the one she had before Agnew came along. However, now with Archie in the barn waiting for her, things were definitely looking up. Since neither Archie nor Valera had ever hung around with the rest of the family after supper, there was no problem for them to meet evenings in the hay barn with no one noticing their absence. At least that's the way it appeared to them.

One evening after they'd been meeting in the barn for several months, they were stretched out on the hay, exhausted after a passionate encounter. They lay side by side, their bodies glistening with perspiration and their eyes closed. After a brief period when neither spoke, Valera turned to Archie. Lifting her body, she leaned over him and said in a quiet voice, "Archie?"

He stared up at the rafters of the barn through half open eyes and didn't bother to answer her. He was more than a little drunk and physically drained. He wished she'd just leave him alone.

She tried again. "Archie, are you listening to me?"

He finally sighed and grumbled, "What do you want?"

"Now, Archie, don't get upset because it's probably just my imagination, but I have to ask you. Did you think your mother was starin' at us in a strange way at the supper table tonight?"

He was instantly sober and sat bolt upright, his eyes wild with fear. "Oh my God, no! Do you think she knows something's going on?" He ran his fingers through his hair then covered his eyes with the palms of his hands. Panic gripped him as he was forced to come to terms with what the consequences of getting caught would be. Then anger followed his panic. He dropped his hands from his face and glowered at her. "Okay, Valera! Look what you've gotten us into! I've told you that you needed to be more careful, that someone might see you coming out here. But, oh no. You just had to keep it up." His face twisted with fury and he clenched his fists and waved them in the air.

Valera cringed and pulled away. He looked wild and the way he was waving his arms around she feared he might hit her. But instead, as she watched she saw the anger on his face slowly melt away. He dropped his fists and then his body slumped as if his bones had suddenly turned to powder. His eyes took on a tortured look. "Oh my God, Valera. What have we done?"

"For heavens sake, Archie. Don't get so upset. I didn't know you'd fall apart just because I didn't like the way your mother looked at me. I shouldn't have even mentioned it. Your mother's always giving me dirty looks. You know that. She hates me. Besides, how could she know? There's no way." She reached over and put her hand on his cheek and cooed, "I'm sorry I upset you over nothing, Darlin'." Then, flashing her most seductive smile, she pushed him back down in the hay. "Just calm down now and forget I said anything. My imagination runs away with me sometimes." She crawled on top of him and stroked his hair gently back from his forehead, then kissed him softly on his lips. With a twinkle in her eyes, she said, "Now you lay right there, Baby, and I'll get you a little drink. Then, I promise, I'll do something for you that will make you forget I upset you."

When she returned with the bottle he grabbed it from her and drained it. In a few minutes he was beginning to relax. He considered what she'd said and replied, "You're right,

Valera. You are inclined to let your imagination run away with you at times. And Dandy is always giving you dirty looks. I overreacted. I'm sure you're right. There's no way she could know." He reached up and pulled her back to him. "Now what was that thing you were going to do to make me forget about being upset?"

CHAPTER 23

The farmhouse at Ardis Heights was always buzzing with even more activity than usual on Sunday mornings and today was no exception. Everyone in the family was expected to go to Sunday school and then take their places in the third row pew of the First Baptist Church in downtown Greenville for the service. This was not optional. Everyone understood that unless they were running a temperature of over 102 degrees, they were to be there.

As Dandy did every Sunday morning, upon arriving at the church, she walked down the aisle of the sanctuary with her back erect, her nose in the air, and her "I'm Mrs. Doctor Swinson" attitude. The entire family followed behind her in procession. Once seated, she turned her head in all directions, surveying the church to see who was there and making sure everyone was aware of her family's presence. After all the grownups and children were settled in their places, Papa took his seat beside Dandy and, as usual, she kept an elbow ever ready to give him a poke any time his eyes fluttered and his chin dropped to his chest.

While Dandy continued to check out the crowd, the members of the family sat shoulder to shoulder in the pew, preparing themselves for the sermon. It seldom varied. The prancing, dancing, stomping, yelling and sometimes crying Brother Boles, the preacher, assured the congregation that when you review the Bible in context, it's clear that most of those present would wind up in Hell. Today's message was no exception.

The preacher went on endlessly with the list of sins. Raising his arms to heaven he pronounced, "Know ye not that the unrighteous shall not inherit the kingdom of God? Be not deceived: neither fornicators, nor idolaters, nor adulterers, nor effeminate, nor abusers of themselves with mankind, nor thieves, nor covetous, nor drunkards, nor revilers, nor extortionists, nor sodomites..." When it seemed he had covered everything possible, he stopped to catch his breath, then added to this list: "nor those who dance, nor curse, nor play cards."

On this uplifting note, the family returned to the farmhouse for Sunday dinner, understanding there was no way they could avoid committing a sin before the sun set that day. But first came dinner and they didn't let awareness of their doom ruin their appetites. Dandy's Sunday menu was nearly always the same: pot roast, new potatoes, carrots cooked in butter and maple syrup, green beans with bacon, and a salad of fresh vegetables when the garden was in season. Peach or apple cobbler with heavy cream followed. After everyone stuffed themselves and left the table, Dandy threw a tablecloth over the food and left it there for supper that evening. This routine had been cast in stone.

After cleanup, having fulfilled their obligations, everyone was free to do exactly as they pleased for the rest of the afternoon. There was a stampede for the door as people headed off in different directions attempting to find a place for privacy.

After everyone departed, Papa and Dandy climbed the stairs to their bedroom. They changed their church clothes and Papa settled down on the bed, surrounding himself with the Dallas Morning News. On the other side of the room, Dandy seated herself in her rocking chair and busied her hands crocheting while her troubled mind dwelled on her newly formed suspicions. She sat for a time, rocking and crocheting while a fire brewed in her belly. Finally, when the fire burst into a full-blown flame, she was unable to keep her thoughts to herself any longer. She rested her crochet in her lap and turned toward Papa, her eyebrows together in a frown and her mouth turned down at the corners.

"Papa."

"Uh huh," he grunted, but continued to read his paper.

"Put down your paper, Papa. I've got something serious to talk to you about."

He shot her wary look and put his paper aside. Obviously resigned to hear her out, he said, "Okay, Dandy. What's on your mind?"

"Well," she declared in that voice she used when she was about to reveal some revelation she'd had. Stopping a moment for dramatic effect, she leaned forward with her back stiff and her chin held high, giving her the appearance of looking down her nose at him. "You know how I told you the minute I laid eyes on that hussy of a wife Agnew brought into this house, that she was big trouble? Remember I told you that?"

He breathed in deeply and answered, irritation in his voice, "Yes, Dandy. I remember."

"Well!" she said huffily. "I don't like one bit what I see going on before my very eyes."

"And what would that be?"

"Mark my words. That woman is making eyes at poor Archie. And," she added with a look of dismay, "you know he's never been able to defend himself."

Papa shifted on the bed and looked at her with disbelief. "Oh, Lula. Is that what you're so upset about? That's just Valera's way. She doesn't mean anything by it. And even if you're right, and she is 'making eyes' at Archie, as you say, and I want to make it clear that I don't think she is, but on the outside chance you're right, I'm sure it's just an attempt to get Agnew to notice her. Maybe you haven't been aware, but Agnew doesn't treat her very nice. In fact, I've been thinking about saying something to him about it. It's not right the way he totally ignores her and makes her feel like she's an outsider in this family."

"Humph! Well! She is an outsider!" Dandy's back stiffened, then she snorted haughtily, "I haven't gotten to be almost sixty years old and raised four sons and a daughter without learning a thing or two about human beings and the way they behave. Unlike you, I recognize trouble when I see it, and believe me, this is big trouble."

After hearing that declaration, Papa sat up straighter and leaned forward. He yanked his glasses off, and looked Dandy right in the eyes. Shaking his index finger at her, he said with a lot more sternness than he usually used with her, "Now listen to me, Lula. I want you to stop and think what voicing this unfounded opinion of yours would do to this family. I'm telling you to keep your mouth shut for once. Admit it. You don't like Valera and you're just looking for trouble."

Dandy didn't say any more to him, but as she picked up her crochet and started to work on it again, she softly mumbled under her breath "Okay. You just wait and see. I know what I know."

CHAPTER 24

Evelyn sat staring at the fading green vines on the wall paper that covered the walls of the bedroom. Clutched in her hands was the letter from her brother she'd received today. The pasted on smile she hid behind had disappeared now that she was alone. After supper cleanup, she'd slipped away without notice from the others who were still on the sun porch. The grownups were playing games at the large dining table and the children were gathered around Dandy at the piano on the other end of the room. She could hear the children's small shrill voices through the wall, singing the same Baptist hymns they always sang.

This evening Archie had come stumbling in just in time for supper, drunk earlier than usual. Everyone pretended not to notice and she had joined in the pretense. That was the easiest way to deal with it. When he came across the room to where she sat at the table and tried to kiss her, she'd turned her head and pulled away from his alcoholic breath. Now a shutter passed through her body even to think about it. She wondered how it was possible to hate someone and still love them at the same time.

Who did Archie think he was fooling? Long experience had taught her to see the signs. Something was going on between him and Valera. They must think she was blind or stupid not to pick up on the way they managed to sit next to each other at the table now, exchanging sideward glances and rubbing each other every chance they had.

She'd watched as Archie slipped out the door as soon as supper was over. No one else seemed to notice or to care. They were probably relieved to have him gone. And maybe no one but her noticed that Valera quietly slipped out the back door as soon as the women finished cleaning up from supper. Evelyn had a good idea where she might be headed.

It was humiliating. But then her whole life with Archie had been humiliating. Embarrassment had taught her to hide behind that stupid smile, a smile she'd become expert at. And 'If practice makes perfect', why not?

Surely everyone in this family wondered why Archie had married such a mousy, spiritless woman as she. She had always wondered as well. A great mystery. When she'd met him he was charming and handsome. He could have had his choice of so many women. Why had he decided on her as his wife?

She knew she wasn't ugly. Her nose wasn't too large or her eyes too small. Everything was in the correct place on her face; it's just that it didn't all fit together to make her anything but plain. She wondered what was missing from the formula that made her turn out as she did. What had been omitted that left her without spark, made her one of the invisibles that travel through life not seen, or if noticed at all, seen as insignificant. Then there were those like Archie who had gifts heaped on them. Maybe that's why he'd married her. Some subconscious guilt about the waste of his gifts that made him need to link himself to someone who'd been given none.

As she sat staring into space, her mother's image began to appear in her mind. She was standing in the doorway of their farmhouse, looking through the screen door as she did every day, waiting for Evelyn's school bus. Evelyn fought to hold back tears as she got off the bus and walked down the dirt road that led to her house. But when she saw her mother waving and smiling at her, the dam broke and she wept bitterly as she ran into her mother's arms.

"Evelyn. What is it child?"

"Oh, Mama. Every girl at school has a date to the dance Saturday night except me. Even Millie Sutton got a date today and she's the most unpopular girl at school, besides me."

Her mother held Evelyn in her arms and tried to comfort her as she sobbed. "Now, now, honey. Don't cry."

Evelyn looked up at her mother through her tears, "Mama, why can't I be pretty? Or if I can't be pretty, why can't I be funny, or clever or smart or something? It just isn't fair."

"Now stop your crying," her mother said as she stroked Evelyn's hair back from her face. "You'll survive this and remember, it's more important to be a good person than to be pretty or popular. You act prettier than any of those other girls. Don't worry, Evelyn. This is just one dance. Your day will come. Just you wait and see."

She did survive missing the dance and after she graduated from high school, she had her choice of staying home and helping out on the farm or taking a job at Phillips Drug Store in downtown Sulpher Springs. The temptation to choose the security of staying home around people she knew and felt comfortable with loomed large. After a week of indecision however, she gathered her courage and decided to take the job in town.

Almost a year passed without incident and one quiet day in the drugstore, Evelyn was straightening merchandise on the shelves. She was so preoccupied with what she was doing that she didn't notice when someone came into the store. Suddenly a man's voice came from behind her, startling her so much she jumped.

"Hello there, beautiful lady," he said, then laughed when he saw her jump. "I'm sorry. I didn't mean to scare you."

Evelyn looked behind her to see who he was talking to. He couldn't be calling her "beautiful lady." But seeing no one there, she turned and stuttered, "Ca-can I help you?"

He removed his hat and bowed. His well-groomed mustache was auburn red, like the curly hair that had been hidden beneath his hat. Dancing blue-green eyes beamed at her and his smile revealed perfect white teeth. She couldn't help it. She caught her breath. This was the most handsome man she had ever laid eyes on. He wasn't a large man, an inch or two short of six feet tall and quite slender, but his vitality made him seem larger than life.

"Can...can I help you?" Evelyn managed to repeat. She felt herself blushing and was sure he must have noticed.

"Yes, I think you can, Sweetheart. Could you direct me to the owner of this store?"

She tried hard to hide her embarrassment as she answered. "Yes. That would be Mr. Phillips." She pointed to the back of the store. "His office is back there."

He winked at her. "Tell you what, pretty lady, if I make a sale to Mr. Phillips, I'll take you out for a night on the town." He paused and looked out through the window on the front of the store to see the few buildings that lined the narrow street. "Such as this town is," he added with a grin. When he saw the look on her face he caught himself. "I'm sorry. That is if you'd like to, and don't already have a date tonight."

Have a date? She almost laughed at the thought. She was nineteen years old and had never had a date. Her face was feeling hotter by the minute. Was this handsome man actually asking her for a date -- calling her beautiful? Looking down at her feet and feeling she might actually faint at any moment, she managed to stammer, "Thank you very much, sir, but I don't even know you."

"Well, let me introduce myself. I'm Archie. Archie Swinson." He held out his hand to shake hers. She hesitantly reached out and put her hand in his.

"And your name is?"

"Evelyn. Evelyn Raeborn." She forced herself to meet his gaze.

"Well, Evelyn Raeborn, that takes care of that. Now we know each other. Tell you what. Even if I don't make a sale, I can't let a girl like you get away. Please. Have supper with me?" When he saw her hesitate, he flashed a winning smile, "Ah, come on. I'm a stranger in town. Don't make me eat alone."

She couldn't suppress a little laugh. He was infectious. How could she say no? She had to see this dream played out before she woke up.

Archie did make the sale. As he pranced by on his way out of the store he stopped and got instructions to her farmhouse. "Okay, Evelyn Raeborn. I'll pick you up at 6 P.M. sharp." Leaving her with a smile and a wink, he was off.

Her eyes followed him as he walked through the store and out onto the street. After he was out of sight, she stood behind the counter motionless as she tried to get her breathing under control. For the rest of the day her eyes searched out the clock every fifteen minutes. Finally, when she could stand it no longer, she went to the office at the rear of the store and stood for a few moments with her fist paused in midair, gathering the courage to knock. She took two deep breaths, lifted her shoulders up and tapped softly on the door.

"Yes, come in." Mr. Phillips looked up from where he sat at his desk. "Why, Evelyn. Come in. What can I do for you?"

"Mr. Phillips," she asked, her voice not quite as timid as usual, "We aren't very busy today and I wondered if I could get off a little early?"

"Well, Evelyn, if it's important to you, I guess so." He looked puzzled. In the year she'd worked there she had never made any such request, had never missed a day or even been late.

"Oh, thank you, Mr. Phillips," she beamed, hardly able to keep from jumping up and down. "I'll make it up. I promise," she said over her shoulder as she raced across the room to grab her purse from the closet where she kept it. As she left she was so excited that she tripped, then looked up at Mr. Phillips with an embarrassed grin as she ran out the door. She left him watching in amazement. He'd never seen Evelyn show exuberance about anything before.

Buelers Department Store was just three doors down the block from the drug store and she practically danced her way down the street. There it was, still in the window, her dream dress: brown chiffon over silk crepe with tiny seed beads sprinkled over the bodice. She had admired it through the store window for days but knew she'd never have a place to wear it, even if she could afford it. Now she must have it even if it meant borrowing money from one of her brothers and eating biscuit sandwiches for lunch for a month.

With newfound confidence, she marched into the store and went directly up to a salesclerk, a young woman who stood behind the counter filing her nails. Evelyn blurted out in her strongest voice, "Miss. I'd like to try on that brown dress in the window."

Evelyn's new found confidence sprung a leak as the clerk stopped filing her nails and looked her up and down. She flushed, suddenly aware of how shabby she must look with her scuffed shoes, run-down at the heels, and a dress her mother had handed down to her that was a little too large. She self-consciously raised her hand to smooth the straight brown hair that hung limp by her face and she felt herself melting under the clerk's condescending stare.

The clerk sighed audibly, made a big thing of removing the pencil from behind her ear and slamming it down on the counter beside her sales book. Apparently she felt it was a lot of trouble to get that dress out of the window and Evelyn could guess she didn't look like a very likely prospect for a sale. After giving Evelyn one last look up and down, seemingly to make sure she knew what an imposition this was, the clerk said in a voice which felt designed to make Evelyn feel even more ill at ease, "Wait here, please." Then she stalked off to remove the dress from the window.

The rest of the day, Evelyn was on pins and needles, worrying that Archie wouldn't show up. What possible reason could he have for asking her out? He must have been playing with her, teasing her. However, promptly at 6 PM, he appeared on her front porch as he had promised.

The town of Sulpher Springs had two restaurants. One downtown: Mike's Café, which the locals called a greasy spoon. The other was on the edge of town in the Sundown

Motel and was short of atmosphere but the food was said to be good. They decided on the latter.

She was terribly overdressed in her new brown chiffon but if Archie noticed, he covered it with compliments and made her feel like a queen. He had a wonderful way of making her forget her shyness and she was surprised by all they found to talk about. Well, actually, he did most of the talking.

That evening was a dream come true. Archie had been a perfect gentleman. He didn't even try to hold her hand. The next time he was in town, he took her out again and this time he kissed her good night on the cheek. But after that, when he took her out he began to make up excuses to stop by his motel room before taking her home. At first she was reluctant to go in, but her resistance didn't last. He assured her he was in love with her and she believed him because she had to. She was hopelessly in love with him.

One morning after she'd been seeing Archie off and on for almost ten months, her brothers came into the kitchen and gathered around her. Her hands were buried in hot soapy water as she washed the breakfast dishes at the kitchen sink. She looked around at them and smiled, then turned back to continue washing the dishes. "What's going on?" she asked after a moment. They stood silent, nervously stealing glances at each other out of the corners of their eyes. Finally, her oldest brother, James, spoke, his voice hesitant.

"Evelyn, you know we love you, don't you?"

She nodded her head and smiled without turning around again.

He cleared his throat and persevered. "Well, we've talked it over and decided we need to tell you some things you aren't going to like hearing." The other two brothers grunted in confirmation.

When she realized how agitated they were, her heart seemed to stop for a second. She withdrew her hands from the dishwater and slowly and deliberately dried them. Then she turned around to face her brothers' serious faces.

"So?" she asked, frowning.

"It's about Archie," James said softly, squirming as he said it.

By now she was trembling inside and struggled to gain control of herself. She already knew she didn't want to hear whatever they had to say. All she cared about was that she loved Archie and believed in him. In a guarded voice she answered, "What about Archie? If you're going to say something bad about him . . . *don't* say it!"

Sam and Bill drew in closer to James for support. "Honey, we're afraid you're getting too serious about this bird and he's a bad apple."

Evelyn said nothing but her chin began to quiver.

Bill spoke up now. "Evelyn, we're sorry but we have it from a reliable source that not only does Archie drink too much, he's a woman chaser as well. After he brings you home, he goes out with other women. Some of 'em are even married. We heard that some husband over in Sherman came home unexpectedly one night and found Archie in bed with his wife. As Archie tried to climb out the bedroom window, the husband took a shot at him."

"Yeah," Sam chimed in. "He was in the hospital for several weeks. That's probably where he was that time when you didn't hear from him for a spell."

Evelyn glowered at her brothers, hatred in her eyes. She wasn't one to anger easily but everyone in the family knew to beware when she did get mad. "Are ya'll finished?" she asked.

They took a step back when they saw the fire in her eyes. "We were just trying to protect you," Bill's thin voice pleaded.

"Yeah. You're our sister and we don't want you to get hurt," James agreed.

"If you loved me you wouldn't make up lies about the man I love," she screamed. The violence in her voice surprised even her as she turned, grabbed a cup out of the dishwater and threw it across the room at her brothers who had been slowly backing up toward the kitchen door.

Ripping off her apron, she threw it at them as she ran past them on her way out of the room. "You just don't want me to leave here. You want me to be trapped here forever to take care of ya'll."

Her mother stood in the kitchen door listening and as Evelyn whipped past her, she pleaded, "Evelyn, please listen to what your brothers are telling you."

Evelyn gave her a hurt look and continued running.

That evening when Archie was on his way to her house, she met him down the road and stopped him. Her eyes were swollen from crying and when he pressed her to tell him why, she broke down and told him all her brothers had said.

He grabbed her hands and held them, looking deep into her eyes. "Evelyn, believe me, none of that is true. I can't imagine why your brothers would tell you those vicious lies about me. Whoever told them those things must have gotten me confused with someone else."

Because Evelyn wanted so badly to believe him, she did. For days she refused to speak to anyone in her house except when absolutely necessary. Then in the middle of the night a month later, without telling anyone her plans, she packed a small suitcase, climbed out her bedroom window and met Archie who was waiting for her down the road. They eloped to Ft. Worth.

The next two years were a fulfillment of all her brothers had tried to warn her about. Archie lost one job after another because of his drinking and they constantly had to move from town to town in search of new employment. He could always charm his way into a job but keeping one was another matter.

Besides that, she knew in her heart of hearts that there were always other women; however when she confronted him about it, his reply was always the same. "Now Darlin', why would I want another woman when I already have the best woman in the world." Then with his most charming smile he would add, "Besides, who else would put up with me?" Next he'd grab her and cover her neck with kisses and convince her that she was just being silly. And again she would believe him because she wanted to so badly.

They lived in Denton, Texas, when the stock market crashed and the bottom began to fall out. Not long after, Archie lost his job as a shoe salesman at Treys Department Store and this time there were no jobs to be had anywhere. By now they had a baby boy to worry about and Evelyn was caught in a losing battle with despair.

One evening Archie came stumbling in the door, reeking of alcohol. Earlier that day, Evelyn had discovered that the money she had managed to hide away in a coffee can was missing. Archie's condition confirmed her fear that it now belonged to the local bootlegger.

He looked around the rundown apartment they were living in, one large room with a wooden icebox and a hot plate on a counter in one corner. A table with two chairs, a highchair for their young son, and a baby bed filled a large portion of the room. The only other furnishings were an old dresser with drawers that refused to close all the way and an iron framed bed.

"Well, Honey," he slurred, his tongue thick, "say goodbye to this luxurious dwelling. We're homeward bound. We've reached the bottom -- that is unless you have more money hidden somewhere."

"No, Archie. No more money hidden." Evelyn's voice was listless. "What do you mean 'homeward bound'? What are we going to do, Archie? What's going to happen to us now?"

"Not to worry, my love. I talked to my dad today and they're expecting us on the bus tomorrow night. He's wiring us bus money."

She looked at him with eyes empty of emotion. No tears fell, none were left. Without a word, she got up from the table where she'd been sitting, walked to the closet and got out the beat up old suitcases she had packed so many times. Opening the dresser drawers, she started to pack their few belongings once again.

Archie, Evelyn, and their young son had been the first in the family to come to live with Papa and Dandy on the farm in Ardis Heights. Now all the bedrooms were occupied as was the little farmhand's house. So many people here, and yet Evelyn always felt alone. Every morning she put on her clothes and pasted on a smile and prepared for another day among strangers who neither knew nor cared to know her.

Sitting in the dark room, thinking about this family, Archie's family, made her realize how blessed she was by the family she'd been born into. But now it was too late. She'd started dozens of letters to them since she'd been gone, all of them winding up in the trash, unable to bring herself to tell them how right they'd been about Archie. But a month ago, she'd felt desperate enough that she'd finally mailed a letter to them, hoping they'd welcome her back. Every day since, she'd anxiously checked the mailbox. At last, today an answer had come. She'd read the letter so many times she knew it by heart.

Dear Evelyn,

What a surprise to hear from you after all this time. I didn't know whether to be grateful you're still alive or mad you've waited so long to write. Both I guess. It's been so long since you went away and so much has happened to our family, I hardly know where to start. I'm sorry to tell you it broke Mama's heart when you left and she was never the same after that.

The rest is a long story but I'll make it short. When the depression hit, we hung on to the farm as long as we could, but there was no market for our cotton and we had to leave it to ruin in the fields. We were broke. The bank foreclosed. Ours was just one of many farms around us to go. Mama and Daddy went to live with Uncle Edmond in Oklahoma City. Mama got sick and died not long after that. Daddy's still there.

Bill, Sam and I had no place to go so we bummed around, riding the rails with thousands of others, looking for work, begging for food, just sort of surviving from day to day. Finally Sam and Bill got on with the Civilian Conservation Corps, building bridges, schools, hospitals, stuff for the government. Thank God for President Roosevelt and his programs -- they saved a bunch of young men from starving or turning to crime. I came back here and am sharecropping a piece of land not far from our old place. That's how I came to get your letter; post office knew I

was here. I'm sorry to be the bearer of such bad news.
Wish it was otherwise.
Love from your brother,
James

Evelyn rocked back and forth in the rocking chair wishing for the relief tears might bring, but they refused to come. Maybe she'd finally used them all up. Resting her hands on her growing stomach, she stopped rocking and felt for movement. Any day now she should start feeling the baby. She wouldn't be able to hide it much longer.

CHAPTER 25

Long before the sun was up, Dandy stood at the kitchen cabinet mixing flour, baking powder and water for biscuit dough. The air that blew into the kitchen through the open window above the sink bore the first signs of crispness. It gave her hope that the sweltering humid air of summer would soon be over. Just yesterday she'd noticed green leaves starting to show signs of golds and reds around their edges. Before long the garden and orchard would be put to rest and would no longer provide their table with fresh food. She groaned as she realized this meant she must push harder. Her daughters-in-law already resented her for being a slave driver, insisting everyday as she must that they harvest and can all the food they could. Seemed to her they were oblivious to the fact that they must depend on the jars of fruits and vegetables that line the shelves of the smoke house to feed the family this winter. She smashed down hard with her fist on the dough. She was so weary of pushing people against their wills to make them do what was necessary for them. She rolled her eyes toward heaven. *Why me Lord? Is this the way I must spend the rest of my days?*

The sound of approaching footsteps jerked her from her lamenting and she glanced up to see Agnew amble into the kitchen. He crossed the room to where she stood and gave her a peck on the cheek that felt to her more like duty than affection.

"Mornin' Dandy," he mumbled as if half asleep.

She acknowledged him with a nod of her head and continued mixing the biscuit dough.

Before sitting down at the kitchen table, he grabbed a cup from the cupboard and poured himself coffee from the steaming pot on the woodstove. The coffee was black and strong, just the way he liked it. He held the cup in both hands and peered into the dark liquid as if searching its depths for an answer to some grave issue. Without raising his head, he continued to stare into the black coffee as he asked, "What's up for today, Dandy?" The eyes behind the thick lenses of his glasses were weary and his question was asked with a total lack of enthusiasm.

From the tone of his voice she could tell he wished he didn't have to hear what lay before him today or maybe any day for that matter. Since he was the oldest son, and the most reliable, he had been made foreman of the farm, an honor he tried to decline but wasn't allowed. This meant every morning he must meet with Dandy in the kitchen before anyone else arrived for breakfast so they could discuss what chores needed to be done on the farm that day.

Dandy put down her rolling pin and turned to look at Agnew as he sat hunched over his cup. She found herself filled with concern for him. It hurt her to see how dejected he looked. She knew no one here was all that happy, but Agnew looked downright tortured.

"What's the matter, Agnew? Are you sick? Is there something going on I need to know about?"

"No, Dandy. Nothing's going on. I'm fine." He was unconvincing.

"You don't look fine."

"Well I am. Let's drop it, please."

"Okay then, if you say you're fine, maybe it's just that you need a haircut and a shave. Doesn't look like you've shaved in days." Or maybe you just need to get rid of that wife of yours, she thought, but had the good sense not to say aloud.

"Yes, Dandy." he answered in a voice marked with surrender. "You're right. I'll take care of it."

She shook her head as she continued to study him. No argument from Agnew ever. He didn't argue. He just tuned you out. She marveled at how such a disobedient little boy turned out to be such a docile man. But one thing hadn't changed. She remembered that even as a child he always held everything in, his thoughts and actions always his private possessions not to be shared with her, or anyone else for that matter. And though he was always in trouble as a boy, she'd suspected even then that Agnew hadn't been the instigator of her sons' boyhood misbehaviors. He'd just gone along with Erby's schemes.

"Ah, Erby," she sighed as her thoughts turned to him. She remembered him as a child, always mischievous from the day he could walk and talk. And unlike Agnew, he held nothing back. In fact, he often told her more than she wanted to know -- even made up stories that were worse than what actually happened just to shock her and see her reaction. When he was young, she used to worry about how Erby'd turn out, to think it would be good if life took some of that spunk out of him. However, to see him now, all deflated, made her long to see some of that old mischievousness in his eyes again.

She wondered if her boys would ever be the same again after this terrible depression was over. Only Raymond, her youngest, seemed to have survived untouched. His medical practice had saved him from the desperation that brought the others to the farm. She stared into the darkness outside the open window. It was as if she could see her four young sons, standing in stair steps, Agnew down to Raymond, looking back at her through the window. Amazing how boys that all grew up in the same house could be so different from each other, she thought.

She loved them all, but if the truth be told, Archie was the son closest to her heart, the one who always needed her mothering, her love and protection. As a child his brothers and kids at school always picked on him because -- for some unknown reason -- he wasn't able to take up for himself. Even Raymond wasn't fair game for his older brother's pranks like Archie. Poor Archie, she thought with a sigh. He'd always seemed to be a helpless victim. Even now. She felt an ache in her heart as she thought about him and how that woman was trying to tempt him.

Returning to her biscuit dough, she pounded it with gusto before rolling it out. Using the open end of a glass dipped in flour, she punched circles in the dough, placed the round biscuits one by one on a cookie sheet and shoved them in the oven to bake. Then before joining Agnew at the kitchen table, she reached in the cabinet for a cup, and poured herself coffee.

They talked about what fences needed mending and which pasture to put the sheep in today, but she longed to change the subject from farm chores. She had to bite her tongue to keep from screaming, *Agnew, how could you marry that---that woman? Can't you see what she's up to?*

She couldn't help but compare Valera with his first wife. Helen Lee was such a lady and had fit in this family so well. When Agnew first arrived back here with Valera as his wife, Dandy tried in vain to get him to tell her what happened between him and Helen Lee. But he'd told her in no uncertain terms he didn't want to talk about it. Ever! And knowing Agnew, she was sure he meant it. She'd let it drop but that didn't mean she'd accepted it.

Their meeting over, Agnew left the kitchen, but thoughts of Valera and Archie continued to invade her peace. She didn't care that Papa didn't agree with her about this. She knew her suspicions had merit and she had to find a way to protect Archie before it was too late.

And that wasn't all that was bothering her. For several weeks now, there'd been changes in Evelyn. She was looking a little green around the gills. Also one of the few things Dandy found to admire about her was her punctuality and now she moped in to breakfast late and when she got there she didn't want anything to eat. Didn't take long before Dandy recognized what was going on, but Evelyn said nothing. Dandy hated it when people tried to keep secrets from her. If she was going to keep this ship afloat she needed to know what was going on.

That night after the dishes were washed and dried, the floor swept, and cabinet tops wiped down, the women were leaving the kitchen to go their separate ways. Dandy gave Evelyn one of her hard looks and with a flat voice said,"Evelyn, would you please stay here a minute before you go to your room?"

"Yes, of course, Mrs. Swinson." Evelyn answered, a concerned look clouding her face.

Dandy turned and walked over to the cabinet and pretended to look out the window over the kitchen sink. She purposely kept her back to Evelyn, making her wait for a minute. Then she turned abruptly and looked squarely at her.

Evelyn stood a few feet away and nervously waited for Dandy to speak, her hands folded tightly in front of her stomach. She bowed her head and tried to breathe deeply.

"Evelyn, look at me. Isn't there something you ought to tell me?"

She lifted her eyes. "Why no, Mrs. Swinson. I can't think of anything."

"Don't toy with me, girl. You know what I'm talking about." Dandy's eyes were glued to Evelyn's stomach.

She stood without speaking for a long moment before she muttered in a voice Dandy could barely hear, "I guess you're talking about . . ." Her eyes dropped to the floor again and slowly the words came out as painful as birth. "It appears I'm going to have a baby."

"I know that." Dandy's voice was filled with disgust. "Do you think I don't know when someone's in a family way? What I want to know is why haven't you told me? I need to know these things."

"I guess because I was so hoping I was wrong. I've been praying it would go away." She looked up pleadingly, as if hoping Dandy could wave a magic wand and make it all a bad dream.

"Have you told Archie yet?"

"No."

"You better tell him. He should know."

Evelyn shook her head. "I don't think he wants to know. He's awfully preoccupied of late." Then she added, "And I hate to tell you this because I know you don't want to hear it, but he's drunk even more than usual."

Though displeased to hear this, Dandy managed not to say anything, but continued to stare disapprovingly at her.

Evelyn studied her folded hands for a short time. Finally, she looked up and her eyes met Dandy's. "Frankly, Mrs. Swinson, I don't see that much of Archie anymore. He gets up and leaves before I do in the morning and he comes in late at night. If I try to talk to him when he gets in, he tells me to leave him alone; that he's too tired to talk. Too drunk to talk is more the truth."

Obviously eyeing her stomach, Dandy said sarcastically, "Well, Evelyn looks to me like he's paid you attention sometime. I've got to tell you, this doesn't sound like Archie to me. You must be doing something to push him away."

Evelyn's hand rose to her cheek as if she'd been slapped but she didn't try to answer this unfair accusation. Her eyelids dropped over her eyes and her head fell to her chest. Then Evelyn raised her head and looked up at her with such sadness and despair that Dandy immediately regretted the way she had spoken to her.

As Dandy watched Evelyn's defeated figure disappear out the kitchen door, she wanted to speak out, to apologize, but her pride wouldn't let her. She knew she'd been wrong to blame Evelyn for keeping secret a pregnancy that she didn't want. She probably would have done the same herself. And why did she always have to blame someone else for Archie's mistakes? She knew in her heart that he was a loser. He'd always managed to surround himself with trouble. Truth was it just hurt her too much to admit it.

What Evelyn had just told her about Archie's recent conduct confirmed her suspicions about what was going on with him and Valera. Thinking about it sickened her. Suddenly, she felt exhausted by her inability to deal with things more rationally. She dropped down in a kitchen chair and stared at a blank wall for a long while, wishing she never had to face people again;

wishing she could hide from the world and everybody in it. Doubling up a fist she pounded on the table.

*   *   *

Morning light stole into the room around the edges of the window shades, painting bright stripes across the flowered rug that covered the bedroom floor. As the light found Dandy, her eyes popped open and she glanced at the clock on the nightstand beside her bed. Nudging Papa with her index finger, she exclaimed, "Papa, wake up! We've overslept a little. We must have slept right though the roosters crowing."

He raised his head and glanced at the clock, took a deep breath and exhaled slowly as he allowed his head to drop back on the pillow for a few minutes before throwing back the covers. After his bare feet hit the floor, he reached for the glass on the nightstand beside his bed, fished in it for his false teeth, put them in his mouth and chomped down several times until they were in place. Then grabbing his glasses, he rushed for the bathroom in an attempt to get there before anyone else. Mornings the schedule for the bathroom was tight and he didn't want to loose his place.

Dandy lay in bed dreading the day ahead. She knew why she'd overslept. She'd been awake most of the night. After her encounter with Evelyn last night, she'd struggled with her conscience over the way she'd talked to her. Evelyn was obviously upset about more than just the pregnancy. Dandy had to wonder if she was aware of what was going on between

Archie and Valera. More and more she feared that saving Archie was no longer a possibility.

She stretched her arms out and groaned. Her body ached. She couldn't feel any worse if she'd been attacked by a vampire who'd drained all her blood. But lingering in bed was not an option. Another day had begun. She had to meet Agnew in the kitchen and breakfast had to be made. It took all the effort she could muster to get out of bed and drag herself across the room to her dressing table. She struggled to get a brush through the tangles in her hair, all the while wondering why she even bothered. "Who cares about the way I look anyhow with all the troubles going on in this family?" she asked the image in the mirror.

Papa paused as he reentered the room and heard the question. "What was that you said? You seem to be in an awfully serious mood for so early in the morning."

She put down her brush and turned to look at him. "I guess I am. I'm so tired of being upset all the time." She moaned and raised her eyes to heaven. "Do you think God will ever stop testing us?"

He came across the room to where she sat, leaned down and planted a kiss on her cheek. "Sweetheart, I know the years of dealing with all the people who live here has been hard for you. And I'm truly sorry. But honestly, I've gotta say, I do feel you're inclined to bring some of it on yourself with your wild notions about everybody and the things you imagine they're doing." When he noticed her face starting to twist into a grimace, he hugged her and changed his tone. "So okay, darlin'. Please don't look that way. Tell me what's got you so upset now?"

"Nothing." she answered curtly. "You never believe me anyhow."

CHAPTER 26

Erby seldom joined the other men in the evening to listen to the radio or play games. The best thing about living in the little farmhand's house was that his family could have time away from the others at night. Inez was usually so tired that she went to bed right after she tucked in their girls and heard their prayers. He looked forward to hearing her say "Goodnight". Since she was convinced that to take even one drink made a person an alcoholic, he had to escape the house to enjoy a drink or two.

Tonight, as soon as she was settled in bed, he went immediately to the place where he kept his bottle hidden under the back porch and cursed when he found it empty. He really, really, needed a drink. His day had been long and hard -- but then weren't they all?

He sat down on the edge of the porch, rested his chin on the palm of his hand and pondered his dilemma. He couldn't go anywhere. His car was out of gas. In order to call the bootlegger to bring a bottle, he'd have to go to the big house to use the phone and if anyone saw him, he might get stuck there for the evening. Besides, what was he thinking? His dad hadn't paid him yet for the farm work he'd done this week. He didn't have money to pay a bootlegger and they insisted on cash. He could walk down the road to the Jones place. They always had liquor for sale. He could promise to pay them later. He shrugged. Probably not. They wouldn't sell liquor on credit either. He might as well face it. No money -- no drink. Then just as he was totally discouraged, he remembered Archie always had a bottle hidden in the hayloft. Archie wouldn't mind if he helped himself to a drink or two.

After he'd figured out where he could get a drink his spirits rose and with new life in his step, he headed down the road that led to the hay barn. Now he was able to see it was a beautiful evening. A full moon peeked in and out of the clouds and a soft breeze blew through the cottonwood trees by the side of the road. As he strolled, hundreds of fireflies twinkled around him like tiny earthbound stars, and shadows moved across the ground and danced in the moonlight. What he enjoyed most about the walks he took on sleepless nights was the way nighttime seemed to transform the world, making it a better place. Sounds, sights and smells lost in the distractions of daylight became obvious in the dark. In the light of day he probably wouldn't have noticed the smell of smoke from the wood stoves and the fragrance of flowers that lingered in the air. Nor would he have been so attuned to the many sounds: frogs croaking at the pond nearby, and baby lambs and calves crying for their mothers. The only thing missing to make the night perfect was a drink and he'd have that soon.

The moon suddenly disappeared behind a cloud and the road was lost in darkness, but his feet knew the way even without moonlight. Over time, they'd become familiar with the dirt road laid bare over the years by horse drawn farm equipment and wagons. As he approached the hay barn, the moon reappeared and once again cast its mellow light on the scene. However, when he pushed the barn door open, the interior was as black as pitch. While he stood in the doorway waiting for his eyes to adjust, he heard strange noises coming from the loft above him. At first he couldn't identify what he was hearing. Then he realized it was heavy breathing. His first thought was that Archie must be having an attack of some kind. Alarmed, he stumbled blindly through the darkness holding his hands out in front of him until he felt the ladder that led to the opening in the loft. He climbed the rungs as fast as he could but half way up the ladder he stopped abruptly. The heavy breathing was now joined by moans that were decidedly female.

His breath caught in his chest as he listened more intently. *Huh oh. That's not the sound of someone having an attack. That's two people. Whatever is going on up there is none of my business and I'm better off not knowing.* However, even as he tried to convince himself to stop his ascent, his curiosity got the best of him and his legs kept climbing the ladder -- only this time as he climbed he was careful not to make a noise.

When he reached the top, he cautiously poked his head through the hole that opened to the loft. His eyes searched in the direction of the noises but at first he couldn't make out anything in the darkness. However as his eyes adjusted he could see that the clumps strewn across the loft floor were clothes. Several feet away, flashes of white skin gleamed in the dark and two bodies thrashed around on the hay. He stood on the ladder, paralyzed, afraid to even breathe while he watched.

When the bodies stopped moving, he heard Archie's hoarse voice. "Wow, Valera," he wheezed as he collapsed on his back. "You're just too much!"

She giggled in response, then cooed, "You're not so bad yourself, Archie."

Erby almost fell off the ladder. *Valera? Was that Valera? Archie with Valera!*

As soon as he recovered enough from the initial shock, he quietly started back down the ladder. He was so disturbed by his discovery that he missed a rung and fell almost four feet to the barn floor. A loud grunt escaped him as his body hit with a thud.

"What was that? Did you hear something?" Valera gasped as she pulled herself up and looked back over her shoulder toward the opening in the loft floor.

"Huh? I don't know. What'd you hear?"

"I thought I heard something hit the floor below. It sounded like a grunt."

"Are you sure?"

"Yes…pretty sure."

Archie jumped up and grabbed the shirt that lay nearby and held it in front of his nude body as he tiptoed over to the loft opening. He peeked over the edge but found it too dark below to see anything. "Who's there? Is anybody there?" he asked, squinting his eyes in an effort to see.

Silence. Then a moan. "It's me, Archie -- Erby." He sat on the floor of the barn holding the painful ankle he had apparently sprained in the fall.

"Goddamnit, Erby. What are you doing here?"

"I just thought I'd come and have a couple of drinks from your bottle. I didn't think you'd care." Then in a voice heavy with disgust, he added," I didn't know you had company. Hell, Archie, she's your brother's wife. Isn't this a new low, even for you?"

To his surprise, Archie started to cry -- big sobs. Erby hadn't heard him cry like that since they were children. However, he knew Archie too well and if this was an attempt to enlist sympathy from him, it wasn't going to work.

"Oh, please, Erby. You can't tell anyone about this. Just think what it would do? It would kill Evelyn." He added, whining, "And Agnew would kill me." His voice frantic now, pleading through tears, "Besides, you just don't understand. Agnew treats Valera so bad, like he wishes she wasn't even here. And you know Dandy hates her. Poor thing. She needs someone to pay her a little attention."

"Well, paying her attention is one thing, but what you're doing with her is a little more than that, don't you think?"

"You're right," Archie dropped the shirt he was holding and hid his face in his hands. Still sobbing he said, "But please. I'm begging you not to tell anyone about this. If Papa finds out, he'll kick me out for sure. Please, please, don't tell."

Erby managed to get to his feet and limp toward the barn door. "I don't know. You should have thought about all that before you got yourself into this. I need to think. I'm not making you any promises. There's got to come a time when you have to suffer the consequences of all the really crummy things you do. And as for Valera, I've been upset with Dandy for the way she's treated her. Now I see she was right all along. I don't know what Agnew was thinking -- marrying that woman. He never should have brought her into this family. She's nothing but trouble. We'd all be better off without either of you."

As he hobbled out the barn door, Archie yelled after him. "Don't go. Please come back and let's talk about this. Don't you want that drink you came for?"

He ignored Archie and kept limping away, his mind in chaos and his hands trembling. He didn't want to be any part of this. Now he didn't just need one drink, he needed a whole bottle.

CHAPTER 27

Today was Monday, washday on the farm in Ardis Heights. Steam rose from large pots of water heating on the electric stove which was called into service on washdays. The bar of P and G soap was shaved into small pieces and the washing machine that usually stood pushed against a wall in the pantry now stood by the kitchen sink in readiness. Dandy and Bess Nell had arrived in the kitchen early and sorted their laundry into piles. Mountains of dirty clothes and linens covered the floor even before the others arrived.

Dandy stood by the sink and wiped beads of perspiration from her forehead. Her curly hair had started to turn into even tighter little kinks from all the moisture in the room. Staring at the clock on the wall and fidgeting, she grumbled under her breath as she waited for the rest of the women to bring in their laundry. She wanted to get started. Doing laundry for fifteen people required a full day. A definite routine had to be followed. Sorting was important since the water in the machine tub needed to be used at least three times before changing. First in would be linens, then underwear, sleeping garments and lightly soiled things. Last would be work clothes. Even though Dandy had the latest in washing machines, a lot of work was necessary. Water must be heated and poured into the tub of the machine. After agitating until thought clean, clothes must be fed into the kitchen sink through rubber wringers attached to the tub, then rinsed by hand before being fed back through the ringers to squeeze out any remaining water. When a basket was full of clean clothes, it must be carried to the clothes line behind the smokehouse and hung to dry.

When Evelyn and Valera finally came downstairs with their dirty laundry, Dandy greeted them with a nod and a disapproving stare. One look at them told her that neither felt well, but she chose not to waste her energy or time pursuing it. She knew what was wrong with Evelyn and didn't care what Valera's problem was.

As they started to sort their laundry and put things in the proper piles, Dandy's eyes searched the room. "Where's Inez? Isn't she here yet? She knows we need to get started right away if we're going to get finished by supper time."

Evelyn and Valera stopped sorting and looked at each other, shaking their heads. Bess Nell, who'd gone to the sun porch to get the children occupied with paper and crayolas came back into the kitchen and heard the question. "I don't know where she is. Her girls haven't shown up either. I was hoping Betty Lou could help keep the little ones out of the way while we washed."

Dandy pursed her lips. "Well!" she huffed. "I better go see what's going on. Ya'll get started. Pour one of those pots of hot water in the machine and put in the first load. I'll be back in a minute."

As she trudged down the path toward Inez's house she heard thunder booming in the distance and noticed the smell of rain in the air. She stopped walking and looked up to see dark clouds gathering. Rain was all they needed with all those clothes to dry. This definitely wasn't starting out to be a good day.

Crossing the backyard, she climbed the rickety steps to the small back stoop of the house, having to remind herself she was supposed to knock before entering. As she opened the screen-door she observed one corner of the screen had torn away from the tacks. "Erby should do something about those steps and that door," she mused aloud. "Looks like I've gotta tell everyone every move they need to make." After a single token knock, she entered the kitchen and saw her two granddaughters sitting at the table, bowls of oatmeal in front of them.

"Girls, where's your mother?" she asked without so much as a greeting.

"Hi, Dandy," Betty Lou said when she saw her grandmother. "Mommy went back to bed. She has a bad headache."

"Where's your daddy? Is he here?"

Betty Lou looked up at her, distress obvious in her eyes. "No. We don't know where Daddy is. He didn't come home for a while and Mommy's mad at him."

Dandy was beside herself. She didn't know why she hadn't been made aware of this before. She knew the others had started keeping things from her so she wouldn't get upset. She hated that, but would deal with it later. The issue at the moment was Erby's disappearance. "What do you mean he didn't come home? You don't know where he is?"

Inez stood in the bedroom door now, clutching a well worn robe around her. Her brown eyes were swollen into narrow slits and obviously she was in pain. "She means exactly that, Mrs. Swinson. We don't know where Erby is. We haven't seen or heard from him for several days." Her hair was in total disarray and she pushed a strand back behind one ear as she added, "And as I'm sure you must know, this is not the first time he's disappeared like this."

Dandy shook her head. Standing in the middle of the kitchen with her hands on her hips, her eyes roamed the room while she tried to think what to do. After a few moments, she turned to Betty Lou and Gloria Nell. "Okay girls," she said with a resigned sigh, "finish your breakfast and come with me. Inez if you feel up to gathering your laundry I'll take it." Aware of how miserable Inez looked, she added, "Then you go back to bed. Do you have anything to take for your headache?"

Inez shook her head slowly and whispered, "No."

"I'll have Dr. Swinson bring something over when he gets home." She felt a little guilty at not offering Inez a pill from her hidden stash but her generosity didn't go that far.

Inez's mouth twisted in an attempt at a smile. "Why thank you, Mrs. Swinson. That's very nice of you." She looked over at her girls to make sure they were eating their breakfast, then disappeared into the bedroom to gather up their laundry, except for Erby's. She left his in a pile in the middle of the bedroom floor."

* * *

Erby woke with a drum beating in his head and a tongue too thick to belong in his mouth. His body felt like he'd been hit by a train. Every bone and every muscle was a source of pain. He didn't know what day it was or where he was. At first when he awakened he thought he was in a strange bed; however, as his bloodshot eyes explored the room, the furniture and wallpaper were familiar. Then he realized this was Tom's house. Since coming back to live in Ardis Heights, he'd spent several nights in this bed when he drank too much. Tom's wife was a lot more understanding than Inez when it came to alcohol. Maybe because she liked to have a few drinks herself. Besides that, his friendship with her and Tom went all the way back to first grade and it was unconditional.

The walls spun around him and waves of nausea overcame him when he sat up on the edge of the bed. His head finally stopped swimming and he spotted his wrinkled pants and shirt lying across the wicker chair a few feet away. After a few minutes he felt steady enough to stumble over to retrieve them and winced when putting weight on his sprained ankle made it start to throb. He had no idea how long he'd been here, but from the smell of his body, several days had passed since he'd bathed. He ran his fingers through his hair, then felt his face where a scraggy beard had a good start. *God, I'm a mess.*

Familiar feelings of self-loathing swam over him as he tried to remember what triggered the binge this time. Then as if a dam had broken it all came flooding back to him -- Archie and Valera and that scene in the hayloft. He moaned and doubled over as his stomach heaved. How could he be so dumb, he asked himself. Would he never learn? Getting drunk hadn't made his problem go away and now he felt like hell to boot.

He limped through the house looking for Tom or Maggie. Apparently they'd gone to work at the café. No one else was here. Coffee was his next thought. He needed coffee. He stumbled into the kitchen and made himself a pot. Two strong cups helped him rejoin the human race, but just barely. His hands were still shaking and his head pounded as if little people with hammers were inside.

Slowly the cobwebs started to clear a little and he sat on the living room couch trying to decide what, if anything, he should do about the scene he'd stumbled on. The more he agonized about it, the more certain he became that he couldn't handle the knowledge of what Archie and Valera were up to all by himself. He needed to talk to his dad.

Tom's house was only a few blocks from downtown Greenville. Though his ankle still hurt, he decided to clean himself up, then try to walk to his dad's office. He needed to talk to him alone, away from the possibility of anyone else overhearing. Glancing at the clock above the living room fireplace he saw it was almost 4 o'clock. He'd have to hurry if he was to catch Papa before he left the office.

*   *   *

Erby grew more apprehensive as the elevator climbed to the sixth floor of the bank building. He hoped he was doing the right thing. The full responsibility of keeping this family together might rest on what he did now. When he entered his dad's office the waiting room was empty of patients. Mildred was shuffling folders on her desk and making preparations for the end of the workday. She looked up to find Erby standing in front of her desk looking down at her with a half smile.

"Hi, Mildred. How are you?" Erby said when their eyes met.

She'd known him since he was a young boy and her face showed shock when she saw how awful he looked. "Oh, hello, Erby" A few uncomfortable moments passed while she studied him. "I haven't seen you for a long while. Uh, are you okay?"

"Yeah, I'm fine. I just need to talk to Papa."

"Oh," she hesitated. "Is something wrong? You know he'll be home shortly."

"I know, but I need to talk to him now."

"Well, okay then. Just a minute. I'll tell him you're here." She rose from her desk and glanced back over her shoulder giving him a long inquiring look. Then she tapped on the door and disappeared into the treatment room.

Shortly, he stood in the small inner office. His ankle throbbed and his queasy stomach lurched at the medicinal smell that hung in the air. A shaded lamp on the roll top desk was the only light in the room and he blinked his eyes in the dim light searching for his dad. Papa sat by the desk, unsmiling, thumping his fingers on the desktop and looking over at him. Erby stood just inside the door waiting for him to speak but after a few moments when it became apparent that wasn't going to happen, he walked slowly across the room and stood before him.

Papa remained silent as he looked him up and down. Then he shook his head and said, "You look like hell, Erby."

"Well, if it makes you feel any better, I feel like hell. But I'm not going to defend myself. I deserve your disapproval."

"It's not only disapproval, Erby. It's more like disappointment." He steepled his fingers and peered over them with a pained look. "It hurts me to see what you're becoming -- what you're doing to yourself and your family."

Erby stood mute, his eyes cast down at the shabby hat he clutched in both hands.

Papa shrugged and waived a hand in the air. "Well, speak up. You're not here for a lecture. Why are you here?"

Erby fidgeted, twisting his hat in his hands. "I wish I didn't have to tell you this. I've been going crazy trying to decide whether I should just forget it or if it needs to be told. All I know is I don't want to be any part of the scene I stumbled on."

His dad's disapproving stare didn't waver. "From the looks of you, it's something you took hard enough to go on another one of your benders. But then, that doesn't take a whole lot anymore, does it?"

Stiffening from the blow of that remark, Erby reacted with words he hoped would be equally cutting. "What I need to talk to you about, Papa, is something that happened on my walk the other night." Raising his eyebrows, he gave his dad a knowing look and added, "As you probably remember, sometimes I run into unexpected things when I walk at night."

If Papa picked up on the fact that Erby was retaliating by referring to the night he caught him burning Dandy's dresses, he chose to disregard it. "All right, enough dancing around. Let's have whatever it is you came here to tell me."

"Okay. I'll spare you some of the details, but the other night when I was taking a walk I found myself at the hay barn. When I opened the door I heard strange noises -- heavy breathing and moaning coming from the loft. It turned out to be Archie. Valera was with him. They were . . . how can I put it . . . engaged. When they discovered I was there, a bad scene followed." Erby swallowed hard. "I was so shocked I didn't know what to do. Of course Archie begged me not to tell. But I can't handle this. I know I don't have any right to throw stones at anyone -- after the things I do sometimes -- but I'd never touch my brother's wife. That is just too unforgivable. I won't be a party to it and if I let it go, I feel like that's what I'd be doing."

237

Erby immediately regretted telling him as he watched Papa's reaction. All the blood drained from his face and he looked up at Erby as if he'd hit him. For a long moment, Erby feared he was going to pass out and he rushed over and put his hands on his dad's shoulders. "Papa! Papa! Are you okay? I'm sorry. I didn't realize you'd take it like this." He stood over him not knowing what to do. Then frantic, he raced out to get help from Mildred, but she was gone. When there was no one to help him, he found a towel, wet it with cold water and put it on Papa's forehead, then stood by wringing his hands.

Papa sat limp, not speaking, not moving for what seemed to Erby an eternity. Finally, he recovered enough for Erby to help him out of the building and down the street to his car. His legs were still shaky and the color hadn't returned to his face when Erby opened the car door on the passenger side. "Let me drive, Papa. You shouldn't be driving."

He jerked away from Erby's grasp and stumbled around to the driver's side. He barely managed to get in the car before announcing, "I'm driving. You've done enough for one day, thank you."

Those were the last words they spoke as they rode out to Ardis Heights. Papa drove even more erratically than usual, but Erby wisely knew not to comment. As they sped down the highway he kept his mouth shut but rammed his feet into the floorboard and clutched the edge of his seat with white knuckled hands. When the car skidded to an abrupt stop in the driveway of the big house, he couldn't hold back an audible sigh of relief at being safely home. Avoiding eye contact, both men got out of the car, nodded a silent goodbye and went their separate ways.

As Erby took slow steps toward his house, the rain that threatened all day broke loose and fell in large drops, drenching him. But he didn't mind. He even welcomed the cooling drops, taking off his hat and raising his face toward the sky to allow them to bathe his cheeks and wet his lips. As the rain washed over his face and soaked his body it seemed to cleanse away some of the remaining heaviness left from his awful day. He regretted his dad had taken the news so hard, but at the same time was relieved to have the responsibility out of his hands. After all, he had his own problems to worry about. He needed to prepare himself for facing Inez after being gone again.

When he reached his back stoop, he stalled for time, shaking the rain from his soaked hat and trying to dry himself off a little before entering the kitchen. When he could delay no longer, he lowered his head and opened the kitchen door.

Inez didn't look up or acknowledge him in any way when he entered. She kept her back to him as she stood at the stove cooking supper for the girls. The table was set for three. His chair had been removed.

When they saw him come through the door, his two girls cried in unison. "Daddy!" They jumped down from their chairs and ran to grab him around his legs. Betty Lou looked up at him with concern, "Where you been Daddy? We worried about you."

He didn't answer the question but returned their hugs and kissed them while his eyes searched across the kitchen to find Inez's back still turned to him. He edged over to where she stood and put his hand in the small of her back. In a soft voice he said, "Inez, please. I'm so sorry. I'm a no good SOB. But there really was a good reason this time. Just wait until I tell you what happened."

No response. She continued frying the potatoes, pretending he wasn't there.

"Inez, please say something. Please forgive me. You know I love you. I promise I won't disappear like that ever again, no matter what happens."

Ignoring his touch, she turned without looking at him to take a bowl to the table. After she filled the girls plates she sat down and started to eat, still pretending he wasn't there.

The aroma from the food made his mouth water. Suddenly he realized he was famished. He couldn't remember when he'd eaten last. He walked over to the table and stood a few feet away, shifting his weight from one foot to the other. Surely if he stood close by, Inez would have to invite him to join them. He was wrong. She continued to ignore him. Feeling like an idiot, he ventured, "Hon, please say something -- even if it's something nasty."

She still refused to either look at or speak to him, but Betty Lou looked up at him and asked. "Aren't you gonna eat any supper, Daddy?"

Inez spoke for the first time. "Never you mind, Betty Lou. Just eat your supper," Then without looking up from her plate she said, "Please pass me the coleslaw."

Betty Lou gave her daddy a forlorn look, then turned to do as her mother asked.

Obviously Inez didn't intend to invite him to join their meal or even to acknowledge he was there. This silent treatment seemed worse than when she cried and screamed and yelled at him. At a loss to know how to deal with this, he shrugged, put his wet hat on his head and walked out the kitchen door, looking back at them one last time, in case she changed her mind.

Wondering what he should do now, he stood on the back porch smoking a cigarette and watching the rain pour down. When he'd finished the last of the cigarette, he threw it on the porch and snuffed it out with his shoe. Then having no place else to go, he headed for the big house. When the rain drenched him this time, the cleansing feeling was gone. Now it just felt wet and cold.

The family was gathering around the supper table when he entered the sun porch. Conversation stopped and they all looked up at him and grunted unenthusiastic greetings. Everyone was aware he'd been on another of his disappearing acts and they were all unhappy with him; the men because they had extra work to do when he wasn't there to do his part and the women because they felt sorry for Inez and the girls.

Erby wasn't surprised that Archie ducked his head and fastened his eyes on his plate when he saw him enter the porch.

And he could have expected the same from Valera, but he was painfully aware of the cool reception he was getting from everyone else in the family. He felt himself sink even lower when he saw Dandy frowning at him from the kitchen door where she stood. She was capable of giving a look that could melt metal and he felt that look focused on him. He pretended not to notice, but he was beginning to desperately feel some need for acceptance from someone. Knowing Dandy's need to feed people, he decided to play on that. "Hi, Dandy. That food smells so good. Mind if I set another plate at the table? I'm starved."

This ploy didn't soften her one bit. "Well, you're hungry are you? Is that why you decided to come home?" Her voice reeked of sarcasm. "What are you doing over here?" Did Inez kick you out?" Then she added in a dry voice, "I hope."

"Please, Dandy. I'd rather not get into that right now. May I just have something to eat?" He was beginning to feel really sorry for himself. Seemed the blows were coming hard and fast, and they felt even more painful knowing he deserved them. However -- deserved or not -- they hurt.

By the time he had food on his plate he'd lost his appetite. He put his napkin down and rising from his chair, mumbled, "Thanks", and without looking at anyone, limped out of the room and into the pouring rain.

CHAPTER 28

That night, after Erby told him about finding Archie with Valera, Papa tossed and turned for hours. At first he'd been upset with Erby for telling him about their affair. But later, when he was thinking more rationally, he realized it shouldn't have been Erby's problem. He couldn't blame him for wanting to be rid of the responsibility of it. He wished he didn't have to deal with it either. *Archie with Valera.* His first impulse had been to throw both of them out, but then he realized that wouldn't be fair to others concerned. Some kind of action would have to be taken but at this point he had no idea what it should be. One thing he knew for sure: if he could avoid it, he didn't want to tell Dandy. The entire weight of dealing with this mess would have to be on him.

Along toward morning, he gave up the battle for sleep and quietly slipped out of bed, being careful not to awaken Dandy. However, she was already awake.

"What's wrong Papa? You might as well tell me. I always know when something's troubling you."

He groaned. The last thing in the world he wanted to do was tell her she'd been right with her suspicions. After a short time of trying to find the right words, he shook his head. "You're better off not knowing, believe me."

"If it's something bad that's going to affect me, you're going to have to tell me eventually. Might as well get it over with."

"All right! If you insist," he snarled. "But remember, I told you that you'd be better off not knowing. It's Archie again. Brace yourself, Lula, because as far as I'm concerned this episode is the last straw. I don't share your tolerance for Archie's shenanigans and I've had it up to my eyeballs with him. You're not going to like this, but one way or another, he has to go."

Dandy sat straight up in bed, her eyes and her mouth wide open. "What in the world are you talking about? Go? What do you mean *go?*"

"I mean *go* -- as in leave here. If it weren't for Evelyn and Sonny I'd throw him out on the street. I swear I would." He shrugged and turned away from her. As he walked over to a window and stared out at the beginnings of sun rise, he continued to ponder the situation. "But I can't do that to his innocent family. I've been awake the whole night trying to figure out what to do with him." He wiped his hand across his slick head and cried out, "The Lord only knows what I've done to deserve this one. It's the worst yet!"

"Now you're scaring me, John. What are you talking about?"

"I really don't want to tell you" he sighed. "You're not going to like it. Are you absolutely sure you want to know?"

"Yes. How many times do I have to tell you?"

"Okay. Guess there's no other way than just to come out with it." He hardened himself for her reaction. "Yesterday afternoon, Erby came to my office; said he had to talk to me in private. Seems he'd walked in on something a few nights ago he didn't know what to do about." He stopped talking and groaned again.

Her voice was strained now. "Yes, go on."

"It was Archie and Valera, together in the barn. They were . . . let's say in a . . . you know what."

Her eyes grew larger. "They were *what*?"

"Lula," he said in a disgusted voice. "You know what. You tried to tell me a while back that something was going on with them and I'm sorry to say I wouldn't believe you." Papa looked across the room at her and snapped, "So there you have it." The words choked him as he admitted, "You were right all along."

"That hussy! I knew it. I told you she was after him. It's all her fault. Now listen to me. You can't blame Archie. It's not fair to even think of throwing him out. You know how he's always been so . . ."

"Stop! I don't want to hear it. I don't want to hear again how defenseless he is, how he was picked on, how he was gassed in the war." He paused and scowled at her. "You know what? You're not blameless in this. You've always spoiled Archie, overprotecting him, making excuses for his bad behavior."

245

"You just don't understand," she countered.

"Your right. I don't understand. That boy has been given every opportunity in this life and he just keeps abusing them." Papa was pacing the floor now and clinching his fists. "You think I don't know you slip him money. And you know how he spends it. He's down at the Jones' place buying liquor. Why, he's their best customer." He stopped pacing and looked at her, puzzled. " I can't understand how you keep giving him money when you know it's going to bootleggers? Don't you care? Well, I'll tell you, I do, and frankly, I'm sick and tired of helping you pull him out of the predicaments he gets himself in. In fact, I'm through."

She bent over in the bed and hung her head as she whined, "I don't care what you say. It's all that Valera's fault. You're not being fair."

"Now you know better than that. Face it. You can't just blame Valera for this. She didn't do it alone. Archie is a grown man." He softened a little when he saw her body starting to shake with sobs. Maybe he was taking out some of his frustrations on her, he thought. He walked over to the bed and sat down beside her and put his hand on her shoulder. "Dandy, Darlin', I know this hurts and I'm sorry. But you have to pull yourself together. I need your support in what I decide to do. How in God's name am I going to handle this without ripping these marriages apart?"

* * *

In the downstairs bedroom of the big house, Archie also laid awake that night, his mind filled with possible scenarios of what his life was about to become -- and none of them were to his liking. He listened as the grandfather clock in the hall struck four. He'd also heard the clock strike one, two, and three. If only he could shut his mind off, even for a few minutes. The way Papa looked at him at the supper table tonight convinced him that Erby must have told him about finding them in the hayloft. Damn Erby. Wouldn't you know he would tell?

He hadn't drawn a peaceful breath since the night Erby caught him with Valera. He felt as if his foot was caught in a railroad track and he could hear the whistle of a train. Even alcohol didn't quell the storm invading his body and mind. Those old childhood feelings of being trapped consumed him once more and he fought panic as he lay in a pool of sweat.

Evelyn's body lay in the bed beside him, rigid, as if even when asleep she dared him to touch her. She was bound to know something was going on, but typical of her, she didn't ask. Apparently, she didn't want to know because then she'd have to deal with it. All the good feelings he'd had for her were gone now and replaced with anger. This whole thing was partly her fault. Having sex with her was almost rape. She not only didn't participate, she resisted. No wonder he'd been vulnerable to Valera and her sexual advances. It was easy for him to understand how he'd fallen prey to a woman who wanted him. He glanced over at Evelyn's unyielding body. Of all times for her to be expecting a baby. It was difficult to believe she could have become pregnant from an act only he participated in. As usual, her timing was perfect. She'd told him about the baby the same night that Erby found him with Valera in the loft. Great night that had been!

There was no doubt that Papa would have to take some sort of action. Tears started to fill his eyes. He was a drowning man, going down for the third time, searching for anything to grab and hang on to. Maybe he could convince Papa it was all Valera's fault. After all, it really was. Hadn't she been the one who came on to him? And hadn't he tried to resist in the beginning? But even though that was true, he knew that excuse would never float with Papa. He'd have to come up with something better than that. His mind continued its frantic search through one excuse after another. Then suddenly, in a flash, he had a glimmer of hope. He'd been looking at this all wrong. Evelyn and the new baby could be his salvation. Yeah, that's it! He breathed the first full breath he'd enjoyed since that night in the loft. There was no way that Dandy would let his dad throw him out with a new baby on the way. With that thought in mind, he felt some of the tension seeping from his body and he reached up and wiped the tears from his cheeks. Able now to surrender to his exhaustion, he closed his eyes and soon the room was filled with the sounds of his snoring. When the clock chimed five, he didn't hear it.

* * *

Upstairs and down the hall in her bedroom, Valera lay curled up in the fetal position. She was also listening to the clock strike out the hours. On the other side of the bed, Agnew lay with his back to her as usual. She stared at his back in the dim light wondering what he would do when he found out. He'd probably be relieved to hear about her cheating -- be glad to have this excuse to get rid of her.

Resigned to wakefulness, she listened to the rain hammering the roof and the occasional thunderclap and had visions of herself on the streets of Greenville -- dirty hair, ragged clothes, no money, no home, nothing. She imagined herself looking for food in trash cans and standing in soup lines, and having no place to get out of the rain. The only way she knew to make a living would probably be of no use to her now. Most men had no money for that sort of thing anymore. She couldn't go home again. Over three years had passed since she'd contacted her mother. Besides, her mother hadn't been able to take care of her when she was a child. Most likely, she needed help herself.

She thought of Archie and swallowed hard. How could she have been so foolish? She'd never had feelings of love for him, nor him for her. And now he avoided even looking at her. No doubt in her mind, he'd never defend her. In fact, she was certain he'd blame her to save himself if it came down to that. But if she was entirely truthful with herself, she knew she couldn't blame Archie. In the beginning he had tried to avoid her. Agnew was the real cause of this whole mess. All she'd ever wanted from him was to feel loved and cared for. And in the years they'd been here he'd pulled farther and farther away from her. Like her daddy before him, he'd deserted her.

Rising up on one elbow, she jabbed hard at her pillow with her fist, then flopped onto her back. She couldn't be positive Erby had told his dad yet, but it was just a matter of time if he hadn't. Dr. Swinson had looked at her in a strange way at the supper table tonight. Since Dandy always gave her dirty looks, that could be no indication of whether she knew. Most likely she didn't or she would have made sure Valera was already gone. And wouldn't the old bitch be thrilled to be rid of her? It would be the fulfillment of a wish she'd nurtured since the day Valera arrived with Agnew.

Her mind sifted through the people who had come together on this farm. She knew she wasn't from a typical family but wondered if most other families were like the Swinsons? They were like a cluster of islands in an ocean, together yet separate, fending off the world as a unit but never becoming one.

She grimaced as she turned over on her side once again and curled up with her knees to her chest. She was sitting on a time bomb and it would blow at any minute and blast her world apart.

CHAPTER 29

The rain stopped sometime toward morning, but heavy clouds blocked the sun and the light cast through the sun porch windows was gray, adding to the gloom in the room. Having suffered a sleepless night, four bleary eyed people sat like zombies at the table staring down at their breakfast. Papa, never particularly talkative mornings, was not only stone silent, but his obvious black mood dropped like a wet blanket over everyone present. Dandy's mood was no brighter and before coming to the breakfast table she could be heard banging pots and pans and slamming cabinet doors in the kitchen, a sure sign things were not going her way.

Bess Nell, one of the few people in the room who'd gotten a good night's sleep, studied the faces around the table and her eyes stopped their journey when they came to her dad. When she saw his drawn look, her brow wrinkled. "Don't you feel well this morning, Papa?"

He looked across the table and rested his eyes on Archie, then glanced down the table at Valera before answering, "No,

Sister. I don't feel well at all." His eyes returned to Archie and he continued to stare at him for several seconds before wiping his mouth with his napkin and rising from his chair. "In fact, ya'll will have to excuse me." Leaving his bacon and eggs untouched to grow cold on his plate, he gave Archie one last long hard look before walking from the room.

After he left, everyone picked at their food without enthusiasm. Even those who were in the dark about what was going on didn't feel much like eating. And Archie coughed and choked on the food in his mouth. It would have been hard for him to miss the look on Papa's face when he passed him on his way out of the room.

Instead of leaving immediately for his office, as he usually did after breakfast, Papa climbed the stairs and went into his bedroom, locking the door behind him. Soon the sounds of his fiddle could be heard throughout the house.

Those left sitting at the table looked at each other with raised eyebrows and sideward glances. Something serious was going on. That proved it. Everyone knew that fiddle music this time of day was a sure sign Papa was perplexed about something.

When she heard the music, Dandy bit her bottom lip and took one last look at her food before laying down the fork she held in her hand. Without speaking a word, she rose from the table and made her way into the kitchen. Bess Nell followed close behind.

"What's going on, Dandy? What's wrong with Papa? And you don't look so good yourself."

Before answering, Dandy pulled out a chair, flopped down at the kitchen table and threaded her fingers together. Deep creases spread across her forehead and her eyes roamed the room before they came back to rest on Bess Nell. When she finally spoke her voice was just above a whisper, "I can't tell you now, but you'll know soon enough. It's very serious is all I can say." Having said that, Dandy looked through the open kitchen door toward the breakfast table where Valera sat looking blankly at her plate. It was all she could do to keep from walking right up in Valera's face and telling her what she thought of her. But she managed to find some self-control. She knew better than to say anything in front of the rest of the family.

As she observed Dandy, Bess Nell's face registered growing concern. She pulled out a chair and joined her at the table, reaching across to take her mother's hand. "Whatever it is, obviously it's really upsetting ya'll. I don't like the way Papa looks. Why don't you go upstairs and check on him? I'll take care of breakfast cleanup."

"Thank you, Sister. I'll do that," Dandy said as she pulled herself up from the table and left the kitchen. She stared straight ahead when she walked past Archie and Valera on her way. She couldn't look at them without thinking about the two of them together in the hayloft. The very thought of it made her sick at her stomach.

Bess Nell was right. This thing was taking its toll on both her and Papa. As she climbed the stairs one slow step at a time her legs felt like they were made of cement. She didn't like the determined look on Papa's face. She'd hoped for time to make her case before any final decisions were made. She needed to come up with some way to save Archie from exile.

When she arrived at the bedroom door, she found it locked. The sound of fiddle music blasted through the door so she wasn't surprised when he didn't hear her first knock. The second time she banged harder and yelled, "Papa, open this door."

The music stopped, followed by a moment of silence. Then Papa's stern voice came through the door. "Go away, Lula. I've got to think and I don't want to be disturbed."

She stood for a full five minutes staring at the closed door before turning to go. Over forty years of marriage had taught her when she could push him and when she must leave him be. Her heart sank as she slowly turned and made her way back down the stairs. She might as well face it. He was going to make this decision without her and there was nothing she could do about it.

* * *

After he was sure Dandy was gone, Papa stood holding his fiddle under his chin for a short time; however, the desire to play had disappeared. It didn't matter. Playing his fiddle was neither settling his nerves nor helping him make any decisions about how to handle this impossible situation. He put down his bow and replaced his fiddle in its case, then crossed the room and released his body to the rocking chair. From where he sat he could see out the bedroom window, beyond the pasture behind the house, to the barns in the distance. Imagined images of Archie and Valera in the hayloft played across his mind and convinced him he had no choice. No way of dealing with this without hurting innocent people came to him, but one thing was certain, he couldn't back down. Archie must go and go soon. He cringed as he thought about Dandy. Knowing her, she wouldn't accept any decision to get rid of Archie without a royal battle so he'd have to be strong.

*   *   *

After the incident in the barn, Archie avoided the hay loft and started joining the men in the family who gathered at the end of the porch after supper. Two days had passed since Papa started showing signs that Erby must have told him. Though he hadn't said anything, he continued to give Archie long hard looks every chance he got.

This waiting for the other shoe to drop was more than Archie could take. He needed a drink. Not wanting to return to the hayloft after being caught with Valera, he'd moved his bottle to the base of a tree out behind the blacksmith shop. Tonight after supper, he stayed around for a while and when he thought no one was watching, he nonchalantly edged his way to the opposite end of the room and slipped out the door into the night.

Papa was secretly watching and waiting to confront Archie. When he saw him leave the room, he rose from his chair by the radio where he'd been pretending to listen to Amos and Andy. After excusing himself, he followed Archie, carefully keeping his distance.

Archie -- too anxious to get a drink to notice being followed -- raced down the gravel road that led to the blacksmith shop. Grabbing his bottle from its hiding place, he stood in the glow of the moon and sighed with pleasure as he downed a big swallow of the amber colored liquid. He raised it to his lips again and dropped the bottle when he heard a voice calling his name.

"Archie." His dad had suddenly materialized a few feet away.

"God, Papa, is that you? You scared the hell out of me."

"Well, Archie, I'd be lying if I said I'm sorry. To tell you the truth, right now I'd like to beat the hell out of you. However, I have something I need to tell you in private. I knew I'd find you where you'd hidden your bottle. Appears I was right."

A deep guttural sound escaped Archie. but he sensed this wasn't the time to offer a defense.

Papa stood with his legs spread and his hands in his pockets. He could just make out Archie's face in the moonlight. "I'm sure you know by now that I'm aware of your latest escapade." He let that sink in for a moment before he continued. "I don't have to tell you how sickening I find it that you would stoop that low. You've not only shown disrespect for your wife and your brother, but also for your mother and me. While you're living under our roof, I expected more -- even of you."

Archie stammered now, looking down and kicking the ground with the toe of his shoe. "Papa, I know it sounds terrible, but you just don't understand. It wasn't my fault. It was Valera. You can't know how hard I tried to get away from her but she wouldn't leave me alone." He started to weep and wiped his runny nose on the sleeve of his shirt. Then he hesitated while he put his most pathetic face on and turned to his dad with a look of despair in his eyes. "I fought hard to avoid her. Really I did. But finally, she wore me down. I felt sorry for her. She's pitiful. Nobody around here likes her or treats her very nice. Especially Agnew." He could tell that his dad wasn't buying this, so he decided to try another track. "Besides, Papa, Evelyn is so cold to me and Valera wanted me. You just don't . . ."

"Stop it, Archie!" Papa said, his voice heavy with anger. "Has anything ever been your fault? Poor Archie, always the innocent victim. Your mother might be taken in by your excuses but I'm not, so just save your 'poor me' act. Besides, I've already made a decision about what to do with you and that's what I'm here to tell you."

Archie caught his breath. He hadn't even had a chance to use the bit about Evelyn being pregnant.

"I've decided we're not going to tell Evelyn or Agnew what you two have been up to. No point hurting them. But you're going to pack up your family and move. I want you out of here."

Archie wailed, "Oh, no! Please no. What about Evelyn and Sonny? You probably don't know, Papa, but Evelyn's going to have a baby. Think what it will do to them if you throw us out."

"Simmer down, Archie. Don't you think I've thought about that? I'm not going to punish your innocent family more than they're already punished having to put up with you. I have some land over by Commerce. There's a little house on it. The sharecropper who lived there left when the cotton market collapsed and he couldn't make a living off the land. I went out there the other day. The house is livable but it needs some repair. I'll pay. You'll do the work. Then I'll expect you to keep things up and farm the land. In the meantime, I'll give the money for your family's necessities directly to Evelyn with explicit instructions that you're not to get your hands on a penny of it." Then he added with unmistakable resolve, "Archie, the end has come. I absolutely will not abide my money being spent on alcohol. And there'll be no more money from your mother so you better start thinking about giving up your drinking."

Archie doubled up and dropped to the ground. Continuing to sob, he said, "I'm sorry. I'm really, really sorry. I'm so ashamed. I know it was an awful thing to do. Let's face it. I'm just no good. Please don't hate me, Papa."

"Oh, Archie. I don't hate you. You're my son and I love you, in spite of the things you do. I just have to ask myself where I went wrong with you. You had so much promise." He stared into the dark shadows cast by the moon for a brief period and his voice broke when he spoke again. "This isn't revenge or even punishment, Son. This is my attempt to wake you up, to give you a chance to get your life together before it's too late." Having said this, he turned and walked away, fighting tears as his feet searched for the path back to the house.

*   *   *

The next morning Papa woke before the sun came up and lay with a knot the size of a baseball already growing in the pit of his stomach. He still hadn't made up his mind about what to do with Valera. *God, will the time ever come again when I can wake up and not dread the day.*

Last night when he'd left Archie still on the ground, he was completely drained. Slipping back through the sun porch and ignoring the curious stares of those still there, he'd trudged up the steps to his bedroom. Dandy had taken to her bed with another headache and when he entered the bedroom, she was sound asleep. He was embarrassed to think it, but her headache had come at an opportune time for him. In order to protect his own sanity, he wanted to avoid talking to her about this until he'd taken the actions he needed to take.

At the first signs of sunrise, he got out of bed and dressed quietly. He deviated from his usual routine, slipping out of the house and leaving for the office without eating breakfast. Food was the last thing on his mind.

At the office, patients came and left and he tried to lose himself in their problems, but without success. Thoughts about what to do with Valera throbbed like a toothache that refused to go away.

By the time he arrived home from the office, the thing he wanted most was to get all this behind him. He'd made his decision. Now he just needed an opportunity to get Valera alone. The evening meal seemed to drag on forever. Finally, supper was finished. and most of the household gathered around the radio. Tonight, President Roosevelt was addressing the nation with one of his Fireside Chats. Bess Nell and Evelyn joined the men by the radio, hoping for some good news. That took care of most of the people in the house and Dandy's headache kept her in bed and out of the way.

He watched to see what Valera would do and was relieved when she disappeared as soon as the kitchen was put in order. Now was his chance. Quietly, he crept up the stairs to the second floor and walked down the hall to Agnew and Valera's bedroom. The knot that was in his stomach this morning was now a lump in his throat. He stood in front of the door for a few moments, reviewing in his head what he planned to say. Then, with conviction, he took a deep breath, held his shoulders back and his head high, and tapped on the door. "Valera. It's me. May I come in?"

She opened the door a crack and looked out. Then she opened it all the way and stepped aside to let him in. Their eyes met briefly, then both looked away.

"You know why I've come, don't you?"

"Yes," her voice was barely audible. "I've been expecting you."

He looked down at her, reached out and took one of her hands in his and held it briefly. "Can we talk?"

She motioned to the one chair in the bedroom and after he was seated, she took a seat on the edge of the bed facing him.

"There's no good way to say this, Valera. I can't tell you how disappointed I am in you and Archie."

"I know," she said, looking down again to avoid meeting his eyes.

"I won't ask you why or how this happened. I don't even want to know. But I'm sure you understand it must be dealt with."

"Yes. I know."

"I've given it a lot of thought and I don't want innocent people to be hurt."

"Neither do I." She raised her swollen eyes to meet his. "I can't tell you how terrible I feel, how much I hate myself. You've taken us in and been so good to us, and this is how I've repaid you."

He cleared his throat and his hand rose to rub his head. "I've already talked to Archie. He and his family will be moving soon. Just outside Commerce, about twenty miles away. That should be far enough that you two will be separated."

"You don't have to worry about that. The last thing in the world I'd ever do is go near Archie again, and I'm sure he feels the same."

"Nevertheless, he needs to get out of here. It's for his own good."

She rose from her seat on the bed and walked across the room turning her back to him. Her throat was tight when she asked, "What do you plan to do with me?"

"I see no reason that we should tell Agnew, or Evelyn for that matter. It would serve no good purpose and would only cause more pain. All things considered, it seems to me it would be best for you and Agnew to stay on here until things in Nacogdoches appear to be right for your return."

She whirled around to face him, dashed across the room, grabbed his hand and kissed it. "Oh, Dr. Swinson. Thank you! Thank you so much. I was so scared you'd tell Agnew and he'd kick me out, and I had no place to go."

He withdrew his hand and held it up to stop her when he saw a smile starting to appear. "Wait now. You're not getting off scott free. My wife knows about you and Archie and I think you can understand she won't be pleased with my decision. In fact, most likely she'll let you know how she feels in no uncertain terms. You'd better prepare yourself for that. It's not going to be easy."

She shook her head. "I know she don't like me. She never has. It'll be even harder for her to have me here now. I understand."

"In the meantime, I can't help but notice the way Agnew treats you and I plan to talk to him about it. Understand that's not an excuse for what you've done. I can't condone that. But I'll remind him that a man treats his wife with love and respect. And maybe the two of you can have some honest talks so you won't feel you need to take other paths to get his attention."

She fell to her knees in front of him. "I'm so ashamed. How can I ever thank you? I promise you, I will never do anything else to make you sorry."

*   *   *

When Agnew came in from the fields the next day he found Papa waiting for him on the sunporch.

"Hi, Son. Do you think you and I could have a talk?"

"Sure, Papa. What's going on?"

"Let's go for a walk."

Agnew looked puzzled but said, "Okay."

Papa led him out the back door and to the gravel road that led to the barns. They both kept their silence for awhile. As they walked, Papa searched for a way to say what he needed to say without giving away that Valera and Archie had been unfaithful.

Agnew broke the silence. "Papa, you seem pretty serious about something. Is it something I've done?"

"Well Agnew, I don't really know how to say this; however I feel I need to say something. I've been wondering if you realize how your behavior toward Valera is affecting her?"

Agnew's face turned red and he answered with resentment, "I don't know what you mean by that, and I'm sorry but that's between Valera and me."

"You're wrong. When people live together as close as we do, everything each of us does affects those around us. You should know that."

His defenses were still up when he answered. "Okay. I'll grant you that, but what do you mean by *my behavior toward Valera*?"

"I can't help but notice that you more or less ignore her. I think you need to look at this. If we are all going to survive this test of living together, we need to show each other love and respect. This goes double for the ones we've chosen to be our mates."

Agnew didn't respond right away. He looked down at the road, watching his feet move across the ground while he considered what Papa was saying. Being able to speak about this truthfully took him awhile. It meant revealing himself as the weakling he felt himself to be. It hurt to face it, but he knew in some corner of himself that he had been unkind to Valera ever since they'd come to live here.

After they'd strolled without speaking for awhile, Agnew said, "I guess you're right, Papa. I've always had trouble talking about my feelings and this is particularly hard because it still causes me so much pain. Helen Lee left me for another man -- a man I considered to be a friend. She broke my heart, took my two sons away from me. Do you know how I met Valera? She was a prostitute. Helen Lee had such class. She was everything Valera is not. I don't think this really hit me until I saw how Dandy reacted to Valera. Can you understand how hard it's been for me to lose everything: my family, my business, my life? I'm forced to show my failures before the world and come here dragging a wife my mother makes me feel ashamed of. How much is a man supposed to take before he just shuts down?"

Papa stopped walking and turned to Agnew holding outstretched arms. "Come here, Son. I'm so sorry." Agnew hesitated only a second before he came into his arms and the years fell away. They clung together, a father comforting his first child. "I understand, Agnew. And I hurt for you. But you made Valera your wife and she's hurting, too. You're a good man, an honest man. Don't get lost in your own grief to the point you bring pain to those who love you. Valera is here among strangers. She needs you."

Agnew buried his head on his dad's shoulder and at long last allowed his pent up emotions to express themselves while Papa held him in his arms.

* * *

When they returned to the house the family had already gathered around the table for supper. Valera didn't look up when Agnew entered. Usually he would have ignored the empty chair next to her, but this time he not only took it, he reached over and gently touched her arm, smiled at her.

Surprised, she jerked when she felt his touch, then when she saw his smile, she shyly smiled back.

After supper he followed her upstairs instead of joining the other men as he usually did. As they climbed the stairs he placed his hand in the small of her back and once their bedroom door was closed he put his arms around her.

She pushed back and looked up at him. "Agnew. What's happened to you?"

"Valera, I'm so sorry I've hurt you. I've been selfish. Selfish and weak. I've let my own hurt blind me to yours. I can see that now. If you can forgive me I promise I'll try to make it up to you." He watched as the tough exterior she showed to the world melted away, revealing the vulnerable, frightened woman she really was.

"You'll never know how I've needed to hear that. I could tell you were ashamed of me and I didn't know what to do about it. I've felt so alone without you. I was afraid I'd lost you forever."

CHAPTER 30

After three days of oblivion with one of the worst migraines she could remember, Dandy woke to the soft light floating into the bedroom and slowly lifted her eyelids. The pain was gone and she felt like a human being again. She yawned and stretched, then rose and sat on the side of the bed rubbing her eyes with both fists. Papa's side of the bed was empty. Shortly, she heard the bedroom door open and looked up to see him tiptoeing into the bedroom, a towel thrown over his shoulders and a little white foam still on his neck from his shave.

He smiled when he saw her sitting there. "Well now, look who's among the living? Hello, Dandy. You must be feeling better."

If looks could kill he'd be on his way to the cemetery. "Just save your sweet talk. Don't think I don't know you've been sneaking in and out of this bedroom like some robber for the past few days. If I hadn't been so miserable I'd have called you on it. Why are you tiptoeing around? Exactly what have you been up to?"

He gave her a sheepish grin. "I can't get by you with anything can I? Even when you're half conscious." His grin grew larger and turned into a full blown smile as he walked across the room, sat down beside her on the bed and took her hand and kissed it.

She turned her face away. "Okay. None of that until you tell me. Something's happened to get you in a better mood." She turned back and studied him for a moment. "You've done something about Archie and that -- that woman, haven't you?"

"Yes. And I'm glad to say it's all settled. I've taken care of that situation and if I do say so myself, I think I've handled it well."

"Handled it well? That sounds final. What have you done without even consulting me?"

The tone of his voice changed and his smile disappeared. He gave her a long serious look, then spoke with authority. "I decided I had to work this out on my own, Lula. You're not exactly rational when it comes to Archie. Besides, you're right. It is final. I hope you'll agree with what I've done, but whether you do or not, I expect you to support my decision."

A wild look sparked in her eyes and she waved her arms in the air. "Oh Lord, I'm afraid to ask. What have you done?"

"Now just hold your horses and I'll tell you the way it's going to be. Next week Archie and his family will be moving into the little house on the section of land we own near Commerce."

She started to object but he put his finger to her lips and stopped her.

"Don't say a word. Just listen. It's for the best. I plan to talk to Evelyn. I won't tell her about Archie and Valera, but I think she'll agree that a move would be good for Archie. Besides, with a new baby coming, I think she'll be ready for her family to have a place of their own to try to find a normal life again -- as normal as life with Archie will ever be," he added. He watched as she clouded up like a brewing storm. Shaking his index finger at her, he said, "Now Lula, wait before you explode. That's not all I have to tell you, and this next part is going to be even harder for you."

She was making muttering sounds now and he could tell she was about to lose control. He held both her hands and looked deep into her eyes. "Before you go off half cocked, I want to remind you of something. You consider yourself to be a good Christian woman, don't you?"

Jerking her hand away from him, Dandy glowered at him and shook her head furiously, "It really makes me mad when you start out like that. The answer, as you well know, is that I am!"

"And the Bible tells us that forgiveness is one of the most important virtues. Yes?"

"Oh John, I hate it when you do this." She rose from the bed, crossed the room, then kicked at the footstool that sat by her chair and screamed, "Yes. Yes, I know that."

" Okay. I'm going to ask you to remember that from now on when you deal with Valera."

She looked at him like she thought he'd lost his mind. "What do you mean deal with Valera? Surely, she's leaving, too."

He shook his head from side to side.

"You can't mean you're going to let her stay here after what she's done," she screeched.

"Yes, that's exactly what I do mean. She and Agnew will not be leaving until things get better and he can make a living again. I want you to have some compassion for Valera. She's not had an easy life and she needs to be treated with some Christian kindness." Seeing the resistance written across Dandy's face, he added, "And I aim to see that she is."

"Well!" she said in a huff. "That's you. What about Agnew? Doesn't he want to kick her out for what she's done?"

"This is important, so listen carefully. I'm not going to tell Agnew about her and Archie and neither are you. It's our secret. I've had a talk with Agnew about the way he treats Valera. After we talked for a while he was able to see he's let himself get down about all he's lost and he figures maybe he's been taking it out on Valera. And something else he admitted to me, Lula, and you need to hear this. He's ashamed of Valera because he knows you look down on her."

"Humph." She puckered her lips and cast her eyes away, refusing to look at him.

He walked across the room to where she stood, reached over, turned her chin up and made her look in his eyes. "Now you've got to promise me you'll act like the good woman I know you to be."

She jerked her head free and studied her knotted fists. Then she turned her back to him and her voice came out low in her throat. "You've done all this behind my back and now you expect me to smile and say, *Job well done...* I can't do that."

"Yes, you can, and you will, because we have to survive this thing." He slid his arms around her waist and pulled her to him.

She yanked away and charged across the floor. "Don't touch me. I'll never forgive you for this."

CHAPTER 31

Archie remained on the ground feeling sorry for himself for several minutes after Papa left. He felt as if his world were coming to an end. Lifting his head, he looked up toward heaven for some sign of hope and at that moment a shooting star streaked across the sky. He brightened with the assurance it must be a good omen. With his hope somewhat renewed by this illusion, he picked himself up and brushed the grass off his clothes. The bottle he'd dropped still lay on the ground by his feet and he grabbed it and put it to his lips, draining the little that hadn't spilled.

As he walked back to the house he thought about his plight. The idea of being stuck in a place in the middle of nowhere with a wife who had become a bore to him was not to his liking. There must be some way out of this and he wasn't going to give in without a battle. His mother had always been his way to get around Papa. He'd go to her; plead his case. Together they should be able to change Papa's mind about who should leave. His spirits rose and his steps hastened as a plan began to take shape in his mind.

The next morning he rose early and appeared at the breakfast table clean shaven and sober. Usually, when he couldn't get out of his assigned farm chores altogether, he went through them with little effort, taking twice as long as necessary to accomplish a job. Today would be different. He'd show himself to be an asset. That way maybe he'd get Agnew on his side. The more people he had behind him the better. Papa wouldn't be able to fight them all.

After he'd put in what for him was a hard days work, he searched for Dandy and found her in the kitchen. Luckily she was alone. He approached her and kissed her cheek. "Hi, Dandy. Anything I can do to help you?"

"Hello, Archie," she answered coolly. She stopped peeling potatoes and turned to look at him. "I'm sorry but it won't work. Your Papa's mind is made up. I've never seen him like this. Believe me, I've tried to change his mind about making you leave. But this thing you've done with that woman has pushed him over the edge. He won't listen to me anymore."

"But you've got to tell him I've turned over a new leaf. I'm going to stop drinking. I worked hard on the farm today. Just ask Agnew. He'll tell you. He needs my help. I promise to work hard every day."

Disgusted, she said, "Archie, you should have been helping like this all along. It's too late now. I've done everything I can do."

He didn't move for a few minutes while the wheels turned in his head. "Okay, then if that's the case, can you at least give me a little money? I have some things I need to take care of."

She walked past him to put the potatoes on the stove and avoided looking at him when she answered, "I'm sorry, Son. I've been instructed not to give you any more money. We both know you'll go spend it on drink. You're just going to have to learn to do without."

"But, Dandy. Please," he begged, putting on his most pathetic look.

"No. Papa's right. I'm not helping you by giving you money. I'm sorry. I can't."

Archie's shoulders drooped. He glanced back one last time checking to make sure his mother hadn't softened before he left the kitchen in defeat. He had no money and no bottle and he hadn't had a drink since last night. His hands were shaking and his entire body was soaked with perspiration. Once he was in the backyard, he stopped walking and looked around him, fighting despair. He'd worry about having to leave later. Right now all he could think about was his need for a drink. Erby would have to help him out. Archie figured he owed him. After all, none of this would be happening if Erby had kept his big mouth shut.

* * *

Two days passed and Papa could see that Archie was making no move toward his departure. It appeared his way of dealing with the ultimatum to leave was to ignore it and hope it would go away. Obviously, he hadn't told Evelyn they were leaving or she would have said something or made some move. When Papa thought about it, the news of their move would probably be better coming from him anyhow. He wanted to withhold the real reason for their departure in order to make it as easy as possible for her. That evening he knocked on the downstairs bedroom door.

"Dr. Swinson," Evelyn said in surprise when she opened the door and saw him standing there.

"May I come in?"

"Of course. Please. I was just putting Sonny to bed."

"Hi, Papa." Sonny smiled up from where he stood beside his mother.

Papa patted him on the head and returned his smile. "Hello, Sonny." As he ran his fingers across Sonny's blonde curls he felt a sense of loss. Up until now he hadn't thought about how much he was going to miss this beautiful boy who ran to meet him everyday when he came home from the office.

Evelyn motioned to a chair and once he was seated she sat in the rocking chair and put Sonny on her lap. "This is a pleasant surprise."

"Not so pleasant, I'm afraid. I need to tell you something and I hope you won't find it too upsetting."

She flinched and the color left her face. "What has Archie done now?" she asked, seemingly resigned to hear the worst.

275

"I don't have to tell you that Archie is drinking more and doing less to help out on the farm."

Her expression didn't change. "I know."

"I think it's too easy for him to get liquor around here and I've been thinking of some way to alter that. I've talked to Archie about this. Apparently he didn't tell you about my plan."

She adjusted Sonny who was squirming on her lap. "No. Archie doesn't share too much with me anymore."

"My hope is you'll agree that he would be better off living somewhere else; somewhere he'll have to depend on himself more."

She nodded and waited for him to continue.

"I have some land with a house outside Commerce. How would you feel about living there?"

She didn't answer immediately. Her eyes studied the ceiling and then her hands. Finally, when she returned her gaze to him her voice was flat. "Honestly, Dr Swinson, I'm open to anything you think might help. Frankly, I'm at my wit's end. Archie seems out of control."

Her eyes showed such misery that for a moment he was without words. He shifted in his chair trying to find a more comfortable position. Failing, he looked past her as he said, "My wife tells me you're expecting another baby."

"That's true." She tried to smile but just the corners of her mouth turned up. Her eyes remained sad.

"This could be a new start. At least that's my prayer. If there's no reason to delay, I think the sooner the better. Do you think you could be ready to move by next week? I don't want to rush you if that's too soon," he added.

"As little as we have to move, we could be ready sooner than that."

"All right then. I'll see to it that the little house has the things you'll need to set up housekeeping. Also, I want you to understand that you will be in total control of the money I plan to give you for your living expenses. Archie is to get none, and I mean *none* of it. I've told Archie this and I want you to stand strong. You've got to promise me that. It's for his own good."

"I understand," she sighed. "It won't be easy but I'll do it." She hesitated. "He'll hate me for it. But lately he doesn't seem to care that much for me anyhow. We'll be ready when you say so. She reached out and touched his arm. "Thank you, Dr. Swinson. This must be hard for you."

He couldn't hide his feelings of dismay and the hurt in his eyes matched that in hers. "I'm so sorry, Evelyn. You're a good woman. I wish you had better."

* * *

The next week Papa spent making sure the house Archie and his family were moving into had adequate furnishings and the necessities for living. On the morning set for their departure, he knocked on their bedroom door. Two suitcases that held their belongings sat on the floor nearby and Evelyn and Sonny were dressed and stood beside them. However,

Archie was still in bed, his back turned toward the door, his head buried in a pillow.

Papa stood in the doorway frowning. All patience gone, he tromped over to the bed, poked Archie with his finger and thundered, "Get up, Archie! It's time to leave."

A groan filled the room but Archie didn't move. Ignoring the order, he continued to face the wall.

"I'm warning you. If you don't get up I'm going to have Agnew and Preacher drag you up."

Archie turned his head and looked up from the pillow. "I'm sick, Papa. I can't move."

Agnew and Preacher had followed Papa down the stairs and stood just outside the door. When he motioned to them they entered the room and between them they had Archie on his feet and dressed in a matter of minutes.

Upstairs Dandy stood at her bedroom window and held back the curtains as she looked out on Papa's car as it pulled away. Evelyn and Sonny were tucked in the back seat surrounded by the suitcases. Archie sat in front, slumped in the seat next to Papa. Even though they were only going less than twenty miles away, she couldn't bear saying goodbye. As she watched them pull out of the drive and on to the highway a feeling of loss and frustration swam through her. She couldn't forgive herself for letting Archie down.

CHAPTER 32

Dandy's lips were pursed and her eyebrows came together in a deep frown as she put the cup she just dried into the cabinet. She knew she'd be in big trouble when Papa found out what she'd done. He just wouldn't stop badgering her until she'd promised to make every effort to be nice to Valera. And she'd tried. God knew she'd tried! For over three weeks she'd been true to her promise -- painful as it was. The first week, she'd managed fairly well to hold her tongue. She'd even been more than nice to her. But by the middle of the second week her resolve had started to seriously deteriorate. The third week had proven too much. She'd bitten her tongue until it was raw and she couldn't hold it any longer. For weeks her feelings had been bottled up and fermenting and threatening to explode. And today they had. All her good intentions had gone down the drain.

Everything had come to a head this morning when she and Valera were together in the kitchen fixing the noon meal. She was at the stove making gravy and glanced over to where Valera was mashing potatoes. When she couldn't stand it any longer she walked over and checked the potatoes to make sure she was doing them right. Then she glared at Valera like she had committed some unforgivable sin and stormed at her, "These mashed potatoes are lumpy. Can't you do anything right?" The minute the words left her mouth she drew in her breath. She'd done it. She'd broken her promise to Papa.

Gazing blankly at nothing in particular, she thought back to this morning and tried to make excuses for herself. Valera had no right to be here. Try as she may, good Christian or not, Dandy just couldn't find it in herself to forgive Valera. Surely God must know it just wasn't fair that she was still here while poor Archie was forced to move out. Every little thing Valera did irritated her. When she worked in the garden picking green beans she yanked too hard on the vines, and she left roots in the ground when she pulled weeds. When she peeled peaches for canning she cut away too much of the fruit. To top it all off, her grammar drove Dandy crazy. How many times had she corrected her when she said "ain't"? But did she stop? No, she did not! Might as well be talking to a wall. Dandy shook her head from side to side as she mumbled to herself. "The truth of it is she's just poor white trash and will never be anything else." It's like Dandy's mother used to say, "You can't make a silk purse out of a sow's ear."

* * *

Rain, shine, snow or sleet, farm work had to be done. Animals must be watered and fed, cows milked, grain planted and harvested, on and on. The chores never ended. This morning at their meeting Dandy reminded Agnew that the fences in disrepair needed mending. Some cows had gotten out and wandered into the road. And among other things, wood needed to be chopped for the wood stoves. He decided to send Erby and Preacher off in different directions to mend fences and accomplish other tasks, purposely arranging it so he could work alone today. Mending fences is a mindless job and left opportunity for soul searching, and he had a lot of that to do. Papa's talk with him about the way he treated Valera had gotten to him. It hurt to admit it but he knew he'd been treating her badly for a long time.

There was also that thing with his mother he needed to ponder. He knew he'd always allowed her too much power over him. She'd looked down on Valera since the day he'd brought her to live here and he had to face that under her influence -- and because of his own weakness -- he had become ashamed of Valera, of her background, her lack of education, all of it. Now he flushed with shame as he remembered that Valera had been his only comfort at the time of his greatest need.

Hours passed while all this occupied his mind. The sun beat down on him and perspiration dripped off his forehead and stung his eyes. He put down his hammer, pulled his handkerchief from his hip pocket and wiped the sweat off his face. He stood for a short time gazing out over the fields and his eyes stopped on the sheep on the other side of the fence. He watched them for a while as they nibbled on the grass. They seemed so free of thought. He wished he could be. Thinking can lead to seeing yourself honestly and he found that to be painful.

He rested for a few minutes more, then went back to work unrolling barbed wire and nailing it to fence posts. His mind refused to be distracted from his guilt as he thought about the change in Valera. In the short time since Papa's talk with him he'd started treating her with a little love and respect and she'd become a different person, sweet and loving, concerned with his every need. Well, to hell with his mother and her judgments, he thought. Papa was right and he was determined to try to make it up to Valera.

The long muggy day finally ended, fences were repaired, wood cut, animals taken care of and the men came in to clean up for supper. Agnew climbed the stairs to his bedroom with renewed determination to show Valera he appreciated her. When he opened the door he was alarmed to find her lying face down on the bed, crying.

"Valera?"

No answer. She hid her head in the pillow and continued to cry.

"Valera, what's wrong? Stop crying and tell me what's happened."

She raised her head from the pillow and whimpered, "I left lumps in the mashed potatoes. Your mother screamed at me because she said I left lumps in the mashed potatoes. And Agnew, I've been trying so hard to please her. You can't know how hard I've been trying. But I just can't win with her. It's hopeless."

He couldn't believe his ears. Incredulous, he said, "Did I hear you right? She screamed at you *because you left lumps in the mashed potatoes?*"

She shook her head.

His head dropped into his hands. This thing with Dandy and Valera had reached a crisis that he was going to have to deal with. This was ridiculous. Obviously, this was to be his test. If he had to choose between his wife and his mother then this was the time for him to untie the apron strings.

He slowly walked over to the dresser where Valera had left a basin of water for him to wash up. He was surprised by a quiver of fear that rushed though him as he washed his face. Having never confronted anyone if he could help it, the idea of confronting Dandy engulfed him in a moment of terror. He sensed Dandy had always thought him a little weak because of this inability to challenge. Maybe she'd been right. But not this time. This time he must prove to her and to himself that he could stand up to her.

He grabbed the towel that hung nearby and dried his face as he crossed over to where Valera lay. She appeared to be all cried out, but he heard an occasional whimper as she lay on her back staring into space. Her beautiful face was swollen and red and she looked so vulnerable. He sat down on the bed beside her, removed his handkerchief from his pocket and handed it to her to blow her nose. After wiping remaining tears from her cheeks with his fingertips, he bent and kissed her softly on the forehead. "Don't worry, Valera. I promise you I'm going to take care of this and she's never going to mistreat you again."

*   *   *

When Dandy woke early the next morning after a fitful night, her mouth was dry and she felt as if an elephant were sitting on her chest. This feeling was more than the aftermath of the pills she'd taken. She knew she'd been wrong to yell at Valera. If there was anything she hated it was feeling guilty, an ugly feeling she'd suffered entirely too much of late.

She'd pretended to be asleep when Papa came to bed last night. She didn't want to chance the possibility he'd found out that she'd broken her promise to be nice to Valera. Venturing a look to where he lay sleeping now, she quietly stole out of bed and tiptoed to her closet, dressed quickly and slipped out of the bedroom. Dealing with his disappointment with her was something she didn't need right now. She felt bad enough. Well, no need worrying about it at the moment, she thought. She'd face that when it happened. Right now she had to go downstairs and wait for the morning meeting with Agnew.

When she got to the kitchen Agnew was already sitting at the table with a cup of coffee in front of him. He glanced up for an instant when she entered, then quickly looked back down at his cup.

"Mornin', Agnew. You're early. I couldn't sleep but I didn't think you'd be up yet. She turned to get herself a cup from the cabinet. "You've already started the fire and made the coffee. Bless you. Smells mighty good."

He kept his eyes on his cup and didn't respond.

She could sense his brooding from across the room. "What's the matter with you, Agnew? You act like you don't feel good."

His eyes met hers for the first time since she'd arrived in the kitchen and they bored into her. "What do you think, Dandy? Do you think there's any way I could feel good?" He waved his hand toward a chair. "Sit down, please. I have some things I need to say to you."

Her face flushed as she took the chair across from him. Agnew had never spoken to her in that tone of voice and her heart beat faster than usual. This confrontation must be about the way she'd yelled at Valera. For the longest time he sat staring into his coffee cup in silence while she folded her hands on the table and resigned herself. Finally, she said, "Okay, out with it, Son. What's on your mind?"

He raised his eyes to look at her and softened a little when he noticed wrinkles in her face that he didn't remember seeing before. Deep circles under her eyes were rimmed with a purple hue and her shoulders seemed to be more slumped than he'd ever seen them. She looked old and tired and it hit him how she'd aged in the last year. This awareness made it even harder for him to be stern with her. "Dandy, as you must know, I love you and I've always tried to honor you."

"I know, Agnew. You're a good son." She peered across the tops of her glasses and waited.

He cleared his throat and looked away. "This is really hard for me, but I've got something to say. I've never challenged you before, but now I must." He rose from the table and walked slowly across the kitchen. "I know that I've been as guilty as you of mistreating Valera, but that's going to change and you need to face it." He turned and walked back to the table and sat down. "Now I know you've never accepted Valera as my wife. But, Dandy, she is my wife. You need to honor that and to treat her with some respect. She can't help it that she's not like Helen Lee, but you've got to face the fact that Helen Lee did a terrible thing to me. I adored her and she took my sons and left me without so much as a warning. She's the one that doesn't deserve your respect. I understand you can't make yourself care for Valera, but you can be civil to her and you haven't been. There's no excuse for the way you yelled at her yesterday over some ridiculous lumps in the mashed potatoes. She may appear to you to be tough but that's just a front. You've really hurt her so many times. I've got to tell you, if you can't respect her, I can't respect you."

This attack was too much for her to bear in silence. Before she knew it she was lashing back. "Agnew, you don't know what you're talking about. There are things you just don't know about Valera that I do." She caught herself and clapped her fingers over her mouth. *Papa would never forgive her. She'd really done it now!*

Agnew's voice rose and he jumped up from his chair almost tipping it over. "What things? What are you talking about?"

"I'm sorry. Forget it. Forget I said anything, please."

"No. If you have something to say, say it!" He grabbed her arm.

"Stop, Agnew. You're hurting me." She'd never seen him so upset.

He released her arm but there was fire in his eyes. "I warn you, if this is another of your attempts to cause trouble between Valera and me, it had better be good."

"It was never my intention to cause trouble. There's plenty of that around here without me adding to it."

"Then what are you hinting at. If there's something you think I should know, tell me."

"I can't say anymore. I promised Papa." Then she glared up at him and added, "If you really want to know, ask Valera. Ask you wife."

He didn't respond, just looked at her with contempt and charged for the kitchen door.

Realizing what she had done, she jumped up and ran after him. "Son, I'm sorry. Please, please forget anything I said. I didn't know what I was saying. I've been so upset lately I'm almost out of my mind."

His face was red with rage when he stopped and turned to face her. "Shut up, Dandy. Just shut your mouth. I'm through with you. I don't want to hear anymore of your insinuations and outright lies about Valera."

He left her standing in the middle of the kitchen, hiding her face in her hands and mumbling to herself, *what have I done now?*

* * *

Valera was in their bedroom dressing for breakfast. When she saw Agnew come through the door, she ran to meet him and threw her arms around his neck. "Darlin', what are you doing here? I thought you were meeting with your mother."

He reached up, removed her arms and pushed her away.

"What . . . What's wrong, Agnew?" Then seeing the look on his face her smile faded. "She told you something that upset you didn't she?"

"Yes, she did. She said I needed to ask you about something she knows and I don't." He searched her face. "Do you know what she's talking about? If you do then you'd better tell me."

All the blood drained from her face. She stepped back a few more steps and looked up at him pleading, "Oh, Agnew, please stop this before it's too late. Things are so good between us now. Please let it go, I beg you."

He shook his head and glowered. "What's going on, Valera? What is it I don't know that Dandy thinks I should?"

She turned and walked across the room, shaking her head while her hands rose palm up in a gesture of hopelessness. "Agnew, you can't know how lost I've felt. You ignored me for so long. Please try to understand. I was so hurt when you turned against me that I . . ." She stopped and whispered, "I can't say it."

He was breathing hard now. "That you what?" he said, his voice loud and demanding. "What did you do?"

The words came out slowly and painfully. "I felt I had to get even with you for treating me the way you were." Then she screamed through tears, "I did the only thing I know how to do. The thing I was trained to do."

It took him a moment to realize what she was implying. When he did, his first impulse was to hit her, but he caught himself and stood speechless while he took in the full impact of her confession. His voice was hoarse when he finally asked, "Who?"

In little more than a whisper, she mumbled, "Archie."

Clasping his hands over his ears, he dropped into the nearby chair. He couldn't stand to hear anymore. Archie's face suddenly loomed before him. Of course, he thought. Papa's insistence on Archie's hasty departure began to make sense now. Agnew closed his eyes and a slow moan that came from deep down in his soul rocked the room. When eventually he opened his eyes again, Valera lay on the floor, her body rolled into a ball. An eternity passed in silence and after all the yelling that had taken place, the stillness in the room felt heavy, oppressive, death like.

* * *

Papa opened the door a crack and stole a look into his waiting room. Patients still lined the walls. He hated to disappoint them. Some had traveled a long way to see him. However, today he just wasn't able to cope with anyone else's problems. He'd gone through the morning like a zombie and it wasn't fair to his patients or him.

He motioned to his receptionist and whispered, "Mildred, would you come in here please?"

She took a quick look around the room at the waiting patients, gave them a half smile, pushed up on her hair and rose from her desk. Before entering the inner office she reached down and smoothed the creases in her skirt. Once there she stood at attention, waiting for the doctor to speak.

"Mildred, I hate to do this, but I'm afraid I've got to go home. I have some pressing problems there and I simply can't get my mind on things here until they're resolved. I'm afraid I won't be back this afternoon but I'll see you tomorrow."

"But Dr. Swinson. What do I tell all those patients? Some have been waiting all morning."

He ran his hand over his head and looked at her without offering an answer. The eyes behind his glasses looked haggard as he shook his head from side to side in a silent plea for understanding.

Seeing his distress, she reached out and put her hand on his arm. "Don't you worry, Doctor. You go on now. I'll take care of everything around here. I'll reschedule the patients. It'll be fine."

"Thank you, Mildred," he said gratefully and without hesitation he grabbed his hat and coat and slipped out the back door. Fifteen minutes later he managed to pull safely into the driveway of his house. He didn't even bother to close the car door before rushing into the kitchen where he found Dandy starting to clean vegetables for the noon meal. He grabbed her by the arm and demanded, "Come on, Dandy. You and I are going for a little drive."

"Are you crazy, John? I'm in the middle of fixing dinner." Then she added with alarm, "What in the dickens are you doing home this time of day anyhow?"

"Forget dinner, Lula. Come with me. We've got to talk and I don't want to be interrupted." She resisted but he gripped her arm tighter and steered her out of the house.

When they got into the car she immediately started to whine. "You heard about me and Valera didn't you. I'm sorry, Papa. I tried. I did. I tried hard to be nice to her. I want to be the kind of woman you want me to be, but truth is I'm not. I'm not loving and kind. I'm not a good Christian." Then she drew in her breath and yelled, "And Valera drives me crazy!" She paused and after a long moment she added, "I guess just about everyone and everything drives me crazy anymore. I tell you, Papa, I'm ready for the loony bin." Pulling her handkerchief out of her apron pocket, she blew her nose, then fell silent.

He didn't respond but started the car, pulled out of the driveway and drove further down the highway until he saw a place where he could pull off the road and stop. He was thoughtful as he looked out the car window at the pasture by the side of the road. Weeds had taken over a field that had once been covered with cotton plants. He wondered if cotton would ever grow here again -- if lives would ever return to normal. His hands were shaking as he looked off into the distance, trying to calm himself before starting to say what must be said. With a deep frown furrowing his forehead, he turned to stare at Dandy who sat waiting, her body tense.

"This isn't just about you yelling at Valera, although I was disappointed to hear about that. This is much worse. Agnew came to talk to me after breakfast this morning and I've never seen him so upset." He stopped and looked at her with raised eyebrows. "You have any idea why he was in such a state?"

Dandy kept her head down and fidgeted with the handkerchief she'd pulled out of her pocket, twisting it and then untwisting it. When she answered her voice was so low he could barely hear it. "I'm afraid so."

"And maybe you would like to tell me why you saw fit to tell him about Valera and Archie."

"I didn't tell him about Valera and Archie." she said, indignant at the suggestion. Then her voice lost its volume and she refused to look at him. "I just suggested that he should ask Valera a few questions."

"Lula, did I not tell you in no uncertain terms that you were never to mention that incident to him, or anyone else for that matter?"

She took in a deep breath and let it out with a gush. "Well, you just don't understand. Agnew attacked me. He accused me of being a trouble maker. I was just defending myself." She twisted her handkerchief some more and continued to look down. When she spoke again her tone of voice had changed. "Papa, I'm sorry. I didn't mean to say anything. It just slipped out before I knew it. I could have bitten off my tongue. I knew you'd be really upset with me." She looked at him beseechingly. "I'm so sorry. I really feel terrible."

"You should. For all sorts of reasons. You've done irreparable damage to the lives of so many people. I swear, do you think you're ever going to learn to control that mouth of yours?"

She studied her fingernails. "It doesn't look like it."

Shifting in his seat, he ran his hand across his pate. "Agnew has some major decisions to make now. It's apparently not going to work for Valera or Agnew to stay here much longer. If he decides to continue with his marriage -- as I have strongly urged him to do -- they can't stay here and have to deal with you."

She flinched, twisted her mouth but didn't try to defend herself.

"I'm sorry, but I might as well say it like it is," he said. "You've stirred up a hornet's nest. I'd like for you to think about how you might have just destroyed two people and a marriage."

He sat for a moment nursing his frustration and trying to think of something positive to say. "Maybe some good can possibly come from all this. Sometimes overcoming trouble can strengthen a marriage if it survives. Ours has certainly had lots of opportunity for strengthening since all our children moved in. I don't need to tell you how much I look forward to the time when everyone can go back to their lives and we don't have to be a part of everything that goes on with them." He reached over and wrapped his hand around the back of her neck and gently squeezed. Then he looked in her eyes and smiled. "Lula, Lord knows you're not easy, and at times I'd like to strangle you -- but I love you in spite of it -- or maybe even because of it, who knows?" Shaking his head at his own vulnerability, he started the car, turned it around toward home and pressed hard on the accelerator.

CHAPTER 33

Valera lost track of time as she lay crumpled on the floor wishing she could die. She didn't know how much time had passed before she'd heard the bedroom door open, then close. Glancing toward the bed she saw Agnew was no longer there. Her eyes searched the room. He was gone. A dagger plunged in her heart couldn't have hurt as much.

As the day went endlessly on the pain wouldn't go away or give her relief. She had never known such desperation, not even when Erby had discovered her with Archie in the hayloft. This felt more final. Every bone in her body ached from lying on the hard floor and finally she managed to get up and drag herself to the bed. As she lay on her back staring into space, her mind whirled. Everyone must know now. How could she ever show her face to the rest of Agnew's family again? The very thought of leaving her room paralyzed her.

Every time she heard someone on the stairs she prayed it was Agnew coming back. She held on to the smallest ray of hope that he might be able to forgive her and would come to tell her so. Several times during the day her heart beat faster when she heard a knock on her door, but it turned out to be Bess Nell.

"Valera, are you okay? Are you sick? Is there anything I can do for you? Would you like me to bring you something to eat?"

"No, thanks," Valera answered and felt relief when she heard Bess Nell's footsteps retreating down the stairs with no further questions.

The light slowly disappeared from the room and in the impending darkness the wind started to whirl around the windows. Wind had always felt like a bad omen to her, a sound that made her feel at risk. She waited and prayed while listening to it rattle the windows in its attempt to break into the room. Bathed in total darkness now, the day gone, she was forced to face the fact her prayers had been ignored. Agnew hadn't returned. She wondered if he ever would.

* * *

After Agnew left Valera lying on the floor of their bedroom, he walked down the stairs and through the porch with his eyes pinned straight ahead. He neither slowed down nor looked around when he passed the breakfast table. Once his feet hit the ground, he walked as fast as his legs would carry him toward the hay barn. Archie had thought it was his secret, but everyone knew where he had gone each evening to hide away and drink. Agnew felt pretty certain that must have been the place for his meetings with Valera. Where else could they go to be alone? As if drawn by some force determined to add to his feelings of betrayal, he arrived at the barn and slowly opened the door. Before entering he looked inside, trying to decide if he was crazy for coming here, but after a few moments of indecision, he crept across the straw covered floor to the ladder. His heart pounded in his ears as he climbed to the loft and stood looking through the opening. A few feet away he could see an area where the hay was packed and he imagined that was where they must have laid together.

How much more was he going to be asked to bear -- his wife with his own brother? What was wrong with him that women always betrayed him, first Helen Lee and now Valera? More questions to gnaw at him. He slowly climbed into the loft, sat down and leaned his back against the wall, then pulled his knees up to his chest. His hands cradled his head and he closed his eyes. He had a lot of decisions to make. *How could he stay in Ardis Heights any longer? He had to figure out a way to leave. And then if he was able to forgive Valera and take her with him, could he ever trust her again? Did he even want to try?*

Minutes turned into hours and finally there were the first signs that light in the barn was beginning to fade. With determination he picked himself up from the loft floor and brushed away the hay clinging to his clothes. Papa would be getting home from the office soon. He'd made some decisions and he needed to borrow his car. His own had been stored in the garage so long the battery was down the last time he'd tried to start it. Wanting to avoid encountering anyone, he took a way back to the house through trees that partially hid him from view and crouched behind the garage to wait for Papa to arrive. When he heard the car pull into the drive, he hurried out to meet him.

"Hello Papa. Would you mind if I borrow your car for awhile?"

"Hi, Agnew. You startled me." Papa looked puzzled. "Where do you want to go?"

"In to town. I have some things I need to take care of."

Papa scratched his head. "You can have the car but I'll need it to get to work in the morning."

"I'll have it back tonight, I promise."

"Okay. And when you get back maybe we can talk more. I've been so concerned about you. I know what you're going through but I urge you not to do anything drastic. Valera has paid dearly for her mistake and I feel she's learned a lesson. She loves you, Agnew. I'm certain that if you give her a chance she can make you a good wife. Don't take this as criticism but just something you need to consider. What would you have done if Valera had treated you the way you've treated her all this time?"

A gust of wind swept through the trees and blew leaves to the ground around them while Papa waited for Agnew to reply. Suddenly they were interrupted by small voices and he looked up to see his grandchildren headed in their direction. Hurriedly he handed the car keys to Agnew and started across the yard to meet them. "We'll talk more tomorrow," he said over his shoulder as he fled, fishing in his pockets for the bubble gum he had bought for them today.

Agnew nodded at his dad without comment as he got in the car, backed out the driveway and headed for town. Papa hadn't said anything Agnew hadn't spent the day considering but he wasn't in any mood to discuss it. Right now he had other things to tend to -- things he needed to do on his own without interference from anyone, not even Papa. As he drove through town he looked for a public phone and found one at the gas station on Lee Street. He dialed the number and waited.

In a few moments a familiar voice came on the line. "Hello." It was his old friend, George Thompson in Nacogdoches.

He deposited the required coins and said, "George? This is Agnew."

"Agnew, Buddy! God, it's good to hear from you. It's been over a year. Why haven't you answered my letters?"

"I haven't had anything good to say, George. Things haven't been so hot for me. How's it with you?"

"Oh, I'm holding on. So, what's up?"

"I'm coming home and I want to know how things are there. Has the bank sold my house?"

"No. It's been sitting empty except for a short period when some people rented it and had to move when they couldn't make the rent payments."

"How's business. Anything going on? Think I could sell glasses again?"

"Well, things are getting better slowly. I'm sure there are people who need new glasses and I've still got all your equipment stored in my shed. It might be a little dusty but I've had a tarp over it so it should be in good shape."

"I thought if I could work out something with the bank on my house, I'd just operate out of there for awhile until I could open an office again."

"It'll sure be good to have you back. I've missed you like hell, Agnew. How's Valera?"

"I can't answer that now, George. We'll talk about that later."

"Okay, whatever you say. If you need a place to stay while you're getting settled, you all are more than welcome to stay with Emily and me."

"Thanks, Friend. I'll probably have to take you up on that offer. Not for too long I hope, but it would be a big help."

"I count on you to let me know if there's anything else I can do. I want you back here."

"Thanks. I'll talk to you again when I know more. Bye for now."

"Goodbye. And hurry home."

Agnew hung up the phone and climbed back in the car. Turning it toward Ardis Heights, he slowly drove the five miles to the farm. He pulled in the drive and sat in the car for a long time, thinking. Not ready to face Valera yet, he decided to sleep in the room vacated by Archie and his family.

* * *

Agnew and Valera became the concern of everyone as their two chairs sat empty at the table all that day. When supper time came, Dandy was unusually quiet and kept stealing glances at Papa who offered nothing to the conversation and refused to look at her. As soon as he finished eating, he excused himself, left the table and went upstairs to his room.

Bess Nell could contain her curiosity no longer. She followed her mother into the kitchen after supper. "Okay, Dandy. Out with it. Strange things are going on around here. Archie and his family leave in a big hurry with no explanation. Now, Agnew's been missing all day and Valera's hiding away in her room and won't open the door. I've been up twice to check on her and I can hear her in there crying. I was outside with the children when Papa got home this evening, and Agnew appeared out of nowhere. Then I saw him drive off in Papa's car. You'll have to admit that's all very curious. I've tried not to be a busy body and to tend to my own business, but this is too much."

Dandy started to wash dishes in the sink and avoided answering her. "Could you hand me those plates over there, please?"

"I want to know, Dandy," she said emphatically as she handed the dishes to her mother. "You've gotta tell me what's going on."

Dandy heaved a deep sigh. "It's such a mess, Sister. And in a way, I'm afraid I might be partly responsible for it. It's very hard to talk about." Her voice trailed off as she continued. "I let Archie down. Papa's disappointed in me. Agnew's mad at me. And not that I care that much, but I'm sure Valera must hate me."

"I'm sorry to hear everyone's mad at you, but that still doesn't answer my question."

Dandy didn't move for a long moment, her hands still in the dishwater. Then she slowly removed them and dried them on the bottom of her apron as she walked over to the kitchen table and sat down. She gestured for Bess Nell to join her. "I guess you have a right to know. Everyone around here is so upset." Her eyes wondered up toward the area of the house where Valera was. "I hate to say this, but it all started when Agnew brought that woman into this house." She stopped and sighed again. "You want to know what's going on? Okay, I'll tell you. That woman -- that Valera -- seduced poor Archie."

Bess Nell clasped her hand over her mouth in disbelief. "No! Are you sure? I can't believe that."

"Of course I'm sure. I wouldn't make up a thing like that. Anyway, your Papa, who was never fair to Archie in my eyes, decided he was the one who should leave. Because of his drinking, he said. And in Papa's wisdom," she said sarcastically with an emphasis on the wisdom, "and against my wishes I might add -- he let that hussy stay here."

"Oh, my gosh! No wonder everyone's upset. How could she do such a thing? And Archie! I can't imagine." She stopped and with a puzzled look she asked, "But then, why is everyone mad at you?"

Dandy made a face before answering. "Because I'm a blabber mouth and I as much as told Agnew about Valera and Archie when I'd promised Papa I wouldn't."

"Oh, I see." She hesitated, "Does Evelyn know?"

"No. Papa got them out of here fast -- before I could let it slip I guess. He didn't want either Agnew or Evelyn to know."

Bess Nell rolled her eyes. What could she say?

CHAPTER 34

When Agnew returned from town he waited in the car until he saw all the lights go off in the house. That was his signal to steal into the downstairs bedroom without anyone seeing him. The room had been closed off since Archie and Evelyn's departure and an eerie quiet sent a shudder through him as he entered the dark empty room. He imagined he could actually feel the unhappiness that had existed here. It seemed to have a life of its own and magnified his feelings of unrest. The very thought of Archie torched his anger and gave him an overwhelming desire to strangle him. Even being in a room where Archie had slept distressed him. But this was his only option for tonight since he wasn't ready to deal with Valera yet.

He undressed in the dark and crawled into the bed. Although he'd never been one to cuddle, in fact always made an effort not to touch or be touched when sleeping, the bed felt lonely and empty with only him in it. He was surprised how he missed the warmth of Valera's body lying beside him.

Was this the way he wanted to spend the rest of his life? Alone in bed? Alone at the breakfast table? A man alone in a world filled with couples? He'd done that after Helen Lee left and he'd hated every minute of it.

He tried to close his eyes but they kept popping open as Papa's words repeated themselves over and over in his mind. His dad's observations always seemed to hit a nerve and made Agnew look at himself in ways he's rather not. *What would you have done if Valera had treated you the way you've treated her?* That was a question he must answer honestly. His future depended on it.

The bedroom where he spent an agonizing night shared a wall with the porch and the next morning, he lay in bed and listened for the family to gather around the breakfast table. When he felt confident everyone must be there and he wouldn't have to worry about bumping into anyone, he cautiously left the bedroom and stole up the stairs to the room he shared with Valera. Slowly he opened the door and stood in the doorway for a few moments before stepping in. The shades were drawn and the room was in semi-darkness. He could just make out the shape of Valera's body in the bed.

When she heard the door open, she turned and looked out at him from under her arm, then silently lifted herself up and waited for him to speak. Her pleading eyes rested on him.

He walked across the room and stood beside the bed. As he observed her swollen face and puffy eyes, he was again reminded of Papa's words: *She's already been punished enough.*

He could see that now. Her suffering was plainly written across her face.

He stood for a moment looking down at her, then whispered softly, "Hi."

"Hi," she replied in a voice hoarse from crying.

"You feel like talking?"

She sat up in bed, smoothed her hair with her hands and sniffed. "Yes."

"Valera, we've both done things we regret and we've caused each other enough misery. I'm tired of it and I'm sure you are, too. I'm willing if you are, to try to leave the past behind us and to start over. Hopefully, we can find a way to make each other happy. I think we've both learned something from our mistakes. I've spent a miserable twenty- four hours since I left you here, and Valera, I don't want to go through the rest of my life alone."

She jumped out of the bed and stood before him, her arms reaching out and her face turned up to him. "Oh Agnew, I prayed to hear those words."

He stepped toward her, pulled her to him, held her close and whispered in her ear, "If you can forgive me, I'll forgive you and we'll go on from here."

* * *

The rest of the family was still at the breakfast table when Agnew and Valera walked in, hand in hand. Papa jumped up and Dandy's mouth dropped open when they entered the porch together.

"Sit down please, Papa." Agnew said. "I'm glad you're all still here. We've come to tell you something." Ignoring the two empty seats at the table, they remained standing and Agnew looked down at Valera and squeezed her hand. She stood beside him, avoiding making eye contact with anyone. Sensing her need for reassurance, he put his arm around her waist.

His next words were addressed directly to Papa. "First, Valera and I want you to know that we appreciate all you've done for us. However, we've been here long enough, and in view of all that's happened recently," he said glaring at Dandy, "we know it's time we returned to our lives in Nacogdoches. I've talked to a friend and he's offered to let us stay with them until we can manage to get back in our house. So, looks like we'll be leaving as soon as we can get everything together."

Papa and Preacher rose from the table and came to where Agnew stood and shook his hand. Bess Nell approached Valera and the two stood facing each other for a moment before Bess Nell grabbed her and gave her a hug. But Dandy remained seated at the table, pursing her lips and withholding any comment.

Early morning, four days later, Agnew's car, with a new battery, sat in the driveway loaded and ready to go. A loan of five hundred dollars was in his pocket, "Just enough to get you started," Papa had insisted. Agnew stood beside the car with a forced smile and Valera sat in the front seat with her head down.

Erby and Inez and their girls had joined the rest of the family on the front porch and all stood waving goodbye as Agnew got in the car, pulled out of the driveway and headed east toward the rising sun and the beginning of a new life. He waved back but Valera never looked up.

As they disappeared down the road Papa turned to Dandy and whispered under his breath, "Well, Lula, are you happy now?"

She didn't reply, just gave him one of her drop dead looks and turned on her heels and disappeared into the house.

The rest of the family stood on the porch for a few more minutes after the car was out of sight. As Erby watched them drive away he was surprised to find he could feel any lower than he already had. He didn't dare look at Inez who stood next to him. Her frustration at seeing another family drive away surely matched his own. Agnew and Valera's escape could have left them with hope that maybe their turn would be next, but Erby was too much of a realist to nourish any such delusion. He stole a look at Bess Nell and Preacher and found their faces looked as glum as his. When they saw his eyes on them they shrugged, then turned to look longingly at the road one last time. A few moments later, one by one each reentered the house before going their separate ways to do their assigned chores.

* * *

The day had been muggy and hot, very hot for October. When Erby came in from the fields that evening, dirty, tired and soaked to the skin with perspiration, Inez was waiting to unload a multitude of grievances on him. She had worked herself into such a frenzy that she didn't stop to think about the presence of her two small daughters who sat at the kitchen table waiting for their supper and witnessing her emotional outburst.

Erby was hardly through the door when she started. "I'll tell you, Erby, I can't stand it anymore! People are leaving! When can we get out of here? I want to go home. I want to go back to Lubbock and be with Mama." She stomped her foot and waved her arms over her head. "How come Agnew and Valera got to go and we have to stay here? It's not fair!"

"I can't answer that, Inez, but you might as well face it. We're going to be here for a while yet." Then he added in a dejected voice, "Maybe a good long while. And even when we get out of here, there's no life for us back in Lubbock. There are no signs that the cotton market is coming back anytime soon and the cotton business is all I know. I don't have a profession like Agnew. I don't even have the personality to be a salesman like Preacher. Prepare yourself for it, Inez -- Preacher and Bess Nell will probably be the next to go."

She stormed around the kitchen, still raving, as if she hadn't registered a thing he'd said. "I'm sick of being stuck with your mother. She's a mean, selfish woman. I don't know how you expect me to deal with all the things she heaps on me. We have no privacy, half the time she comes barging in here without notice and today when I went over to get the milk, she'd skimmed all the cream off ours again. Just look at our skinny little girls. They need that cream, but Dandy wants it all to go to Bess Nell and her butterball kids. Why do you think hers are so fat and ours so thin? It's sickening how partial she is to that family."

Inez's diatribe was interrupted when she heard footsteps on the back stoop and turned to see Dandy opening the kitchen screen door, rapping her knuckles lightly on the door frame as an after-thought. As usual, she launched right in with no words of greeting. "Inez, I need to go into town in the morning. Be over at the house a little earlier than usual so you can drive me. Bess Nell will watch the girls. We might be gone most of the morning. I have several things I need to take care of."

Inez stood in the middle of the kitchen with her mouth open. Before she had a chance to respond, Dandy turned to Erby. "Now that Agnew's gone, you'll have to take his place at the meetings before breakfast so I can tell you what needs to be done on the farm. Since there's just the two of you left, I've told Preacher to be there, too." As she headed out the door she turned and instructed, "See you both in the morning. Now don't be late." Then she stopped for a second and glanced over at the two little girls, nodded and gave them her version of a smile before scooting through the screen door and down the steps of the back stoop. Inez and Erby exchanged glances, then watched as she raced down the path toward the big house.

Exhausted by her explosion and by the hopelessness of her interactions with her mother-in-law, Inez put supper on the table for the three of them and then disappeared into her bedroom, leaving Erby to deal with the two befuddled little girls.

Erby had been on his best behavior since the drunken bender that followed his encounter with Archie and Valera in the hay loft. The reception he'd gotten from Inez and the rest of the family when he'd returned home from that misadventure made the price of a repeat performance seem too costly. Besides, he had been determined to make it up to Inez and his girls for his errant behavior. However, after a day that started with seeing Agnew and Valera escape, then all the extra work on the farm in the heat, coming home to Inez's fit and now this with Dandy, his resolve to stop drinking was more than seriously threatened. Because of his girls, he suffered through supper pretending to be in control. But the truth was his heart beat faster while he waited for the time to put the girls to bed so he could seek out the bootlegger and try to numb the devastating frustration he felt.

1935

CHAPTER 35

Thunder rumbled shaking the earth and the sky was electric, lightning darting in all directions. Large drops of rain beat down on Preacher as he raced through the back yard and onto the small back stoop. He stopped for a few seconds to shake off his slicker before entering the house. Removing his dripping hat, he ran his fingers through his straight brown hair as he stepped into the sun porch and looked around to see if anyone was there.

Bess Nell sat on the floor at the other end of the room with their two children and Inez and Erby's girls. They were busy building houses with Johnny's wooden blocks. She jumped up when she saw him come in and ran to where he stood. "There you are! Thank goodness! I was worried sick about you when I heard the thunder and saw all the lightning. Sounds like it's really going to storm. I'm relieved you came in before it gets any worse."

Preacher shook his head wearily as he walked over and fell into a nearby chair. He untied his wet shoes and slipped them off, then removed a handkerchief from his pocket and wiped the rain from his face. Leaning back deeper in the chair, he laced his fingers over his head, stretched his legs out in front of him and let out a low moan. "You know. I think I must have prayed for this goddamn storm. I'm so glad to have an excuse to rest. I'm exhausted."

"It's hard on you without Agnew to help with the farm chores. No wonder you're tired." She reached over and stroked his arm. "It's too much that all the work has fallen on just you and Erby now."

"Yeah" he smirked. "Me and Erby. That's a joke. Lately, more times than not, he's off on one of his drunks. In fact he's gone now. Poor Inez. I know I'm no prize but I don't understand how she puts up with that goddamn guy."

"It's really sad. That's why I have her girls today. She's in bed with one of her headaches again. Every time he disappears it seems to bring on a migraine." She dropped her eyes as if to study her hands and her forehead wrinkled as she thought about it. "I feel so bad about Erby. Watching someone you care about fall apart breaks your heart. I hate what he's doing, but I hate what has brought him to this point even more. He's another tragedy of this depression." Her eyes glazed over for a moment and then she said. "Oh, I almost forgot! This came for you in the mail today." She reached in her pocket and pulled out a letter.

"Bess Nell! Why didn't you tell me?" He jumped up from the chair and grabbed the envelope from her. He held it in his hands for a full minute, staring at the return address in the upper left hand corner:

Big D Carpets and Floors
4200 Mockingbird Land
Dallas, Texas

He could hardly get his breath. The letter he clutched in his hands could determine their whole future.

Bess Nell stood watching. "Well, aren't you going to open it?"

"I'm afraid to. There's something I haven't told you because I didn't want to get your hopes up. A week or so ago when I was really feeling desperate, thinking about how Archie and Agnew had been gone for almost a year and we're still stuck here, I decided to write my old boss again. I checked with him after they left and things weren't good. I thought I'd see if he'd been able to hang on to the store and, if so, if he was any nearer to needing a salesman." He waved the envelope in the air. "This is his reply."

She raised her hands to her cheeks, then crossed her fingers and held them up on either side of her face. "Oh, Preacher. Pray that this will be our way out of here."

With shaking hands, he tore open the envelope, slowly pulled the letter out and unfolded it.

"What does it say? Preacher, come on. Read it to me!"

"Okay. Keep those fingers crossed." He cleared his throat and began reading.

October *14, 1935*

> *Dear Preacher,*
>
> *I was pleased to get your letter and to know that you have survived this terrible depression. A lot of people have really suffered in the past several years; however there are those here in Dallas and elsewhere, I guess, who seem untouched by it all and can still afford new carpet. Because of them I've managed to scrape by. I am beginning to see there are definite signs that the economy is starting to improve. Certainly not to the degree we'd like but at least there's a ray of hope.*
>
> *Preacher, you were the best salesman I ever had and the person I most hated to see go. After receiving your letter it made me think about starting to hire back a few of my best people. I'd like to start with you. Let me know when you would like to return to work. It will be good to have you back.*
>
> *Sincerely yours,*
> *Charles B. Duncan*

When he finished reading the letter, he and Bess Nell stood mesmerized for a moment, staring at each other, unable to believe what they'd just read. Then they shrieked in unison and danced around the room, whooping so loud they drowned out the thunder from the storm outside.

Even though it was a little premature, as soon as the initial excitement was over Bess Nell gathered up her children and sent Betty Lou and Gloria Nell home before racing upstairs to start packing. Preacher was so elated he could do nothing but pace back and forth and wring his hands. He almost wore a groove in the floor while he anxiously waited for Papa to get home. The minute he saw him walk through the door, he raced to meet him waving the letter in the air. "Dr. Swinson. I have great news! I got my old job back."

"Preacher, how wonderful!" Papa's face was one big smile as he grabbed Preacher's hand and shook it.

"We're so excited. I can't believe I've got a job again," Preacher said. Then his grin disappeared for a second. "The thing we hate about going is leaving you without anyone but Erby to work the farm."

"Oh! Please, don't worry about the farm. There are lots of farmhands looking for work and I was thinking of hiring someone anyway. I'm aware there was too much work for just you and Erby. I'm grateful to you for what you've done these last months to hold down the farm by yourself. I know farming isn't you're choice of work. I'm pleased for you and Bess Nell to be getting your lives back again. When do you think you'll be leaving?"

"As soon as we can work out all the details of a place to live and all that."

"We're gonna miss ya'll. I've gotten used to the children greeting me every evening and it won't be the same without them. But Dallas isn't that far away. We'll see lots of each other in the future." Papa shook Preacher's hand again. "It's going to seem awfully quiet around here but we're happy for you. We wish you all the good luck in the world."

"Thank you, Dr. Swinson. We know you do." Preacher flashed him another smile, then turned and dashed toward the hall and up the stairs that would take him to their bedroom for one of the last times. Taking the steps two at a time, he hummed as he went.

* * *

Papa stood saying a little prayer of gratitude after Preacher left the room; then he turned toward the kitchen, the smile still on his face. He found Dandy starting preparations for an apple pie.

"Isn't that wonderful news?" he asked as he burst into the room.

"What news?" she continued pealing an apple without looking around.

"You don't know?" he asked.

"Papa, what in the world are you babbling on about?"

"I'm talking about Preacher getting his old job back."

She stopped in the middle of peeling the apple and threw it in the sink. Her face was a storm of emotions when she turned to look at him. "How do you know that?"

"Preacher just told me."

"Are you sure? Preacher told you? When did he find out?"

"He got a letter in the mail today."

Dandy raged around the kitchen, opening and then slamming cabinet doors. She just couldn't accept it. Bess Nell and her children were leaving? Even the fact that Preacher would also be going didn't console her. What added to the hurt was Bess Nell hadn't been the one to tell her. She'd had to find it out from Papa.

He stood watching her with his mouth open. "Why are you stomping around like that? They're getting their lives back. And think about it. We're getting our house back. It will finally be empty except for you and me after all these years. I thought you'd be happy."

"You thought I'd be happy?" she screamed, giving him a look only she could give. "How could I be happy? I'm losing my daughter and her children."

"You knew they wouldn't be here forever, that they'd be leaving some day."

"Yes, but I didn't know it would feel like I was losing my daughter all over again." She put her hands over her face and sunk into a kitchen chair.

Papa shook his head and threw up his hands. "I give up!" he said. Then he left the kitchen without another word.

She rested her fingers on her temples. Her head was starting to throb. Maybe if she took one of her pills she could avoid the headache she felt coming on. She rose from the table and fled to her room, blinded by tears as she stumbled up the stairs. Once she was in her bedroom, she searched the sewing table drawer and found her stash of pills. Under the circumstances one pill didn't seem enough. Maybe she should take two, or even three, for good measure. After all, this was an emergency.

*   *   *

The rain had stopped and dark clouds opened up enough to show the setting sun in the west as Tom pulled his car to a stop in front of Erby's house. "Take it easy, Erby. I'll see ya' later," he said as he put the car in gear and started to leave. Noticing Erby weave a little, he hesitated and asked, "You okay?"

"Yeah, Thanks. I'm fine." Erby replied as he stumbled across the ditch in front of his house, grasping the bucket of fish they'd caught. He had to admit he was a little woozy. Both he and Tom knew these fishing trips were just an excuse to drink; but he thought if he brought home fish that exonerated him a little. They'd caught a whole string today, in spite of the rain. Too many fish for his small family to eat. As a ruse to delay facing Inez, he decided to take some over to his mother.

The minute he walked into the kitchen at the big house, he could tell by the way Dandy's eyes failed to focus that she'd been into her pills again. Then he noticed tears rimming her eyes. He put the bucket of fish in the sink beside the half peeled apple and crossed over to the kitchen table where she sat with her hands clutched. A cup of cold coffee sat on the table in front of her. He took the chair opposite her and tried to meet her eyes.

"Dandy, have you been crying? What's going on?"

She glared at him. "Little you care. You're never around anymore, anyhow."

"Well, I do care. Why've you been crying?"

Her face clouded up even more. "Your sister's leaving," she whimpered. The words dissolved her control and she burst into tears again.

"Leaving? Where's she going? How can she leave?"

"Preacher got his old job back. They're going back to Dallas. She's upstairs packing right now. She hasn't even bothered to tell me she's going."

If someone had thrown ice water in his face it would not have caused more of a reaction. This development sobered him up in a hurry. Only he and his family were left behind now. His whole body cringed when he thought about how Inez would react to learning everyone else had escaped.

He rose from the table and walked around to where Dandy sat and put his hand on her shoulder and squeezed. "You've still got us, Dandy." Then he said in a voice so low it couldn't be heard. "We'll probably be here forever. Nobody wants to hire a drunk."

CHAPTER 36

Inez and the girls were at the kitchen table eating supper when she heard the backdoor slam. She looked up to see Erby standing inside the door. He stood stone still, his head down, his shoulders sagging and his arms hanging limp by his sides. At first she thought this was an act, a new version of the same old apology she'd experienced every time he returned home from one of his binges. She turned away from him for a second, silent while she tried to decide whether to ignore or attack him for being gone overnight again. She was sick of this game they'd been playing for years. However, when he raised his head and she saw his ashen face and hollow eyes, fear overcame her desire to throw her plate at him. Obviously something terrible had happened. She jumped up from the table and rushed to where he stood. "Erby, what's wrong? Are you sick? Has there been an accident?"

"Worse. I wish I didn't have to tell you this. I know how much it's going to upset you and -- God, Inez. I'm sorry. I'm so sorry for everything. I don't know why you've stood by me all these years." He closed his eyes. "I don't blame you if you hate me"

"I admit, sometimes I do hate you, Erby," she said, standing with her hands on her hips studying him with narrowed eyes. But she felt herself mellowing as she observed the state he was in. Her forehead creased and she added, "However, not always." She reached out and touched his arm. "I've never seen you look so distraught. What in the world has happened? Erby tell me. You're scaring me."

"I just came from Dandy's. Inez, please take it easy when I tell you this. Preacher got his old job back today. They're leaving." He leaned against the door and waited for her tearful explosion but to his surprise it didn't happen.

After her tirade about being left behind when Agnew and Valera went back to Nacogdoches, she'd realized throwing a fit didn't change anything. It only made her and everyone around her miserable. It had been a bitter pill, but she had finally come to accept the fact that Bess Nell and Preacher would be the next to leave. She'd promised herself no more tantrums, no more recriminations. It was what it was. Everyone else would leave before them.

When she heard the reason for his dismay, she was both relieved and disgusted. She dropped back into her chair at the table and sighed. "Really, Erby. I'm not going to have a fit and I don't understand why you're taking this so hard. It's not as if we didn't expect it. You've told me over and over we'd be the last to go. Besides, I should think you'd be glad they're leaving. Dandy's favoritism to Bess Nell is a constant source of irritation to both of us."

"It's not that I care about them being gone. I was afraid of how you'd take it. Everyone else is getting their lives back and we're stuck here, Inez." He paused for a moment and looked away. "And I can't help but feel it's my fault. To make matters worse, I can't see any way out of here for us -- ever." Looking down at the frayed cuffs of his shirt and his worn shoes, he mumbled, "Just look what I've brought us to." Then he turned, walked out the door and sat down on the steps of the back stoop, hiding his head in his arms.

* * *

Several days passed before the reality of having everyone gone hit Inez full force. Even though she thought she'd prepared herself, it turned out she hadn't. Anger slowly took hold of her like a cancer invading her body and depression soon followed. She was stuck here--left behind--left with a husband she no longer knew and a mother-in-law who seemed bent on making her life hell on earth.

On many of the days that followed, she thought she would surely go crazy. Wandering through the house, shoeless on the bare wooden floors, she took in her miserable surroundings like someone seeing them for the first time. She snatched down the only mirror in the house and turned it to the wall, unable to endure the image that gawked back at her, the drab person with dead eyes she'd become. How could she be this person with faded hair, the henna long gone, frizzled and dry from a home permanent she had given herself--a permanent she'd bought with nickels and dimes scraped together over weeks? The shapeless housedresses that hung from her shoulders to below her knees reminded her of days long gone when she was always dressed in something fashionable. Where was that person whose life had been filled with nice things, pretty clothes and fun times, with laughing and dancing? She felt herself shrinking, becoming smaller and smaller as she searched her whole being for the person she'd been before coming to Ardis Heights, but that person was gone, was no more. She wondered how it was possible that at one time in your life you can be one thing and then later, in that same lifetime, disappear completely.

One day after roaming the house like a zombie, she flopped down on her bed and crossed her arms over her face, feeling empty, drained, used up. She didn't cry. She was beyond emotion. She laid there only a short time before she heard small voices calling "Mommy". She dropped her arms and looked up to find her two little girls standing by the side of the bed, their eyes mournful and their faces twisted with concern. In that moment her selfish indulgence died.

*   *   *

Bess Nell and Preachers departure meant different things to different people. Dandy suffered it as a loss and went to bed for several days as her protest. But to Erby it signified personal failure and left him overwhelmed with guilt. Obsessed with a desire to make the situation better for Inez and his girls, he tried hard to stop drinking again and his disappearing bouts ended for a while. When he was the only one left to work the farm, Papa hired a farmhand and when he was no longer expected to contribute much there, Erby started once again to earnestly look for a job.

The economy seemed to be looking a little better. President Roosevelt and Congress had enacted several programs to help with unemployment in the country. One of the programs, The Civilian Conservation Corps was restricted to young men, much younger than Erby. However, he had hopes he might find a job with The Works Progress Administration which was designed to create jobs for men to build highways, roads, bridges and airports as well as for artists, writers, and musicians. Even though the WPA paid only $47.57 a month, those jobs were immediately grabbed by men even more desperate than he. And since Greenville was more agricultural than industrial, new jobs were few and far between and he was not one of the lucky ones. After several weeks of going out each day and returning home with no prospect of a job, he grew more and more despondent and when a job kept eluding him for another month, he finally gave up and returned to drinking and fishing and doing only what he absolutely must on the farm.

1936

CHAPTER 37

Inez was in the living room darning socks when she heard the back screen door open and close. Her first thought was that it must be the girls coming in from the backyard where they had been playing; however when she looked up she found Erby coming through the door with a smile replacing his usual grim expression, and to her surprise, he seemed to be sober.

Her heart stopped for a second when she heard him exclaim "Inez, guess what? We're going to be moving!"

She jumped out of her chair letting the sock she'd been darning fall to the floor. Her hands flew up to clutch her cheeks and she cried, "We are? Where? When?"

"Don't get too excited," he said. "We'll still be here on the farm but further away from Papa and Dandy's house. You know that place down the road about a fourth of a mile, the one on the edge of this property? I'm to redo it for us."

She closed her eyes as her hopes sank. "Erby, you can't mean that old dilapidated place." The energy drained from her body as she envisioned the rundown house she'd passed numerous times, sitting off the road, vacant for who knows how long, no paint, windows broken out or boarded up. Horrified, she asked, "Why? Why on earth would we move there? In fact, why would we move anywhere if we're not leaving this farm?"

"Because it's not working out for the farmhand Papa hired to be living off the property. Papa thinks he needs to live on the farm so he can keep a better look on things. Rather than have him live way down there so far away from the barns and animals, he wondered how we'd feel about giving the farmhand and his family this house. Papa said he'd pay for me to totally redo that one. I went down to look at it. It's larger than this and has lots of possibilities." His enthusiasm dampened when he saw her reaction. "Oh, Inez, please don't look like that. You just have to use a little imagination. Honestly, I can fix it up so you'll like it much better than this place."

"I'll have to think about that," she said, but as she looked around at her present surroundings, she decided any change would have to be good. It wasn't as if this place was so wonderful. Besides, it had been a long time since she had seen Erby show excitement about something.

He threw himself into this new project. When he found it difficult to find all the materials he required locally, he realized there was a need for another lumber yard in the Greenville area. This discovery planted a seed which grew in him, creating a dream and once he had a dream again, his drinking bouts almost disappeared. As he worked on the new house and made plans for building a lumber yard nearby, he appeared to be happy for the first time in years.

No matter how much Inez begged, he wouldn't let her come to see what he was doing until his project was almost finished. Then one afternoon he came home drunk -- with excitement, not alcohol. "Okay. Come on. I'm ready to show you the new house." He held her hand as they walked past Papa and Dandy's house and across the grass field that separated it from their new place. Their girls were caught up in his excitement and followed behind them, laughing as they chased butterflies and picked bouquets of the wild flowers that grew in the field, Indian paint brushes and buttercups.

When the house came into view, Erby walked faster, pulling Inez after him. "Come on Inez. There it is waiting for you."

She stopped and stared in disbelief. The transformation that had taken place from the rundown old house that she remembered to the gleaming white house she saw now was amazing. Still in shock, she crossed the freshly painted front porch and entered the living room. New wallpaper covered the walls and the hardwood floors in the front room shined with polish. The floors in the rest of the house were covered with new linoleum. Her eyes lit up as she entered the kitchen where new cabinets hung on the walls and a porcelain sink sat on a cabinet beneath a large window. But all this was quickly eclipsed when she walked into the bathroom Erby had built onto the house. A sparkling white bathtub sat on clawed feet, and on the other side of the room was a toilet more beautiful to her than any queen's throne. This wasn't their Lubbock house, but after what they'd been living in, it seemed a palace.

Inez glowed at Erby who stood watching her response. "I can't believe this. I just can't believe this is that same old house. Erby, you've done a wonderful job."

"Thanks," he said beaming. "I still have a few things to do, but do you think you could be ready to move in a week or so?"

Inez shook her head. She couldn't stop smiling. "I've got to tell you. I owe you an apology. I didn't think this was possible."

He laughed and grabbed her hand again. "Now come with me. I want to show you the spot where I plan to build the lumber yard."

*   *   *

The next day, Inez drew aside the curtain and looked out the small kitchen window of the house they'd lived in since coming to Ardis Heights. Three of the Leggett children were in the backyard playing hide and go seek with her two girls. She flinched a little when she saw that Gloria Nell was "it" again. Any minute she'd surely come in crying and complaining. Seemed the youngest in the group was "it" most of the time. She'd talked to the older kids about it but some things don't seem to change.

As evidence of that, Inez's eyes followed the smoke that rose in circles from the yard next door. She could see Mrs. Leggett bent over her large black kettle adding a log to the fire underneath. After the fire was kindled she picked up her broom handle and returned to stirring the clothes in the pot, an act Inez had seen her perform hundreds of times over the four years they'd lived side by side. Inez was touched with sympathy as she watched. There was little hope Mrs. Leggett's plight could ever change. It made her doubly grateful that, at last, there were changes coming in her own life, and it appeared they would be for the good. She said a little prayer of gratitude as she thought about their new place.

While she stood observing all this, Dandy came into view, hurrying down the path from the big house, carrying something in her hands. Inez left the window and walked out to wait for her on the back stoop.

As she rushed up, Dandy announced, "Picked the last of the peaches this morning. Thought ya'll might like some peach cobbler. I made way too much for just Papa and me." She held out the dish.

"Why thank you, Mrs. Swinson. That was thoughtful of you. I have some coffee on the stove. Would you like to come in and have a cup?"

"Don't mind if I do," she answered without hesitation.

Inez held the screen door open and stood aside, trying to hide her surprise at Dandy's acceptance of her invitation. She watched with raised eyebrows as Dandy marched in and dropped into a chair at the table. Inez got two cups from the cupboard, filled them with coffee, and joined her.

Ignoring the coffee, Dandy said, "Still seems strange cooking for just Papa and me. I miss all those kids."

"It's hard to believe it's been over a year since Bess Nell and her family left. Heard anything from them lately?" Inez asked politely.

"Got a letter just the other day. Said Preacher's job is going well and they like their house. Seems everything's fine with 'em. They're happy, I guess."

Dandy sat for a while without saying anything more, letting her eyes roam the room. Inez could tell something was weighing on her mind. There seemed a strange urgency about her and it wasn't like Dandy not to come out with what she had to say. Inez grew uneasy as she waited for her to speak.

Finally, Dandy's eyes stopped wandering and she announced, "We also got a letter from Agnew. Said he and Valera are doing well." She raised her eyes and Inez was astonished to see they were brimming with tears. Her voice appeared to break a little when she continued. "It's the first letter since they left that he's addressed to me as well as to Papa. Seems he's finally forgiven me for the way I treated Valera."

Without thinking, Inez found herself reaching across the table to cover Dandy's hand with her own. Their eyes met and Inez saw a very vulnerable woman looking back at her, all the confidence and unstoppablity gone.

As if embarrassed by her daughter-in-law's gesture, Dandy bent her head and appeared to be studying the table. "I've had a lot of time to think since everyone left. I'm afraid I'm a prideful old woman. It's hard for me to admit when I'm wrong. It's taken me all this time to face up to how I behaved all those years when the depression was so bad and the house was filled with my displaced children." Her voice was just above a whisper. "I've got to tell you I don't feel good about the way I handled it all. I haven't been very considerate of other people's feelings and I have a need to make amends." When she raised her head and looked up at Inez the tears that had rimmed her eyes before were now sliding down her cheeks. She reached up and quickly wiped them away with the back of her hand. "That includes you, Inez. Appears you and Erby won't be leaving here any time soon. I'm hoping you'll forgive me and we can start over on new footing."

Inez had been noticing the change in Dandy's behavior over the months as she got her life back and was free of all the strife. She'd gradually become less demanding, even more considerate at times. And she and Erby had noticed Dandy didn't seem to be under the influence of her pills so much anymore. Yes, there had been signs of change but never had Inez expected her to apologize like this. She was at a loss for words so she just smiled back at Dandy and squeezed her hand.

Dandy's mission apparently accomplished, she rose from the table, left her coffee untouched and headed for the kitchen door. As she left, she looked back at Inez and nodded solemnly. Then without another word she was down the steps and racing back down the path toward her house at her usual fast pace.

Inez followed her out onto the stoop and watched as she disappeared. Touched by Dandy's unexpected need for forgiveness, she was reminded of her own need to forgive. Suddenly, she felt lightness, as if something heavy that had been pressing on her chest for a long time was gone. As she looked around her, over at Mrs. Leggett on the other side of the barbed wire fence, down the path to the outhouse, then at the water tank that hugged the side of the house, she thought back on the worst years of her life in Ardis Heights and realized she'd come a long way. She'd learned that even when you're no longer the person you used to be, it's possible to find new meaning, and if you try hard enough, to live fully again.

She smiled as she stood watching the children running to seek places to hide. Relieved when she noticed Betty Lou was "it" now, her smile broadened. She wouldn't have to smooth Gloria Nell's feathers after all.

ABOUT THE AUTHOR

Betty Richards lives in Wichita, Kansas with her husband of fifty-five years and her dog, Dilly. She is a painter and jewelry designer who also loves to write. This is her first novel.

Printed in the United States
125498LV00001B/1/P

9 781434 336613